RECONSTRUCTING REALITY

OXFORD STUDIES IN PHILOSOPHY OF SCIENCE

The Book of Evidence
Peter Achinstein

Science, Truth, and Democracy
Philip Kitcher

Inconsistency, Asymmetry, and Non-Locality: A Philosophical Investigation of Classical Electrodynamics
Mathias Frisch

The Devil in the Details: Asymptotic Reasoning in Explanation, Reduction, and Emergence
Robert W. Batterman

Science and Partial Truth: A Unitary Approach to Models an Scientific Reasoning
Newton C.A. da Costa and Steven French

Inventing Temperature: Measurement and Scientific Progress
Hasok Chang

The Reign of Relativity: Philosophy in Physics 1915–1925
Thomas Ryckman

Making Things Happen: A Theory of Causal Explanation
James Woodward

Mathematics and Scientific Representation
Christopher Pincock

Simulation and Similarity: Using Models to Understand the World
Michael Weisberg

Systematicity: The Nature of Science
Paul Hoyningen-Huene

Causation and Its Basis in Fundamental Physics
Douglas Kutach

Reconstructing Reality: Models, Mathematics, and Simulations
Margaret Morrison

RECONSTRUCTING REALITY

Models, Mathematics, and Simulations

Margaret Morrison

OXFORD
UNIVERSITY PRESS

OXFORD

UNIVERSITY PRESS

Oxford University Press is a department of the University of
Oxford. It furthers the University's objective of excellence in research,
scholarship, and education by publishing worldwide.

Oxford   New York
Auckland   Cape Town   Dar es Salaam   Hong Kong   Karachi
Kuala Lumpur   Madrid   Melbourne   Mexico City   Nairobi
New Delhi   Shanghai   Taipei   Toronto

With offices in
Argentina   Austria   Brazil   Chile   Czech Republic   France   Greece
Guatemala   Hungary   Italy   Japan   Poland   Portugal   Singapore
South Korea   Switzerland   Thailand   Turkey   Ukraine   Vietnam

Oxford is a registered trademark of Oxford University Press
in the UK and certain other countries.

Published in the United States of America by
Oxford University Press
198 Madison Avenue, New York, NY 10016

Library of Congress Cataloging-in-Publication Data
Morrison, Margaret, 1954-
Reconstructing reality: models, mathematics, and simulations/Margaret Morrison.
pages cm.—(Oxford studies in philosophy of science)
Includes bibliographical references and index.
ISBN 978-0-19-938027-5 (hardcover: alk. paper)   1. Science—Mathematical
models.   2. Physics—Mathematical models.   3. Mathematics—Philosophy.   I. Title.
Q158.5.M667 2015
501—dc23
2014010524

CONTENTS

CONTENTS

PART II
WHERE MODELS MEET THE WORLD: PROBLEMS AND PERSPECTIVES

PART III
COMPUTER SIMULATION: THE NEW REALITY

ACKNOWLEDGMENTS

My greatest institutional debt is to the Social Sciences and Humanities Research Council of Canada, not only for financial support of the research required for this book but for their generous and consistent support of my work since graduate school. Without the many research grants I have received, this work would have taken a lot longer than it has. . . which means it might never have been completed. I would also like to thank the Philosophy Department at the University of Toronto for financial support in preparing the manuscript for publication.

Personally, my greatest thanks go to Colin Howson, who was relentless in pestering me to both start and complete the book. His sense of humour and good advice are unsurpassed, and I am grateful beyond words to be the beneficiary of both. Because the book is a combination of ideas and material that have been reconfigured from past work as well as new ventures, the number of people who have contributed, in one way or another, to the end product are too numerous to mention. Peter Ohlin has been encouraging all the way and over a very long period of time. I am also grateful to participants at all the many talks and conferences, to referees for written comments on earlier versions of this work that appeared in journals, and of course to the referees for the book manuscript itself. I have benefitted enormously from all of their input. Special thanks for various comments, suggestions, and conversations about specific issues/ arguments that have made their way into the final manuscript go to Sorin Bangu, Robert Batterman, Paul Humphreys, Wendy Parker, and Eran Tal. The first version of the work on simulation was presented at the Oberlin Colloquium in the Philosophy of Science held in April 2008, and I would like to thank Martin Jones for the invitation and his generous hospitality. Other parts were presented at a workshop in June 2008 and a conference in June 2011 at IHPST Paris, where I was the beneficiary of the hospitality of Anouk Barberousse, Jacques Dubucs, Marion Vorms, and Julie Jebeile. Themes and ideas from chapter 2 were presented at The Twenty-fifth Annual International Workshop on the History and Philosophy of Science entitled "Mathematical Knowledge and its Applications." The workshop was in honour of Mark Steiner and held at Tel Aviv University and the Van Leer Institute, Jerusalem, December 12-14, 2011. I would like to thank the organisers, Yemima Ben Menachem, Leo Cory and Carl Posey for their hospitality, and Mark Steiner for his generosity over the years. The material on simulation and the Large Hadron Collider was presented at a conference on methods of data collection held in March 2013 and sponsored by the University of Wuppertal group on history and philosophy of particle physics. I would like to thank Koray Karaca and all of his colleagues there for their discussion and feedback. Last but not least I would like to thank Emily Sacharin at Oxford University Press for her expert help with various administrative issues, Molly Morrison for her efficiency on the production end and Kevin Kuhl for compiling the index.

RECONSTRUCTING REALITY

Introduction

How do reconstructive methods and practices of science, specifically those associated with mathematics, modelling, and simulation, impart information and knowledge of the world around us? An answer to that question defines my goal for this book. It has been 15 years since *Models as Mediators* (1999) was published, and since then debate about the role of models in science has evolved into a subdiscipline of its own. Scholars are now interested in specific aspects of modelling practice, the kind of knowledge we extract from models, and, more recently, how simulation fits into the modelling debate. What this work offers is an insight into particular problems that arise in the context of modelling as well as the role mathematics plays not only in model construction and interpretation but as a method for producing physical understanding in its own right. Simulation extends this framework by reconstructing the world in new and complex ways. Although that reconstruction is by no means a straightforward process, an examination of the strengths and weaknesses of simulation reveals how it can be used to legitimately extend the boundaries of both theoretical and empirical knowledge.

We are all familiar with the remark of Galileo in *The Assayer* that the book of nature is written in the language of mathematics. He claims that if we are to understand the universe then we need to describe it correctly, and mathematics was, for Galileo, the basis for

1

that description. If we take his example that the distance of free fall of an object is proportional to the square of the interval of time, what we see is that the pattern of free fall motion can be described by measuring a parameter—distance. The measurement and assigned value can be said to illustrate the pattern, namely that the distance varies as time squared, in a way that is not otherwise obvious.[1] The mathematisation of the problem consists in our being able to specify the relation between distance and time in a precise way, a specification that is not possible using qualitative language. But note here that the relation between the *qualitative* concepts of distance and time plays an important role in what we call the 'mathematisation' of the problem. This notion of a physical attribute being signified by a numerical symbol, as Duhem put it (1954, 108), presupposes that the attribute involves a quantity or, in the case of geometry, a magnitude. In order to describe acceleration as a second derivative we need to first have some physical notion of acceleration as a property that applies to a moving object. A somewhat different but nevertheless mathematical argument occurs with the unification of light and electromagnetic waves by Maxwell, where the realisation of their identity resulted from the calculation of the velocity for the then unverified electromagnetic waves.

What these types of examples reveal is that an important part of scientific investigation involves reconstructing or recasting nature in a specific form and investigating how it behaves or might behave under certain circumstances. Although we can use mathematics to do this, the notion of 'reconstruction' can also be instantiated in other ways. Both modelling and experimentation serve as examples of how we can reconstruct or reconfigure physical or biological systems in a way that facilitates probing certain features that may not lend themselves to investigation outside a well-defined and circumscribed context.

---

1. This and several other examples are discussed in Sarukkai (2005).

The search for the Higgs boson is one of the more extreme cases of this; the particle will only appear at certain energies that have to be created inside the collider, and it requires an enormous amount of data to determine whether the observed events are signatures of a standard model Higgs. However, the type of reconstruction that culminated in the discovery of the Higgs particle had its origins not just in the notion of experimental reconstruction but also within a complex mathematisation of nature, a methodology that provides the foundation for theoretical (and now experimental) physics.

The argument for the existence of the Higgs particle (field) has its foundations in the mathematics used to model features of quantum field theory. Indeed, it is no exaggeration to say that the entire history of theoretical physics involves the development of mathematical notions and structural concepts used to model the physical phenomena in question. The identification of symplectic geometry as the underlying structure of classical Hamiltonian mechanics and the identification of group theory as the underlying structure of particle physics and field theory are two such examples. What is interesting, however, is that from the uses of mathematics as a type of tool for reconstruction emerges a representational framework with a life of its own, one that is capable of generating hypotheses and physical explanations that go beyond the physical phenomena it models. For instance, predictions associated with the discovery of elementary particles often arise from symmetry arguments, as in the case of the Eightfold Way developed by Murray Gell-Mann and Yuval Ne'eman. Part of my project in this book involves explaining how mathematics is used to represent phenomena but also how it contributes to the physical understanding of the world.

It is important to point out that my aim is not one of engaging with or attempting to explain what Wigner referred to as the 'unreasonable effectiveness' of mathematics (e.g. the use of the second derivative to describe acceleration) but rather to enquire more deeply into the *relation* between mathematics and physics. My interest in explicating that relation stems from an attempt to understand how the abstract nature of mathematics can nevertheless yield concrete physical information; how a reconstruction of reality by abstract mathematics can help us solve physical problems. I take it as a given that this relation is mysterious, but the mystery needn't prevent us from attempting to uncover at least some of its features. In other words, we can hopefully understand *how* mathematics can deliver physical information without understanding *why* it does. Although the book divides systematically into three parts—mathematics, modelling, and simulation—each is concerned with a variant of the 'reconstruction' issue, and in each case mathematics has a role to play. It lies at the heart of most instances of scientific modelling and forms the foundation for computer simulation (CS) techniques. So, although the discussion is directed specifically toward mathematical explanation in part I, it occupies a background role in the remaining parts.

Part I of the book addresses the relation between mathematics and reality by examining two different but related issues: the first is how abstraction and idealisation in model construction enhances rather than detracts from our understanding of specific features of physical and biological systems; the second is how mathematical explanation can deliver physical information more generally. Several scholars working specifically in the philosophy of mathematics (Batterman, Bangu, Pincock, Steiner, Baker, and others) have addressed the mathematics-reality relation on a more global scale, incorporating philosophical arguments related to the indispensability of mathematics for physics as well as general questions surrounding the notion of applicability. My concern here is not so much to engage with these arguments directly, although I do so in a limited way, but rather to highlight the different ways that abstract mathematical models can *define* what it means to understand and explain the phenomena being investigated. In keeping with that goal I also show how abstract mathematics can function in ways that go well beyond simply representing phenomena for the purposes of exact calculation and prediction. To illustrate the point I discuss not only phase transitions in physics but also the Hardy-Weinberg (H-W) law and various models used by R. A. Fisher in the development of population genetics. In the case of Hardy-Weinberg, both the abstraction and idealisation present in the law actually embody a great deal of information that allows us to understand *why* the law functions as a successful predictive device. Even in biological contexts, where details of complex phenomena are thought to be important, mathematical abstraction can, surprisingly, function as the source of concrete information about the behaviour of these systems.

Because a good deal of the knowledge we have of both physical and biological systems comes to us via abstract mathematical models, the "mediated" knowledge those models provide needs to be properly positioned in the epistemic hierarchy. To simply rule out "nonrealistic" descriptions and principles as unexplanatory would be to render incomprehensible much of what contemporary science currently purports to understand. Hence we need some account of how those nonrealistic explanations function. Chapter 2 extends that discussion to the more general point about how mathematics can provide us with physical information, specifically how the *mathematical* explanation of physical phenomena also yields *physical* information. While the focus of chapter 2 is not on models per se, the argument is nevertheless applicable to the conclusions about the mathematical character of models in chapter 1, namely their ability to produce understanding and explanation despite their high degree of abstraction.

The second part of the book (chapters 3–5) focuses more directly on modelling and some of the problematic issues arising from the depiction or reconstruction of physical systems via the practice of modelling. One of my goals in chapter 3 is to introduce distinctions among the processes involved in constructing a fictional model, an idealisation, and a mathematical abstraction. Each of these categories transmits knowledge despite the presence of highly unrealistic assumptions about concrete systems. Although there is a temptation to categorise any type of unrealistic representation as a "fiction," I argue that this would be a mistake, primarily because the category is at once too broad and too narrow and tells us very little about how different types of nonrealistic representation can furnish information. That said, fictional models can function in a significant way in various stages of theory development. However, in order to uncover the way these models produce knowledge we need to pay particular attention to the specific structure given by the model itself. In other words, my claim is that there is no general method that captures how fictional models function or transmit knowledge in scientific contexts; each will do so in a different way, depending on the nature of the problem. By separating these models from other cases of unrealistic representation we can recognise what is distinctive about each and how each, in its own way, provides concrete information about the world.

Chapter 4 discusses the representational function of models and how it relates to their role as a mediator. For several reasons I have chosen to focus the discussion on modelling in relation to the Bardeen, Cooper, and Schrieffer (BCS) theory of superconductivity. First, as an example it is particularly rich in detail and exposes the various intricacies involved in model construction. But an equally important reason is that it has been discussed in the literature by several philosophers, including Cartwright (1999) and Cartwright and Suarez (1995), as well as French and Ladyman (1997). Because my views on representational models are mostly at odds with those in the literature, the BCS theory is a particularly useful focal point for highlighting those differences and thereby illustrating what I take to be the important aspects of representation.

I do want to stress, however, that although my focus in chapter 4 is the role of representation in the context of modelling, my intention is not to address specific arguments related to the larger issue of scientific representation. The latter is a widely discussed topic in the literature, so much so that an adequate treatment would require a book-length treatise. My own views on scientific representation, and indeed representation generally, are best characterised as 'deflationary,' in the sense that I am sceptical about the ability to formulate a theory of scientific representation that will adequately cover the diverse ways that theories and models can be said to represent target systems. That is not to say, of course, that there are no philosophically interesting issues related to how specific models or theories represent; rather my claim is that what is illuminating from the representational perspective of a particular model or model type may not be so for others. To that extent I see chapter 4 as providing some insight into how representation can be understood within the modelling context without an accompanying theory that constrains its boundaries. Put differently, by highlighting various aspects of the representational features of models I hope to also show why, in the end, we don't need a philosophical theory of representation to either illustrate or appreciate them.

The final chapter in this part deals with a problem that has plagued realism debates related to modelling and theory construction, specifically, how the use of inconsistent models or theories can provide explanatory information. If we look at examples from nuclear physics and turbulent fluid flows, which are among the most challenging and difficult areas of modern physics, we see that each uses what appear to be inconsistent models. However, if we compare the nuclear case with turbulence models we see that they differ significantly with respect to the way these models are employed. In the latter context having different models for different features of a phenomenon needn't involve outright inconsistency. Different turbulent models are employed to treat different types of flows, sometimes for calculational expediency and other times because a specific problem can be addressed by either ignoring certain features of the fluid or adding back properties that have been omitted in other models. The interesting thing about these models, however, is that while they appear contradictory, they do not embody different fundamental theoretical claims about the nature of fluids and hence do not furnish conflicting information.

Nuclear models exhibit a radically different approach. Here we have exactly the same phenomenon (the atomic nucleus and its constituents) modelled in entirely different ways depending on the data that need explanation. However, in most cases these models go beyond mere data fitting to provide some type of dynamical account of how and why the phenomena are produced. Because there are over 30 fundamentally different models that incorporate different and contradictory assumptions about structure and dynamics, there is no way to determine which of the models can be said to even approximate the true nature of the nucleus. In other words, there is no reasonable interpretation of "approximate" that would make sense of even a minimally realist claim. Although we are able to extract information about the nuclear phenomena from these models, we have no way of assessing the epistemic status of that information over and above its success in accounting for certain types of nuclear data. I chose to discuss these two examples to emphasise that in some contexts none of the "isms" prominent in philosophical debates—realism or perspectivism—has anything interesting to tell us about the way models are used to reconstruct physical systems. While the apparent inconsistencies in the turbulence case can be reconciled, there is simply no philosophical interpretation under which the nuclear models can be made compatible. Their inconsistencies point to a scientific problem that pervades the very foundations of nuclear physics but also illustrate the limits of philosophical analysis in resolving interpretive issues related to those inconsistencies.

Each of the chapters in part II deals with a specific kind of problem associated with how models are used to reconstruct phenomena we want to understand. There is also another way that the notion of reconstruction can, quite literally, be employed to investigate, explain, and predict phenomena that would be otherwise inaccessible. Here I am referring to the use of simulation as a way of not only modelling phenomena but experimenting on them as well. While it is tempting to think of simulation as an enhanced form of modelling, a closer look at the way it is used suggests a rather different story. But, however useful CS has become, the epistemic problems that arise in the context of modelling are typically magnified in the context of simulation. Not only does one have to worry about whether the theoretical model one starts with accurately represents the target system, but the discretisation process required for making the theoretical model amenable to numerical solution can involve significant changes in the informational content of the original model. So, in addition to worries about whether the model has actually been solved correctly, there is the problem of determining to what extent the solved simulation model can be taken as a more or less accurate representation of the target system.

The epistemological problems that arise when evaluating simulation data are addressed in chapter 7, but in chapter 6 I put forward an argument highlighting why we should take certain types of simulation seriously as a method for providing experimental knowledge. I use the word "experimental" here to indicate that in some cases and under certain conditions it is legitimate to claim that simulations can measure theoretical quantities. While this may sound like a rather extravagant and counterintuitive claim, it appears less so when we examine what is actually involved in certain features of experimental measurement. Once those practices are properly analysed, we can see that under the right circumstances simulation functions in ways that are sufficiently similar to experimental measurement to render their results epistemically comparable. The argument(s) in favour of that conclusion need to be supplemented by a careful evaluation of issues related to assessment of the reliability of the simulation itself, both as a model of the target system and in terms of a numerical tool. In chapter 7 I discuss some of the problems and solutions associated with assessing the reliability of simulation, as well as the ways in which simulation knowledge can acquire the legitimacy necessary for it to function as an indispensable part of scientific inquiry.

That indispensability is perhaps nowhere more evident than in the experimental searches for the Higgs boson conducted at the Large Hadron Collider (LHC). Although it is obvious that no simulation can prove that the Higgs particle exists, experiments and equipment designed to discover the Higgs rely heavily on knowledge produced via simulation. Hence, to say that the discovery of the Higgs was only possible using simulation is by no means to overstate the case. Not only is simulation required to process the experimental or 'signal' data but simulation provides the foundation for the entire experiment. To put the point in a slightly more perspicuous way, simulation knowledge is what tells us where to look for a Higgs event, that a Higgs event has occurred, and that we can trust the predictive capability of the collider itself. In that sense the mass measurement associated with the discovery is logically and causally dependent on simulation.

Moreover, as I will show in chapter 8, simulation data are combined with signal data in the analysis of various events, rendering any sharp distinction between simulation and 'experiment' practically meaningless. This is not to say that signal data from actual runs of the collider are unnecessary in establishing the existence of the Higgs particle; rather, my claim is that those data alone would not only have been insufficient for the discovery but the data themselves would be impossible to understand without simulation. The inability, in this context, to sharply distinguish simulation and experiment in the traditional way is especially significant, since the LHC experiments are often cited as the paradigm case where experiment affirms its authority over simulation. As I will show in part III, the melding of the two suggests a shift not only in the way experiment and are characterised but also in the way we evaluate the knowledge acquired in these types of contexts. Given the integral role played by simulation in the context of the LHC, the *contrast* with experiment is the wrong perspective from which to evaluate the role of simulated data.

Finally, what can the extensive use of simulation in the LHC experiments tell us about a more general account of simulation and the information it provides? And, perhaps more important, how does the methodology of verification and validation (V&V) help us to evaluate the epistemic status of simulated data when there is a lack of experimental data available for comparison? Does this change the nature of validation in the context of LHC experiments? All these questions will be addressed in the final three chapters.

PART I

MATHEMATICS, EXPLANATION, AND UNDERSTANDING

1

Abstraction and Idealisation
Understanding via Models

INTRODUCING THE PROBLEM(S)

One of the most common themes in the literature on scientific modelling involves the connection between the abstract nature of models and their ability to provide explanations of the phenomena they depict. It is commonly thought that the greater the degree of abstraction used in describing phenomena, the less understanding we have with respect to their concrete features. As a result, it is often puzzling how mathematical models that embody highly abstract descriptions can assist us in knowing and explaining facts about physical, biological, and economic systems. And, while mathematical models may be indispensable for prediction, their contribution to *physical* understanding is often thought to be extremely limited. In this chapter I want to challenge that myth by showing how mathematical abstraction of the sort used in modelling can aid our understanding in ways that more empirically based investigations sometimes cannot. What I mean here by "understanding" is simply having a theoretical account/picture of how a system or phenomenon is constituted that enables us to solve problems and explain why the phenomena in question behave in the way they do. Although much of my discussion

will focus on the role of mathematics in biology, specifically population genetics, I also want to look at some examples from physics to
highlight the ways in which understanding via mathematical abstraction in these two fields can be strikingly similar. That the similarities are there, of course, is no accident, since a good deal of the early
work in population genetics, especially that done by R. A. Fisher, was
based on mathematical techniques drawn from statistical mechanics
(SM) and thermodynamics. But what is puzzling is why these same
techniques should work in contexts where the phenomena under
investigation are so diverse.

Many philosophical accounts of understanding link it to explanation. While some (Hempel 1965; van Fraassen 1980) claim that
understanding is a pragmatic notion and hence epistemically irrelevant to assessing the merit of a theory, most others see understanding as an important goal of science but define the notion in a variety
of different ways. One option is to link understanding with unification (Friedman 1974; Kitcher 1989), where the explanation that
best unifies the phenomena is the one that produces the greatest
understanding. Salmon (1984) on the other hand sees knowledge of
causal mechanisms as the feature that furnishes understanding of the
physical world. What both of these accounts have in common is that
they privilege a particular type of explanation as the vehicle for producing understanding. More recently de Regt and Dieks (2005) have
criticised these monolithic accounts of understanding and instead
define it in the following way: A phenomenon P can be understood
if a theory T of P exists that is intelligible (and meets the usual logical, methodological and empirical requirements; 151). Intelligibility
involves having a theory that enables one to recognise "qualitatively
characteristic" consequences without performing exact calculations.
This is achieved using a variety of conceptual tools that are relevant to
the problem at hand. Their point is that in some cases causal knowledge will be relevant to understanding, and in some cases it will not;

the tool kit contains a number of different resources that, depending on the context, will produce understanding. An important feature of their account is that its pragmatic quality in no way compromises the epistemic relevance of understanding for scientific investigation. The intelligibility of a theory will depend not only on its virtues but on background knowledge and beliefs of the scientists, thereby making the theory intelligible in one context but maybe not so in another.

An example of this account of understanding is taken from Boltzmann's (1964) introduction of the kinetic theory in *Lectures on Gas Theory*. It involves a purely qualitative analysis where a gas is pictured as a collection of freely moving molecules in a container. deRegt and Dieks claim that this picture can give us a "qualitative feeling for the behaviour of macroscopic properties of gases" because "heat can be identified with molecular motion and it follows that an increase of temperature corresponds with an increase of the (average) kinetic energy of the gas molecules" (2005, 152). It also provides a qualitative explanation of the fact that a gas exerts pressure on the walls of its container because if a molecule collides with a wall it results in a push. The total effect of the pushing produces the pressure. Similarly, if one adds heat to a gas in a container of constant volume, the average kinetic energy of the moving molecules as well as the temperature will increase. These and other conclusions can give us a qualitative expression of Boyle's law without involving any calculations. Instead we have only general characteristics of the theoretical description of a gas; but these enable us to understand the phenomena and make qualitative predictions about their behaviour.

My own sympathies lie with the type of contextual analysis provided by de Regt and Dieks; it seems entirely reasonable to assume that any account of understanding, because of its very nature, will involve context specific features. Moreover, there are many different levels and ways that we can understand scientific phenomena, different ways that theories of the phenomena can be intelligible. But

I would put the point in slightly more negative terms. It isn't clear to me that having a general criterion for what counts as understanding while at the same time claiming that the criterion can be understood in a variety of ways gets us beyond the original problem. The motivation for having a "theory" or criterion of understanding is to have some canonical account of what it means to 'understand,' but if the details of that account are highly contextual then it isn't clear how it can function in a canonical way.

That does not mean we cannot explain what it is to understand why a particular phenomenon behaves as it does or what we mean when we say someone understands a mathematical concept.[1] Rather, my claim is that there is no canonical account of what it means to understand that is not context specific; and if it is context specific then there will always be disputes about whether certain conditions are satisfied. I would suggest the same holds for explanation. Very often in science we desire explanations that are causal, but that is not to say that this is the only form of explanation that is acceptable, or that we must give a "theory" of explanation that centres on causal relations. On the contrary, whether something has been successfully explained will depend on the question and the stock of available answers, answers that come from our background theories and models. We simply cannot specify in advance what qualifies as an explanation or what form it will take.

An exception to this of course is van Fraassen's (1980) pragmatic (why-question) account of explanation, which defines it as involving a three-way relation between a theory, a fact to be explained, and a context. He outlines specific structural features that need to be accounted

---

1. For example, we understand a mathematical concept if we can apply it to solve problems in ways other than simply reproducing the example used for learning the concept; and we understand a phenomenon like the weather if we are able to make predictions and explain the reasons for those predictions. The point here is simply that in some cases prediction is a feature of understanding and not in others.

for in defining an explanation, things like the relevance relation and the contrast class. For E to be an explanation of P requires that the contrast class for P is specified. This typically involves a set of events that did not occur; hence to ask why P occurred is also to ask why its alternatives did not occur. The relevance relation determines which, among many, causal factors are salient in a given context. While I see this type of structural approach as helpful in providing constraints on the general notion of explanation, my worry is that its demands are too stringent to be met by complex theoretical explanations in the sciences. For example, we may not be able to specify an adequate contrast class for a given problem (it may simply be too large) while at the same time feeling that we have provided some type of explanation of the relevant fact. Many explanations invoking string theory and supersymmetry (SUSY) involve so many possible alternatives and relevance relations that it becomes very difficult to fit them into a neatly structured framework.

My scepticism about general 'theories' of explanation is motivated not only by their susceptibility to counterexamples but by the daunting task of furnishing a theory of explanation that can account for the causal, the structural, and the many other forms that scientific explanations can take. That said, I do think explanation and understanding are linked in the intuitive sense that one often accompanies the other; that is, we demonstrate our understanding by being able to offer explanations of the object/concept in question, and the success of our explanations is typically a function of how well we understand what we are trying to explain. But I don't think one needs a philosophical theory to substantiate that claim. My position is a minimalist one in that I claim that neither understanding nor explanation is capable of being successfully codified into a philosophical theory.[2]

---

2. I realise, of course, that de Regt and Dieks may not agree with my interpretation of their position. My intention here is not to argue for my view of explanation or understanding but simply to state how I see the relation between the two for the purposes of this chapter.

Bound up with the question of how mathematical abstraction enables us to understand physical phenomena is the role played by models. In Morrison (1998, 1999) I articulate how models can provide knowledge by focusing on what I call their mediating role. That is, models function as *autonomous* (or semiautonomous) mediators between theory and applications (the model provides simplifications of the theory's equations so they can then be applied) or between theory and the world (the model is an idealised or abstract representation of some phenomenon or physical system). In this latter case we then try to compare the abstract representation with its concrete counterpart (i.e. some specific object/system). This of course leads us to the very problem I want to address in this chapter—how a comparison can be made between abstract models and concrete physical systems such that the former is capable of yielding information about the latter. Any attempt to answer that question requires some specification of how the notions of abstraction and idealisation function in model construction and interpretation.

The distinction between idealisation and abstraction I will adopt for the purposes of this chapter is roughly the following: abstraction is a process whereby we describe phenomena in ways that cannot possibly be realised in the physical world (for example, infinite populations). And, in these cases, the mathematics associated with the description is necessary for modelling the system in a specific way. Idealisation on the other hand typically involves a process of approximation whereby the system can become less idealised by adding correction factors (such as friction to a model pendulum). In the latter case, the idealisation is used primarily to ease calculation, since the factors that have been idealised will not, in general, be immediately relevant for the type of problem at hand. In their original state both abstraction and idealisation make reference to phenomena that are not physically real; however, because the latter leaves room for corrections via approximations, it can bear a closer relation to a concrete physical entity. This distinction will become important in showing how mathematical abstraction enables us to understand certain features of empirical phenomena in ways that are different from the more straightforward features associated with idealisation simpliciter.

It is important to note here that my use of the terms "abstraction" and "idealisation" differs from many of the accounts in the literature, for example, those of Cartwright (1999a) and Thompson-Jones (2005). Instead of defining abstraction as leaving out properties that belong to the system in question and idealisation as the distortion of certain properties (for example, point particle) I have chosen, instead, to focus on the kind of mathematical abstraction that we often find embedded in models, abstraction that is not amenable to approximation techniques. My goal is to show how certain types of mathematical abstraction can be necessary for representing and understanding the behaviour of physical systems/phenomena. My reason for changing the terms of reference here relate to what I see as the inability of standard accounts to capture the way mathematical abstraction functions in explanation. As I noted, most accounts of idealisation and abstraction involve adding back properties that were left out of the description or deidealising in order to make the system more realistic or concrete. However, there are many instances where this type of deidealisation isn't possible (e.g. the thermodynamic limit) and standard accounts say nothing about how we should understand cases where the abstract mathematical representation is *necessary* for representing the target system. Because of the importance of this latter type of abstraction for mathematical modelling, some account of how it functions in our understanding of the model systems is required. I will have more to say about this distinction in chapter 3, where I discuss the issue of fictional representation.

The role of mathematical abstraction in model construction figures importantly in characterising the autonomy of models.[3] For

---

3. In Morrison (1999) I claim that what makes a model autonomous is not simply that it is not derived from theory or phenomena but that it involves elements from a variety of different

example, in cases where the system or phenomena under investigation may be inaccessible due to large distances (galactic phenomena) or size (microstructures), the model occupies centre stage and takes on the task of representing how we *assume* the system is constituted. And, because direct comparison between the model and the system is not possible, the model supplants the system as the object under investigation; in that sense it functions as an autonomous object. Models of stellar structure in astrophysics fit this category. In these cases, the model fulfills its role by serving as a source of *mediated* knowledge, that is, by functioning as a type of secondary representation rather than as direct knowledge of the system under investigation. This typically involves a good deal of mathematical abstraction (and idealisation), structure that itself becomes the focus of investigation. Hence, our knowledge of real-world situations is mediated by this structure. Below I discuss examples of this sort, where the mathematical model supplants the physical phenomena as the object of investigation. In each of these cases the degree to which the model produces understanding comes via its abstract mathematical structure. The interesting

sources that, taken together, make the model a unique kind of entity. It is by virtue of this uniqueness that they can and do play a mediating role. With models, and in other situations as well, mediators need to occupy a relatively independent position if they are to properly fulfill the function they are assigned. But their roles as mediators can vary widely. Indeed, in some cases the structures constituting the model fail to provide any clues about the physical nature of the system in question, and the model also fails to point to specific relations/reduction to some background theory. Instead, models may be used simply for their predictive power or to account for specific kinds of behaviours without interpreting them as having any realistic representational power whatsoever. In these latter cases, the models do not really provide us with any *understanding* of the system/phenomena in question; they save the phenomena without answering questions about why the system behaves as it does. An example is the liquid drop model used for nuclear fission. While I still believe these considerations are important in characterising a model's autonomy, other features also play a crucial role—one such feature is the way a model represents the system of interest. My concern in this chapter is how mathematical abstraction represents systems in a way that enables us to understand fundamental features about their behaviour.

philosophical question is how we should understand the relation between this abstract structure and the concrete physical systems that this structure purportedly represents.[4]

While this type of scenario is common in theoretical physics and many of the natural sciences, its acceptance as an appropriate method for biology is much more recent and by no means uncontroversial. In other words, the kind of mathematical abstraction commonly found in physical models was, for many years, not typically associated with biological investigation. Here we associate the experimental context with fieldwork and the mathematical foundations of biological theory with statistical methods used to analyse experimental findings. But the increasing use of abstract mathematical models in biology is not simply due to the rise of subdisciplines like molecular biology. Since the development of population genetics in the early part of the twentieth century, the use of mathematical techniques such as diffusion equations has resulted in new ways of characterising populations. Instead of the natural or "real" populations studied by field biologists, populations are now often mathematical constructs that can be manipulated using sophisticated mathematics. In this context, the model, rather than the real-world environment or system (that is, populations of living things), becomes the object of inquiry. Because conclusions about the role of selection in Mendelian populations were simply not available using empirical methods, this new form of mathematical modelling marked an important turning point for understanding the genetic features of natural populations.

4. Space does not allow me to deal with the often thorny issues surrounding what constitutes a representation in the context of models and theories. For a brief discussion of this, see Morrison (2007b) and chapter 4. For my purposes in this chapter I do not necessarily require a well-worked-out notion of representation in order to address some of the concerns surrounding the relation between understanding and mathematical abstraction.

As I noted, one of the difficulties with this kind of "mediated" knowledge is that it often involves a good deal of mathematical abstraction, taking us further away from the kind of empirical contexts we are frequently interested in. Moreover, we typically prefer models to provide at least a partially realistic representation of the system under investigation. In fact, it is partly because theories function at such an abstract level that we require models for the application of theory to concrete situations and to fill in the details where theory is silent. However, as I will show and contrary to what we might expect, increasing levels of mathematical abstraction often provide the only way to understand concrete physical and biological systems. One prominent example of this is R.A. Fisher's work on population genetics where he was able to explain human variation only by invoking a very *unrealistic and abstract* model of a population.

To flesh out the details of my argument let me begin with a brief example from physics, specifically the abstraction involved in taking the macroscopic limit in thermodynamics, a technique necessary for understanding phase transitions. From there I discuss the H-W law and how the mathematical abstraction built into this law allows us to understand fundamental features of biological populations. I conclude with an account of how the abstract mathematics used by R. A. Fisher produced tremendous advances in our understanding of the genetics of natural populations. Although these examples have all been discussed in the philosophical literature both by me and by others, those discussions have often been motivated from a rather different perspective, specifically, issues related to general concerns about the nature of models. I want to revisit these examples here to especially highlight their common features regarding the explanatory role played by mathematical abstraction as well as to articulate the way my views of this topic diverge from many of those presented in the literature.

WORRIES ABOUT LIMITS

Even without bringing mathematics into the equation the very notion of what it means to "understand" is by no means straightforward. As I noted, philosophical attempts to understand understanding are usually linked to the equally controversial notion of explanation, more specifically, the task of conveying information in a way that will answer a 'why' or 'how' question. Scientific understanding, especially in physics, often involves the application of both general principles and more specialised models that enable us to describe, predict, and explain specific types of behaviour. This is not to say that an appropriate answer to every question must invoke both strategies but simply to recognise that certain kinds of questions demand certain kinds of answers. In other words, the idea that explanation can be achieved solely on the basis of fundamental laws and initial conditions, as described by the deductive-nomological model, is now thought to be insufficient for understanding much of the physical world. We need a variety of things—fundamental theory and different kinds of models as well as laws (e.g. symmetries) that constrain the kinds of behaviours that systems display.

The important question here is how the abstraction (as opposed to idealisation) built into theories, models, and laws enables or in some cases might prevent us from understanding physical systems. To counter the idea that understanding is inhibited by abstraction we only need to look to scientific textbooks to see the role it plays. The kind of models that serve as exemplars in the Kuhnian sense (the quantum harmonic oscillator, the infinite potential well, and so on), as well as entities like virtual particles, embody a great deal of abstraction and yet are the cornerstone of understanding essential features of physical systems. This is because they enable us to conceive of systems as being of a particular type, exhibiting certain kinds of behaviour that allow us to classify them in terms of their *general* features. All of these factors enhance our understanding.

But understanding via abstraction is not simply limited to general features of physical systems. In many of these cases, abstract representations also provide the kind of *detailed* knowledge required to answer causal questions. For example, if we ask why a particular metal exhibits superconducting properties, we can explain it in terms of zero resistivity and the accompanying thermodynamic phase transition, something that is only possible in certain kinds of metals. And if we want to know the details of what happens at the subatomic level, we can invoke the BCS model, complete with its description of electron-phonon interactions, Cooper pairing, and the BCS wavefunction. Although these models involve abstraction and approximation, they allow for a rather peculiar situation: from them we can derive *exact* results associated with superconductivity; properties such as infinite conductivity, flux quantisation, and zero resistivity that are exact for all superconductors regardless of their atomic and molecular constitution.

The puzzle is how one can derive these exact consequences from models that are approximations. What features of the models enable them to work so well? The reason is that we can also understand a superconductor as a material in which electromagnetic gauge invariance is spontaneously broken and these models contain, as a fundamental assumption, the breakdown of electromagnetic gauge invariance. The detailed dynamical theories and models like BCS are required to explain why and at what temperatures this symmetry breaking occurs, but not to derive the kinds of consequences mentioned above; those exact properties that define superconductors. In other words, those properties can be derived directly from the assumption of the spontaneous breaking of electromagnetic gauge invariance and so are consequences of general principles rather than of specific approximations embodied in the model.[5]

But how, exactly, is mathematical abstraction involved here? The situation is far from straightforward. The spontaneous breakdown of electromagnetic gauge invariance involves a phase transition that is associated with the superconducting state. The occurrence of phase transitions requires a mathematical technique known as taking the "thermodynamic limit" $N \to \infty$; in other words, we need to assume that a system contains an infinite number of particles in order to explain, understand, and make predictions about the behaviour of a real, finite system. Very briefly, the situation is as follows. Theory tells us that phase transitions, for example the point where magnets become superconductors, occur only in infinite systems. A defining characteristic of a phase transition is an abrupt change, noted mathematically by a singularity. In other words, thermodynamic observables characterising the system are not defined or "well-behaved"—infinite or not differentiable. All thermodynamic observables are partial derivatives of the partition function, hence a singularity in the partition function is required to obtain a singularity in the thermodynamic function. Although the partition function is analytic, it is possible for systems with infinite N to display singular behaviour for nonvanishing partition functions. The problem then is that in SM the solutions to the equations of motion that govern these systems are analytic and as a result, there are no singularities and hence no basis for explaining phase transitions. Note that the problem here is not that the limit provides an easier route to the calculational features associated with

---

5. The existence of these "universal" properties indicates that superconductivity is a thermodynamic phase. For more on this, see Morrison (2006a, 2012) and Weinberg (1986). While there is some discussion in the literature as to whether electromagnetic gauge invariance rather than global phase invariance is actually the symmetry that is broken in a superconductor, I don't want to address those issues here. A full treatment of the problem would require a separate paper.

understanding phase transitions; rather, the assumption that the system is infinite is *necessary* for the symmetry breaking associated with phase transitions to occur. In other words, we have a description of a physically unrealisable situation (an infinite system) that is *required* to explain a physically realisable phenomenon (the occurrence of phase transitions in finite systems).

The question is whether this procedure yields the kind of explanation that produces understanding. Although one might want to claim that within the *mathematical* framework of SM we can causally account for (explain) the occurrence of phase transitions by assuming the system is infinite, it is nevertheless tempting to conclude that this explanation does not help us to *physically* understand how the process takes place, since the systems that SM deals with are all finite. Doubts of this sort have been expressed by Earman (2004), who argues against taking the thermodynamic limit as a legitimate form of idealisation: "a sound principle of interpretation would seem to be that no effect can be counted as a genuine physical effect if it disappears when the idealisations are removed" (191). Callender (2001) and others (Callender and Menon 2013; Butterfield 2011a and b) also discuss the problem with objections similar in spirit to those raised by Earman. In other words, we should not assume that phase transitions have been explained and thereby understood if their occurrence relies solely on the presence of what they term a mathematical idealisation.

Initially this seems an intuitive and plausible objection, but if we reflect for a moment on the way mathematical abstraction is employed for explanatory purposes in scientific models or theories, it becomes clear that this line of reasoning quickly rules out explanations of the sort we deem acceptable in other contexts. Although Earman refers to the thermodynamic limit as an idealisation, it is here that the distinction I introduced at the beginning between abstraction and idealisation becomes especially important. Specifically, we need to distinguish between the kind of mathematical abstraction required for a theoretical representation and the more straightforward kinds of mathematical idealisations that are used simply to facilitate calculation. In the former case, the abstraction becomes a fundamental part of how the system is modelled or represented and consequently proves crucial to our understanding of how it behaves.

For example, consider the intertheoretical relations that exist in fluid mechanics between Navier-Stokes (N-S) equations and the Euler equations, or between theories like wave optics and ray optics, and classical and quantum mechanics. Because of the mathematical nature of physical theories the relations between them will typically be expressed in terms of the relations between different equations or solutions. In each case we are interested in certain kinds of limiting behaviour expressed by a dimensionless parameter δ. In fluid dynamics δ is equal to 1 / Re (Reynolds number), and in quantum mechanics it is Planck's constant divided by a typical classical action ($\hbar$ / S). But in fluid mechanics (as in the other cases listed above) the limit $\delta \rightarrow 0$ is singular, and it is this singularity that is responsible for turbulent flows. Similarly, in the ray limit where geometrical optics accurately describe the workings of telescopes and cameras the wavelength $\lambda \rightarrow 0$. Because ψ is nonanalytic at $\lambda = 0$, the wave function oscillates infinitely fast and takes all values between +1 and −1 infinitely often in any finite range of x or t.[6]

A good deal of asymptotic behaviour that is crucial for describing physical phenomena relies on exactly these kinds of mathematical abstractions. What we classify as "emergent" phenomena in physics such as the crystalline state, superfluidity, and ferromagnetism, to name a few, are the result of phase transitions whose theoretical representation requires singularities; hence their understanding depends on just the kinds of mathematical abstractions described

6. For an interesting discussion of these phenomena see Berry (1994).

above. Moreover, it is equally important to mention that in many of these cases it is possible to note changes in the system's behaviour as it approaches a critical point, gradually approximating the kinds of changes associated with the phase transition. In that sense, we do have physical "indicators" for the kind of behaviour the mathematics predicts, even though the transition is only exact in the infinite volume limit. While it may, initially, sound odd to say that understanding requires singularities, the point here is that there is no theoretical foundation for phase transitions without this mathematical framework. Hence, insofar as we are able to predict their occurrence and explain their behaviour from within a theoretical perspective, as opposed to just cataloging observable behaviour, our understanding of phase transitions is inextricably linked to the mathematics of singular limits.

What this means is that if we subscribe to the Callender/Earman view we are forced to ignore large portions of the mathematical foundations of our theories and models since so many rely on exactly this type of abstract representation. Consequently, we need to ask why the thermodynamic limit is considered illegitimate, as opposed to other uses of singular limits. Here the distinction between idealisation and abstraction offers some help. We typically think of an idealisation as resembling, in certain respects, the concrete phenomenon we are trying to understand. We usually know how to correct or compensate for what we have left out, or idealised, in the description. That is, we know how to add back things like frictional forces that may not have been needed for the problem at hand. Or we know how to change the laws that govern a physical situation when we introduce more realistic assumptions, as in the move from the ideal gas law to the van der Waals law.

Contrast this with the kinds of mathematical abstractions described above. In the case of the thermodynamic limit, we do not introduce abstractions simply as a way of ignoring what is irrelevant to the problem or as a method for calculational expediency. Instead, the mathematical description functions as a necessary condition for explaining and hence understanding the phenomena in question.[7] Thinking of abstraction in this way sheds a different light on the problem Earman mentions. If we think of idealisations as calculational devices, then yes, they should not be associated with genuine physical effects; but the case of abstraction is different in kind. Undoubtedly it also requires us to think differently about what constitutes "understanding," and it demands that we be able to somehow link mathematical abstraction with physical effects. Given the mathematical character of our theories and models, these demands are unavoidable if we are to properly integrate mathematics and physical understanding. Since many physical phenomena are described in terms of mathematical abstractions, it seems reasonable to expect that their explanations will be given in similar terms. In the following chapter I discuss these issues in more detail by providing an in-depth discussion of the thermodynamic limit and the ways mathematical calculation is sometimes bound up with explanation. For now, however, I would like to move on to another problem related to the link between understanding, explanation, and mathematics—the use of what are sometimes referred to as "false" laws or models.

EXTRACTING TRUTH FROM "FALSE" LAWS

While we might reluctantly accept the role of abstraction in physics, one is likely to be even less enthusiastic when it comes to explanation in biology. The degree of complexity associated with biological phenomena is largely thought to rule out explanations that embody

---

7. For an excellent discussion of issues surrounding the notion of reduction and the thermodynamic limit, see Batterman (2005).

abstractions as simply uninformative; they do not tell us what we need to know in order to understand the behaviour of biological phenomena. Moreover, the reductionist assumptions that underscore many explanations in physics are thought to be inappropriate for biology. It is assumed that by ignoring the individual nature of biological phenomena, we draw the wrong kinds of conclusions about complex living systems, which in turn can be used to justify undesirable social and political practices.[8] Instead, biological explanations need to be "closer to the ground" and to appeal to the specific nature of individuals or species and their interactions with their environments.

A notable exception to this is population genetics, a highly mathematical branch of biology that deals with the genetic basis of evolution. The objects of study are primarily the frequencies and fitnesses of genotypes in natural populations. Some population geneticists even define evolution as the change in the frequencies of genotypes over time, something that may be the result of their differences in fitness. Or to put it more accurately, we can model evolution by assigning fitnesses to genotypes and then following the changes in allele frequencies. The problem is that while genotype or allele frequencies are easily measured, their change is not. Most naturally occurring genetic variants have a time scale of change that is on the order of tens of thousands to millions of years, making them impossible to observe.[9] Fitness differences are likewise very small, less than 0.01 percent, also making them impossible to measure directly. What this means is that although the state of a population can be observed, the evolution of a population cannot be directly studied; hence the need for mathematical models.

---

8. See, for example, Mayr (1982).

9. As Sabina Leonelli has pointed out to me (personal written communication), there are several types of fast evolving populations (such as viruses) whose evolution can be observed and measured, but modelling these systems does not provide the basis for general models of evolving populations in the way that more mathematically based approaches do.

One investigates most systems that are not directly accessible by constructing mathematical models of the evolutionary process and then comparing their predictions with the behaviour or states of the system, in this case populations that can be directly observed. As I will show in later chapters, much of this activity also involves the construction and running of CSs. While simulations are also important for studying various different types of systems, I want to keep the present focus on mathematical modelling. This is partly because I eventually want to argue that simulation represents a different kind of inquiry from both modelling and experimentation and that while it bears similarities to both, it has its own distinct methodological and epistemological merits and difficulties. Because one simply cannot know the genetic structure of a species (not only would we need a complete description of the genome but also the spatial location of every individual at one instant in time, which would then change in the next instant) mathematical models are the focus of inquiry. They incorporate certain idealising assumptions that ignore the complexities of real populations; for example, they focus on one or a few loci at a time in a population that mates randomly or has a simple migration pattern. The success of these models has been remarkable, and indeed the birth of population genetics resulted from the application of mathematical techniques that invoked infinite populations and ideas from statistical physics. To that extent, then, the methods of population genetics look very much like the methods of physics. And indeed the claim by many population geneticists is that allele-based models are what constitutes our *understanding* of much of the mechanics of evolution.[10] What this seems to suggest is that, at

---

10. My claim here is not that population genetics captures all of mathematical modelling in biology; rather, that many population geneticists see their methods as providing the foundations for understanding the genetical basis of evolutionary change. There are many areas of evolutionary biology that consist of loosely connected models that are not part of any unifying theoretical framework, but that point is irrelevant for how we understand what

least in the domain of population genetics, understanding in physics and biology is very similar.

In fact, one only needs to look to the very early developments in population genetics to see how mathematical abstraction plays a role in enabling us to understand certain features about populations. The H-W law is a simple example of a fundamental law that makes assumptions not realised in any natural population. So in what sense do we want to say that this law is explanatory? One of the things that renders laws explanatory is the fact that they are general enough to apply to a diverse number of phenomena. In other words, they enable us to understand specific features of phenomena as similar in certain respects; for example, universal gravitation shows that both terrestrial and celestial bodies obey an inverse square force law. Cartwright (1983) claims that this generality is a reason for thinking fundamental laws like these are false; their generality results in their being unable to fully describe the situations they reportedly cover, or they deliberately omit aspects of the situation that are not relevant for the calculation at hand. In that sense they do not accurately describe concrete situations. The problem, then, is how could they possibly impart understanding? The question is, in some ways, similar to the one raised about models: how do abstract mathematical models impart concrete information about the physical world?

Part of Cartwright's reason for claiming that covering laws are false is to contrast them with phenomenological laws or models that supposedly give us more accurate descriptions of the physical world. But since all scientific description embodies a certain amount of abstraction/idealisation, it is difficult to know where to draw the line. Ignoring things that are seemingly irrelevant and idealising objects/relations that are too complex to describe in detail are necessary

happens when we combine population-level processes (such as selection) with the rules of transmission genetics.

features of science and part and parcel of the ways that laws, theories, and models are constructed. While it is certainly true that we distinguish between phenomenological and more fundamental laws, it is usually the former that are thought of as giving an incomplete description of the relevant phenomena. This is because they fail to appeal to underlying micro-processes of the kind necessary for understanding much of the behaviour of physical systems. What the H-W law shows is that embedded in what Cartwright would call a "false" law is a great deal of accurate information about biological populations, information that constitutes an important part of the synthesis of Mendelian heredity and Darwinian natural selection. To that extent, it serves as an example of how mathematical abstraction can enhance our understanding far beyond simple predictive capabilities.[11]

As I will show, the H-W law enables us to understand fundamental features of heredity and variation by establishing a mathematical relation between allele and genotype frequencies that embodies the very gene-conserving structure that is the essential feature of Mendelism. Hence, the claim that the law is false misses the point if our concern is understanding and conveying information. What is important for my purposes here is to show why the unrealistic nature of the law's assumptions in no way affects the significance of either the conclusions it provides or the information implicit in its formulation. And once again, within the context of the H-W law we can differentiate the mathematical abstractions from other types of idealising assumptions that figure in its formulation. This enables us to show why the former are essential for understanding the basis of the mechanics of evolution.

The H-W law is often described as a consequence of Mendel's law of segregation, or a generalisation of Mendel's law as applied to populations. It relates allele or gene frequencies to genotype frequencies

11. Why this is an instance of abstraction as opposed to idealisation will be discussed later.

and states that in an infinite, random mating population, in the absence of external factors such as mutation, selection, sampling error, and migration, one generation of random mating will produce a distribution of genotypes that is a function solely of allele frequencies and does not change over subsequent generations, provided all conditions are held constant. In other words, if we have a pair of alleles A_1 A_2 at a particular gene locus, and the initial ratio of A_1 to A_2 is p to q, then for every succeeding generation the ratio will be p to q, and regardless of the distribution of genotypes in the initial generation, the distribution for all succeeding generations will be

$$p^2 A_1 A_1 + 2pq A_1 A_2 + q^2 A_2 A_2$$

So p^2 is just the probability of getting an $A_1 A_1$ homozygote, which is the probability that the egg is A_1 times the probability that the sperm is A_1 (by the product rule for independent events). Both of these probabilities are p because in its simplest form the law assumes that the species is hermaphroditic. Since the heterozygote can be formed in two different ways, the probability is $2pq$ (by the addition rule for mutually exclusive events). So, if you know the value for p, then you know the frequencies of all three genotypes.

Since random mating does not change allele frequencies, all that is required to calculate the genotype frequencies after a round of random mating are the allele frequencies before random mating. In populations where each individual is either male or female with different allele frequencies, it will take two generations to reach H-W equilibrium. From this we can see the relation between the stability of the frequencies and Mendel's law of segregation. With random cross-fertilisation there is no disappearance of any class whatever in the offspring of the hybrids; each class continues to be produced in the same proportion.[12]

---

12. The law of segregation refers to the fact that the characters that differentiate hybrid forms

But, and here is the important point, what *is* significant about the H-W law is not so much the binomial form of the genotype frequency and the prediction of genotypes based on the stability of the population, but rather what the stability actually shows or presupposes. Despite the unrealistic assumptions, the stability allows us to comprehend something about Mendelian populations that is significant for understanding heredity and variation. In other words, certain conditions must be present for the stability to be possible. Thus, the predictive success of the law is intimately connected with certain basic claims about genetic structure. What the H-W law says is that if no external forces act, then there is no intrinsic tendency for the variation caused by the three different genotypes that exist in a population to disappear. It also shows that because the distribution of genotype frequencies is independent of dominance, dominance alone cannot change them. In other words, there is no evidence that a dominant character will show a tendency to spread or allow a recessive one to die out. Instead, the genotype frequencies are maintained in constant proportions. The probabilistic genetic structure is conserved indefinitely; but should it be influenced by an outside force, for example, mutation, the effect would be preserved in a new, stable distribution in the succeeding generation.

This was crucial for understanding the problems with blending inheritance as advocated by the Darwinians, and to that extent we can see why the "falsity" of the law is somewhat irrelevant. Under blending inheritance, variation was thought to decrease rapidly with each successive generation, but H-W shows that under a Mendelian

---

can be analysed in terms of independent pairs; that is, each anlagen acts separately—they do not fuse. We can also understand this as stating that any hybrid for a given character produces an offspring distributed according to definite proportions. If the pure parental forms are A_1 and A_2 and the hybrid A_1A_2, then the offspring of the hybrid will be distributed according to the ratio $1A_1:2A_1A_2:1A_2$. Pearson (1904) was probably the first to show the relation between the law of segregation and the stability of a population in the absence of selection.

scheme it is maintained. This pointed to yet another fundamental aspect of Mendelism, namely, the discontinuous nature of the gene and why *it* was important for the preservation of variation required for selection. How was it possible for the genetic structure to be maintained over successive generations? The reason for the stability could be traced directly to the absence of fusion, which was indicative of a type of genetic structure that could conserve modification. This condition was explicitly presupposed in the way the law was formulated and how it functioned. In that sense, one can see the H-W law as the beginning of a completely new conception of the role of mutation and selection and how they affect our understanding of evolution.

Appealing to the abstraction/idealisation distinction can also clarify our understanding of how deviations from the conditions or assumptions specified by the law affect its applicability. Essentially we can divide the assumptions associated with the H-W law into two groups. The first involves assumptions that do not allow for relaxation without violating H-W equilibrium, such as infinite population size and random mating. The second includes the absence of selection, migration, and mutation. These assumptions affect allele frequencies but not random mating. Violations of these latter conditions will not rule out H-W proportions; instead, the allele frequencies will change in accordance with the changing conditions. In other words, these conditions function as idealisations that may or may not hold but whose effect on the system can be straightforwardly calculated. Put differently, we can think of them as external factors that isolate basic features of a Mendelian system that allow us to understand how variation could be conserved.

Contrast that situation with the requirements of infinite populations and random mating. Infinite populations are crucial in that one must be able to rule out genetic drift, which is a change in gene frequencies that results from chance deviation from expected genotypic frequencies. That is, we must be able to determine that detected changes are not due to sampling errors. In theory, the population doesn't need to be exactly infinite, and one can obtain reliable results in very large populations where there is a smooth approximation (unlike the singular limits in SM) to the limit. But the point is that deviations diminish our ability to rule out drift; hence the notion of an infinite population (or one closely approximating it) is crucial. Although random mating seems like the kind of restriction that is typically violated, we can see how its violations affect gene frequencies: in the case of assortative mating, there will be an increase in homozygosity for those genes involved in the trait that is preferential, such as height or eye color. Traits such as blood type are typically randomly mated. Similarly in the case of inbreeding there will be an increase in homozygosity for all genes. Because both of these assumptions are necessary for H-W equilibrium they cannot, in general, be corrected for and hence are fundamental for the formulation of the law. In other words, they ought to be considered abstractions rather than idealisations because they are necessary for explaining how the law enables us to understand particular features of Mendelian populations. We can see here that the significance of the H-W law extends beyond understanding the role of dominance. By defining the relation between allele frequencies and genotype frequencies it laid the foundation for modelling evolution: given certain conditions it is possible to show that a distribution of genotypes is a function solely of allele frequencies.

While the H-W law is based on rather simple mathematics (basically just multiplication and probability) the conceptual revolution it began was extended by R. A. Fisher, who introduced not only the analysis of variance but also the more abstract mathematics of diffusion theory, Markov chain models, and branching processes to achieve a unification of genetics with Darwinian evolutionary theory. While some results in modern population genetics do not require abstract mathematics, there are some that could not have been arrived at nonmathematically, such as the results in the multi-locus and the stochastic theories. Moreover, the fact that selection could operate in Mendelian populations could *only* be shown using the kind of abstraction characteristic of mathematical modelling.

INFINITE POPULATIONS: FROM STATISTICAL PHYSICS TO MATHEMATICAL BIOLOGY

Despite remarkable theoretical success, some eminent biologists and philosophers have voiced criticism about the mathematical nature of the models used in population genetics. For example, in responding to R. A. Fisher's (1918) first technical paper on the topic, a paper that marks the origin of the synthesis of Mendelism with Darwinism, the referee Reginald Punnett complained that it displayed the hallmarks of treating weightless elephants on frictionless surfaces.[13] Ernst Mayr complained in 1959 (1976) that population genetics, to the extent that it treats evolution as mere changes in gene frequency (as an input or output of genes), is like beanbag genetics involving the addition and removal of beans from a bag. Here Mayr was echoing an earlier remark made by Waddington (1957), who claimed that the mathematical theory of evolution had not led to any noteworthy quantitative statements or revealed any new type of relations or processes that could explain phenomena that were previously obscure. Mayr (1982) also remarked that one cannot really understand the workings of natural selection unless one understands the uniqueness of the individual, something that population genetics clearly ignores. Moreover, Provine (2001) has claimed that the mathematical models of the 1930s, still widely used today, are an impediment to the understanding of evolutionary biology.

13. As quoted in Norton and Pearson (1976).

As I mentioned, what motivated many of these criticisms is the view that the abstract mathematical methods of population genetics, with their emphasis on reduction and gene selection, simply ignore many of the important factors that figure in evolutionary development. They are just not explanatory in the sense that they provide us with a proper understanding of the evolutionary process. All of this seems to presuppose that the uniqueness of biological individuals must be taken account of in explanations in the way that the uniqueness of physical objects need not. Idealisation and abstraction can supposedly be informative and aid in our understanding of physical systems, but not in the case of biological populations. A closer look reveals that not only is this *not* the case, but it is difficult to see how it *could* be the case. The fact that the mathematics of population genetics has established results that were impossible using direct observation and other types of empirical methods is certainly sufficient for claiming that it has increased our understanding of evolutionary processes. As I will show, Fisher's mathematisation of selection created a new framework in which its operation was understood as an *irreducibly* statistical phenomenon, a reconceptualisation that emerges in conjunction with the application of specific *mathematical,* as opposed to purely statistical, techniques.[14]

Karl Pearson's statistical account of selection (biometry) formed the basis for much of Fisher's thinking about Darwinism. However, because the Darwinian foundations of biometry provided

14. As I have argued elsewhere (Morrison 2000, 2002), the synthesis of Mendelism and Darwinian selection was accomplished through the employment of mathematical techniques that allowed its founders (R. A. Fisher, Sewall Wright, and J. B. S. Haldane) to establish the operation of selection in Mendelian populations. To that extent, the synthesis produced an enhanced understanding of selection as something compatible rather than at odds with Mendelism. But the interesting aspect of the synthesis was that while its authors, particularly Fisher (1922) and Wright (1922, 1929), agreed on the general conclusion, each had a very different account of *how* selection functioned and the conditions under which it would be most effective.

no understanding of variation, Fisher's goal was to unite the two approaches into a consistent theory of genetical inheritance. Fisher's (1918) aim was to determine the extent to which characteristics such as stature were determined by a large number of Mendelian factors (genes). Studies had shown that in the case of brothers the correlation coefficient is around .54 (amount of variance due to ancestry), which leaves 46 percent of the variance to be accounted for in some other way. Fisher wanted to establish how much of the total variance was due to dominance, how much resulted from other environmental causes, and how much was from additive genetic effects. If one could resolve observed variance into these different fractions (that is, expressing these fractions as functions of observed correlations) then one could easily determine the extent to which nature dominated over nurture. Using the analysis of variance, Fisher not only succeeded in distinguishing between genetic and environmental variance but also between the different components of genetic variance itself (additive and dominance).

In order to perform this kind of statistical analysis, Fisher made a number of explicit assumptions that were clearly at odds with some of Pearson's (1904, 1909a and b) earlier investigations regarding a possible compatibility of Mendelism and Darwinism. Although Pearson believed that biology differed from physics in the sheer number of variables one needed to take account of in any single case of inheritance, he did think that there were certain features of a population that needed to be specified in order to arrive at a proper statistical description.[15] Perhaps the most important difference between Fisher and Pearson was Fisher's assumption of an indefinitely large number of Mendelian factors, an assumption that was not only out of the region of experiment using Mendelian methods but could

---

15. "The causes of any individual case of inheritance are far too complicated to admit of exact treatment" (Pearson 1896, 255).

not be incorporated into the methods of biometrical statistics. The mathematical difficulties arose because Pearson assumed that for each Mendelian factor one needed to know specific information such as which allelomorph was dominant and the extent to which dominance occurred. In addition, one needed to know the relative magnitudes of the effects produced by different factors, whether the factors were dimorphic or polymorphic, to what extent they were coupled, and in what proportion the allelomorphs occurred in the general population.

If these conditions were required, it is immediately obvious that an analysis involving a large number of genes was virtually impossible using biometrical techniques. In addition, there were other more general considerations that needed to be taken into account, such as the effects of homogamy (preferential mating) as opposed to random mating, and selection versus environmental effects, all of which needed to be treated separately if one was to determine the genetic basis of the inheritance of particular characteristics. Pearson thought that if one assumed an indefinite number of Mendelian factors then the nature of the population could not be specified in any complete sense, thereby undermining any statistical result that might follow. In other words, we need certain kinds of information about individuals that make up a population in order for our methodology to give us reliable results.

However, if one takes as a model the velocity distribution law in statistical physics (which Fisher did), then just as a sufficiently large number of independent molecules would exhibit a stable distribution of velocities, a sufficiently large number of Mendelian factors or genes in a population will enable one to establish general conclusions about the presence of particular traits. Contra Pearson, Fisher did not assume that different Mendelian factors were of equal importance, so all dominant genes did not have a like effect. Fisher also assumed random mating as well as the independence of the different factors and, finally, because the factors were sufficiently numerous, some small quantities could be neglected. So, not only did Fisher differ from Pearson with respect to specific assumptions about the *nature* of Mendelian factors (that all were equally important, for example), but assumptions necessary to characterise a Mendelian population were much more general. By assuming an indefinite number of factors it was possible to ignore individual peculiarities and obtain a statistical aggregate that had relatively few constants. Underwriting these results is, of course, the central limit theorem.

Once the causes of variance were determined, Fisher (1922) went on to specify the conditions under which variance could be maintained. This was especially important since in a Mendelian system loss of genetic variability would be significantly less than with blending inheritance and due only to finite population size and consequential stochastic losses. So how would the rate of loss compare with the gains through mutation under differing assumptions about selection? How would gene frequencies change under selection pressures and environmental conditions?

To answer these questions, Fisher began with a discussion of equilibrium under selection. He first demonstrated that the frequency ratio for the alleles of a Mendelian factor was a stable equilibrium only if selection favored the heterozygotes. He then showed that the survival of an individual mutant gene depended on chance rather than selection. Only when large numbers of individuals were affected would the effect of selection override random survival, and even then only a small minority of the population would be affected. To do this he introduced stochastic considerations and examined the survival of individual genes by means of a branching process analysed by functional iteration and then set up the "chain-binomial" model and analysed it by a diffusion approximation.[16] He was able

16. For more on these techniques, see Edwards (1994) and Ewens (2004).

to calculate the amount of mutation needed to maintain the variability, given a specific amount of selection, and found that to maintain variability in the case of equilibrium in the absence of selection, the rate of mutation had to be increased by a very large quantity. So, the presence of even the slightest amount of selection in large populations had considerably more influence in keeping variability in check than did random survival. Consequently, the assumption of genotypic selection balanced by occasional mutations fit the facts deduced from the correlations of relatives in humans.

By making assumptions about the large size of the population and its high degree of genetic variability, Fisher was able to demonstrate how his stochastic distributions led to the conclusion that natural selection acting on genes (rather than mutation, random extinction, epistasis, and so on) was the primary determinant in the evolutionary process. He found that mutation rates significantly higher than any observed in nature could be balanced by very small selection rates. The distribution of the frequency ratios for different factors was calculated from the assumption that the distribution was stable. The kind of statistical independence that figured prominently in the velocity distribution law was applicable to the effects of selection in Mendelian populations.

In keeping with the idealisation/abstraction distinction I have been maintaining throughout, we can see why Fisher's modelling assumptions and techniques fall into the category of mathematical abstraction. Without the requirement of an infinitely large population of genes and the mathematical techniques necessary for dealing with it in the context of other aspects of the population, Fisher would have encountered the kind of problems that Pearson envisaged using straightforward statistical analysis. In that sense, mathematical abstraction became a necessary feature for understanding basic features of Mendelian populations.

What does this analysis enable us to say about the understanding of selection that emerges from Fisher's work? The distribution of the gene ratio provides the ultimate expression of selective effects because the gene remains the only trace of the existence of an individual in a population.[17] Given that selection acts on the heritable, what is important is the mean effect of each allele. Although we cannot know the state of each of the genes in the population, we can know the statistical result of their interaction in the same way that gas laws can be deduced from a collection of particles. Selection is mass selection, taking into account only the additive effects of genes; stochastic factors can be ruled out because of population size. Selection became irreducibly statistical because: (1) it applies only at the level of large populations and is defined in terms of gene frequencies, and (2) this kind of (large) population is necessary if one's statistical methodology is to deliver objective results (that the outcome is in fact the result of selection and not an artifact of small sample size). Consequently, evolution could be understood as the modification of genetic structure, with the gene ratio constituting the real state of the species. Indeed, one can think of all observable processes of evolution as described in the language of the statistical distribution of genes. The natural population is redefined as simply an aggregate of gene ratios.[18] In that sense the processes of mathematical abstraction transformed the notion of a population into a construct capable of being analysed in a way that natural populations aren't.

17. That is, the Mendelian mechanism ensures that although a population may be said to have continued existence, the individuals that constitute it do not. The variability that passes from one generation to the next through reproduction is related to but not identical to phenotypic variability.

18. Of course not everyone subscribes to this view. Not only is it unpopular among the authors I mentioned above but there is an ongoing philosophical debate surrounding the interpretation of selection and whether it should be understood statistically or in causal terms, i.e. analogous with a force. The latter view is advocated by Sober (1984), Bouchard and Rosenberg (2004), and others, while the statistical view is championed by and originated with Walsh (2000) and Matthen and Airew (2002).

Fisher's differences with Pearson are, to be sure, ones that result from bringing Mendelism into the equation; but these differences go well beyond any dispute about the status of Mendelism as a theory of heredity. For Pearson, selection was always about the kind of individual differences that were important for Darwin; however, because we cannot have a proper science of individuals, selection has to be established by using statistical techniques to analyse the occurrence of traits in a population. Although Pearson defines selection statistically, it was still thought to function at the level of individuals.[19] But this is largely a methodological issue about what constitutes proper scientific investigation rather than a substantive matter about the way selection operates. In other words, although Pearson's account of selection became absorbed into the theory of correlation, it retained the fundamental core of the Darwinian account—that its task is to explain why individuals, understood as members of a population, have the traits they do. However, in the hands of Fisher, selection becomes *irreducibly* statistical because the mathematics used to describe it no longer facilitates an explanation of the occurrence of individual traits. Selection is now understood as a population-level phenomenon explained in terms of changing gene frequencies. In that sense, the mathematics used to formulate an account of how selection operates and the assumptions used for modelling a population determined the way selection should be understood in the context of Mendelian populations.

A good deal of Fisher's methodology, including his understanding of selection, forms the foundation of modern population genetics. There remain, however, debates about whether selection operates most effectively in the large populations, and the role that random drift (sampling error), migration, and genetic interaction play in

19. For an excellent discussion of the various issues surrounding Pearson and the development of biometry see Gayon (1998).

affecting gene frequencies. However, what is most important for the purposes of understanding heredity is that selection can now be defined in terms of changes in gene frequencies and that this reconceptualisation resulted largely from the impact of mathematical modelling in describing that process. A full discussion of the details surrounding the nature of selection would require a more in-depth study of the claims of people like Mayr who argue that the methods of population genetics provide little in the way of understanding evolutionary development. However, what I take my analysis to have shown is that this is at least prima facie incorrect. While it is true that our understanding of selection has departed from the traditional Darwinian one, it is also the case that a properly mathematical account of selection as the mechanism of evolutionary change provided the foundation for this departure.[20]

MATHEMATICAL ABSTRACTION, UNDERSTANDING, AND EXPLANATION: BACK TO THE BEGINNING

What I have tried to do in this chapter is first to highlight similarities in the use of mathematical abstraction for characterising and understanding features of physical and biological systems. Part of my purpose in telling that story has been to emphasise the point made at the outset, that what it means to understand and explain certain types of behaviour and phenomena can be different in different contexts. But what is common to each of the examples I have discussed is that the use of abstract mathematical models often defines what it means to understand and explain the phenomena in question. In keeping with that goal I also wanted to show how abstract mathematics can function in ways that go well beyond simply representing phenomena

---

20. For a longer discussion of these issues, see Morrison (2006b).

for the purposes of exact calculation and prediction. This point was made with respect not only to phase transitions in physics but also to both the H-W law and the models used by Fisher in the development of population genetics. In the case of H-W, both the abstraction and idealisation present in the law actually embody a great deal of information that allows us to understand not only how the law functions as a successful predictive device but *why* it does. Even in biological contexts, where the details of complex phenomena are thought to be important, mathematical abstraction can function as the source of concrete information about various types of behaviour.

Because much of the knowledge that we have of both physical and biological systems comes to us via abstract mathematical models, the "mediated" knowledge those models provide needs to be properly positioned in the epistemic hierarchy. To do this, one needs to recognise and properly explicate the role mathematical abstraction plays in producing explanation and understanding. To rule out mathematical representations because they rely on "nonrealistic" descriptions and principles is to render incomprehensible much of what contemporary science currently and justifiably claims to understand.

In the next chapter I want to extend this discussion to the more general point about how mathematics can provide us with 'physical' information, specifically how the *mathematical* explanation of physical phenomena can also gives us *physical* explanation. While the focus of that chapter is not on models per se, the argument is nevertheless applicable to the kinds of conclusions I have drawn about the mathematical character of models in this chapter, namely their ability to produce understanding and explanation despite their high degree of abstraction.

2

From the Pure to the Concrete

How Mathematics Yields Physical Information

MATHEMATICAL EXPLANATION AND PHYSICAL FACTS: PROBLEMS AND PROSPECTS

In the last chapter I showed how abstract mathematical models can often furnish the kind of physical information that is not available using methods of empirical investigation. In that chapter I didn't properly address the question of what actually constitutes a mathematical explanation of a physical fact. Instead I gave examples of how models of physical and biological systems that incorporated abstract mathematics could be seen to provide physical explanations and understanding via the mathematical structure. In these cases one might argue that despite the presence of a mathematical framework, the explanations we extract from the models are physical/biological because the model is really a physical or biological representation of the system under investigation. In other words, the representation is simply expressed in mathematical language, but it is the underlying conceptual or theoretical account that is doing the explaining, not the mathematics. Hence, the model is not a mathematical explanation of a physical (or biological) fact but simply a physical explanation represented mathematically. And using mathematics as a representational vehicle doesn't necessarily mean we have given a mathematical explanation. In the cases I discussed I tried to show that the fundamental features of the explanations emanated from the mathematical features that were introduced into the models to account for certain types of behaviour, behaviour that seemed inexplicable without the relevant mathematical representation. Although I see this as sufficient for claiming that the mathematics functions as the explanatory vehicle, I recognise that its embedding in the larger model leaves it vulnerable to claims of the sort mentioned above, namely, that the explanation is, at best, a combination of mathematical and physical features that cannot be neatly separated within the model itself. Consequently, what I want to show in this chapter is that stripped of any physical adornment, mathematical techniques/frameworks are capable of generating physical information in and of themselves.

A good deal of the recent literature in the philosophy of mathematics (Baker 2005, 2009; Pincock 2007, 2012; Bangu 2008; Batterman 2002, 2010; and others) has focused attention on the question of what constitutes a mathematical explanation of a physical fact. The question is important not only because much of contemporary science, especially physics, is expressed in mathematical language but also because new phenomena are sometimes predicted on the basis of mathematics alone (e.g. the π meson). In that context mathematics functions as the engine of discovery, so it becomes increasingly important to determine whether, or to what extent, mathematics can embody physical information. Mark Steiner asked the same question more than 30 years ago. At the time he answered in the following way:

> The difference between mathematical and physical explanations
> of *physical* phenomena is. . . in the former, as in the latter, physical and mathematical truths operate. But only in mathematical
> explanation is [the following] the case: when we remove the

physics, we remain with a mathematical explanation—of a mathematical truth! (Steiner 1978, 19)

Baker (2009) has criticised Steiner's characterisation, claiming that the 'mathematics' test doesn't need to be passed for mathematics to play a role in scientific explanation. In other words, we don't need to have a mathematical explanation of a mathematical fact as the basis for a physical explanation. Baker's famous example, the one often cited in the literature, centres on the life cycle of the periodical cicada, an insect whose two North American subspecies spend 13 years and 17 years, respectively, underground in larval form before emerging briefly as adults. The life cycle of these creatures has evolved into periods that correspond to prime numbers, so the obvious question is why should this be the case. The answer can be given as follows. It is a biological law that having a life-cycle period that minimises intersection with other (nearby/lower) periods is evolutionarily advantageous. It is a theorem of number theory that prime periods minimise intersection (compared to nonprime periods). "Hence organisms with periodic life cycles are likely to evolve periods that are prime" (Baker 2005, 233). This law is a mixture of biological and mathematical information, so its form will figure importantly in assessing whether the explanation is truly mathematical. There is a further ecological constraint that is crucial for the explanation: cicadas in ecosystem-type E are limited by biological constraints to periods from 14 to 18 years (ibid.). Hence, these cicadas are likely to evolve 17-year periods.

Baker takes this to be an example of an *indispensable, mathematical explanation* of a *purely physical phenomenon*; in other words the 'mathematical' aspects of the explanation are a necessary feature. He then uses this claim as the basis of an argument that one ought rationally to believe in the existence of abstract mathematical objects. Moreover, the indispensability of the mathematical features turns out not to be limited to cicadas; there are other explanations that rely on certain number theoretic results to show that prime cycles minimise overlap with other periodical organisms. Avoiding overlap is beneficial whether the other organisms are predators, or whether they are different subspecies (since mating between subspecies would produce offspring that would not be coordinated with either subspecies). The form of these explanations suggests that the mathematical form of the cicada example is more than just a coincidence.

This seems to bear all the hallmarks of a mathematical explanation of a physical phenomenon, but it is questionable whether it meets Steiner's criterion. Baker mentions (2009, 623) two lemmas that lie at the heart of the explanation.[1] The first is that the lowest common multiple of m and n is maximal if and only if m and n are coprime. The second is that a number, m, is coprime with each number $n < 2m$, $n \neq m$ if and only if m is prime. Baker claims that neither proof is particularly explanatory, but that may be, in part, because the results established by the lemmas are so basic. One needs only a brief reflection to see why they must be true. Consequently, as mathematical truths they don't provide any explanatory information regarding the cicada life cycle. And since Steiner requires that the mathematical truth is the basis for the explanation, the cicada example fails the condition. Baker takes this as evidence against Steiner's view, not only because the cicada example is clearly explanatory but also because evidence from scientific practice indicates that the internal explanatory basis of a piece of mathematics is largely irrelevant to its potential explanatory role in science.

At an intuitive level this seems right; why should we require mathematical *truths* to underpin physical facts, especially since the focus of the questions seems to be whether mathematics actually provides us with physical information. But Steiner undeniably has a

---

1. The mathematical results can be found in Baker (2005).

point here: without a mathematical truth as the explanatory foundation, can we really claim that the explanation is *purely mathematical* rather than simply a physical explanation that is couched in mathematical terms? And the cicada example seems to fit the pattern, especially since the basis for the explanation is a law that combines mathematical and biological information. Put differently, a physical explanation that is simply given in mathematical language is not necessarily a mathematical explanation of a physical fact. In the former case the mathematics simply represents elements of the physical situation that are doing explanatory work.

As I have shown, one of the motivations for the debate about mathematical explanation is the issue of mathematical realism or, more generally, the ontological status of mathematical entities. If there are genuine mathematical explanations of physical facts, this is seen as providing evidence for the reality of mathematical entities. The argument takes the form of a classic inference to the best explanation. The best explanation of the ability of mathematical entities to deliver physical information is that those entities are real as opposed to fictional representations. It is also a version of the famous 'no miracles' argument: it would be miraculous if mathematical entities were simply fictitious and at the same time able to reveal truths about the physical world. These types of arguments have been the subject of severe, and to my mind successful, criticism in philosophy of science, so I see no reason to think they can be successfully applied in philosophy of mathematics.[2]

But I want to suggest that there are other reasons besides the status of mathematical entities for thinking it important to answer the question about the nature of mathematical explanation, reasons that

---

2. Leng (2005) has argued that one can uphold the 'mathematical explanation' thesis without being a mathematical realist. On her view fictionalism about mathematical entities is completely compatible with accepting a mathematical explanation of a physical fact.

shift the focus away from the mathematical aspects of the explanation to the physical features. That is to say, instead of asking whether we have given a *mathematical* explanation of a physical fact, I want to ask whether and how mathematics, in and of itself, is capable of providing genuine *physical* information, where the latter is characterised as information about phenomena that could not (at the time) be furnished by physical hypotheses or models and emanates solely from a mathematical method or framework. So the worry isn't whether the explanation is truly mathematical but rather whether there is any genuine physical information over and above the calculation or prediction of numerical values for specific parameters or effects. The concern that accompanies this change of focus, and indeed all questions about mathematical explanation, is how to draw a genuine dividing line between the mathematics and the physics, allowing them to be successfully decoupled. Although there will often be a grey area regarding the division, there are also clear-cut cases. Hence, the question remains an important one, not just for the philosophy of mathematics but for more general issues in the philosophy of science.

The example I want to consider in addressing this question focuses on the RG methods and how, as a purely mathematical technique, RG nevertheless appears able to provide us with information about the behaviour of a system at critical point—information that is simply not available using the resources of the relevant physical theory, often SM or thermodynamics.[3] I have chosen this example because it is free from the type of ambiguities that sometimes plague the kind of theoretical/mathematical models I discussed earlier, specifically, whether the mathematics is simply the language in which physical or biological information is expressed. No such ambiguities

3. Renormalisation group methods are used in a variety of fields both within physics, especially high-energy physics, and outside physics, in fields such as economics and finance.

can arise in the context of RG because it is a straightforward mathematical technique, pure and simple. (Or maybe not so simple!)

That is not to say that models are not important but rather to stress that RG is a technique that is *applied* to specific kinds of models; it isn't part of the basic structure of the model per se. Some examples of such models include, for instance, molecules in a gas in SM where the particles move about in $\mathbf{R}^3$ or some subset thereof. There are also models in which the degrees of freedom are tied to a lattice. For a crystal structure the degrees of freedom could be the spin of an electron at each site in the crystal. The Ising model, the prototypical model for magnetic phase transitions, and percolation which was originally introduced to model fluid flow in porous materials, are models that have a discrete variable associated with each site. There are also various random walk models, including self-avoiding walks, which are meant to model polymers in solution, as well as Ising models in which there are degrees of freedom at each site in the lattice but where the variable at each site will be continuous with some symmetry. Physically, all of these models exhibit phase transitions in which an infinitesimal change in a parameter (e.g. temperature) produces a qualitative change in the system. In these types of systems RG is used to explain features of critical behaviour.

I begin with a brief discussion of what the RG is and how it is used in physics, particularly quantum field theory (QFT) and statistical physics. Although its use in these two different domains suggests a structural similarity between them, this is not where its explanatory power is most obvious. To illustrate the latter I provide a more specific account of the role of RG in treating critical point phenomena and an analysis of what, exactly, is explained using these techniques, in particular the kind of 'cooperative behaviour' associated with phase transitions. For example, how do short-range interactions between a magnetic moment and its immediate neighbor lead to a long-range ordering of the moments in a ferromagnet, an ordering that is without any external cause. Gitterman and Halpern (2004, 4) put the point very nicely when they compare the ordering in a ferromagnet to a question raised by King Solomon (Proverbs 30:27) as to why the locusts who have no king nevertheless advance together in ranks. As I will show, one of the things RG methods enable us to explain is how it is possible to obtain long-range correlations from short-range interactions.

WHAT IS THE RENORMALISATION GROUP?

The RG is, in short, a method for establishing scale invariance under a set of transformations that allows us to investigate changes in a physical system viewed at different distance scales. As I have noted, one of the most significant things about RG techniques is that they have produced an understanding of critical phenomena in statistical physics as well as features of QFT that were not possible prior to their introduction. The important question for present purposes is whether these features are physical in the sense of revealing knowledge of phenomena or are simply calculational features that allow us to complete a theoretical picture. It is tempting to think that their diverse application indicates that RG methods are a purely formal framework for solving particular types of problems. While this is certainly true, RG techniques also show deep structural similarities between these various domains. To get a sense of the difference between what we learn from these structural similarities and the physical information concerning cooperative behaviour in statistical physics, let me first look briefly at the relation between the different uses of RG and what exactly each tells us.

The first systematic use of the RG in QFT was by Gell-Mann and Low (1954). As a consequence of their approach it was found that quantum electrodynamics (QED) could exhibit a simple scaling behaviour at small distances. In other words, QFT has a scale invariance that is broken by particle masses; but these masses are negligible at high energies or short distances provided one renormalises in the appropriate way. In statistical physics Kadanoff (1966) developed the basis for an application of RG to thermodynamic systems near critical point, a picture that also led to certain scaling equations for the correlation functions used in the statistical description. That method was refined and extended by Wilson (1971) into what is the contemporary real-space approach to RG.[4] If we think about these two very different applications of RG, which involve, in some sense, different methods, then two issues arise. First, does each different application of RG furnish different physical information relative to the context of use, and second, does their use reveal any similarities regarding these two seemingly diverse types of systems?

Initially one can think of QFT and statistical physics as having similar kinds of peculiarities that give rise to certain types of problems, for example many degrees of freedom, fluctuations, and diverse spatial and temporal scales. The RG framework is significant in its ability to link physical behaviour across different scales and in cases where fluctuations on many different scales interact. Hence it is crucial for treating asymptotic behaviour at very high or (in massless theories) very low energies (even where the coupling constants at the relevant scale are too large for perturbation theory). In QFT when bare couplings and fields are replaced with renormalised ones defined at a characteristic energy scale μ, the integrals over virtual momenta will be cut off at energy and momentum scales of order μ. As we change μ we are in effect changing the scope of the degrees of freedom in the calculations. So, to avoid large logarithms, take μ to be

---

4. There are essentially two types of RG: the real-space approach developed by Kadanoff, Wilson, and others that is applied to discrete systems on a lattice in physical or real space, and the k-space approach, which is field-theoretic RG and is applied to continuous systems, with the analysis being done in momentum (or Fourier) space.

the order of the energy E that is relevant to the process under investigation. In other words, the problem is broken down into a sequence of subproblems with each one involving only a few length scales. Each one has a characteristic length, and you get rid of the degrees of freedom you don't need.

In the Kadanoff version, reducing the degrees of freedom gives you a sequence of corresponding Hamiltonians that can be pictured as a trajectory in a space spanned by the system parameters (temperature, external fields, and coupling constants). So the RG gives us a transformation that looks like this:

$$H' = R[H]$$

where H is the original Hamiltonian with N degrees of freedom and H' the transformed one. A wide choice of operators R is possible. The initial version, the Gell-Mann/Low (G-M/L) formulation, involved the momentum-space approach and hinged on the degree of arbitrariness in the renormalisation procedure. They essentially reformulated and renormalised perturbation theory in terms of a cutoff-dependent coupling constant e (Λ). For example, e, measured in classical experiments is a property of the very long-distance behaviour of QED, whereas the natural scale is the Compton wavelength of the electron, which is roughly 2×10^{-12} meters. G-M/L showed that a family of alternative parameters e_λ could be introduced, any one of which could be used in place of e. The parameter e_λ is related to the behaviour of QED at an arbitrary momentum scale λ instead of the low momenta for which e is appropriate. In other words, you can change the renormalisation point freely in a QFT and the physics won't be affected. Introducing a sliding renormalisation scale effectively suppresses the low-energy degrees of freedom.

The real-space approach is linked to the Wilson-Kadanoff method. Kadanoff's account of scaling relations involved a lattice of interacting spins (e.g. ferromagnetic transition) and transformations from a site lattice with the Hamiltonian $H_a(S)$ to a block lattice with Hamiltonian $H_{2a}(S)$. Each block is considered a new basic entity. One then calculates the effective interactions between them and in this way constructs a family of corresponding Hamiltonians. If one starts from a model of lattice size a one would sum over degrees of freedom at size a while maintaining their average on the sublattice of size $2a$ fixed. Starting from a Hamiltonian $H_a(S)$ on the initial lattice one can generate an effective Hamiltonian $H_{2a}(S)$ on the lattice of double spacing. This transformation is repeated as long as the lattice spacing remains small compared to the correlation length, which is the distance over which the fluctuations of one microscopic variable are associated with another. The key idea is that the transition from $H_a(S)$ to $H_{2a}(S)$ can be regarded as a rule for obtaining the parameters of $H_{2a}(S)$ from those of $H_a(S)$. The process can be repeated with the lattice of small blocks being treated as a site lattice for a lattice of larger blocks. So from a lattice that looks like figure 2.1a, we get one that looks like figure 2.2b. This technique is important for statistical physics because the goal is to reduce the amount of information required to describe a system, going from a micro state of roughly 10^{23} numbers (individual position and momenta of all molecules) to five or six (pressure, density, temperature, etc.). The coarse graining provides the bridge between the two states in the operation, the micro to the macro, and also between each state in between, where an exact distribution is replaced with the most probable one. Once the description of the system is coarse grained, the basic variables are rescaled in an attempt to restore the original picture.

Close to critical point the correlation length far exceeds the lattice constant a, which is the difference between neighbouring spins. What this means is that distance points become correlated, and long-range behaviour (as opposed to short-range correlations) begins to dominate, resulting in the kind of cooperative behaviour I mentioned earlier. In other words, fluctuations of microscopic variables are correlated

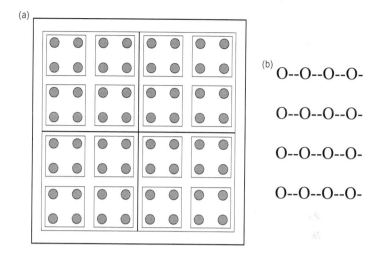

Figure 2.1: The initial lattice (a) and (b) the result of the coarse-graining process. (Source: (a) Courtesy of Javier Rodríguez Laguna at http://commons.wikimedia.org/wiki/File:Rgkadanoff.png)

with each other over large distances. As we move from small to larger block lattices we gradually exclude the small-scale degrees of freedom by averaging out through a process of coarse graining. So, for each new block lattice, one has to construct effective interactions and find their connection with the interactions of the previous lattice. What Wilson (1971) did was show how the coupling constants at different length scales could be computed—how to estimate values for critical exponents (e.g. critical temperature) that describe the behaviour of physical quantities near continuous phase transitions. This, in turn, enables us to understand universality, the fact that phenomena as different as fluids and magnets exhibit the same type of behaviour near critical point— they exhibit the same values for critical exponents.[5]

5. I will have more to say about this later in the discussion of SM; here it is sufficient to point out that universality can be seen to follow from the iterative nature of the RG process

Initially these different ways of using RG seem to suggest that one is doing very different things; in the context of critical phenomena one is interested only in long-distance rather than short-distance behaviour. In the case of QFT the renormalisation scheme is used to provide an ultraviolet cutoff, while in critical behaviour the very short wave numbers are integrated out. Moreover, why should scale invariance of the sort found in QFT be important in the context of SM? To answer these questions we can think of the similarities in the following way. In the Wilson-Kadanoff version the grouping together of the variables referring to different degrees of freedom induces a transformation of the statistical ensemble describing the thermodynamic system. Or one can argue in terms of a transformation in the space of Hamiltonians. Regardless of the notation, what we are interested in is the successive applications of the transformation that allows us to probe the system over large distances. In the field-theoretic case we don't change the 'statistical ensemble,' but the stochastic variables do undergo a local transformation whereby one can probe the region of large values of the fluctuating variables. Using the RG equations, one can take this to be formally equivalent to an analysis of the system over large distances.

This formal similarity also provides some clues to why RG can be successfully applied to such diverse phenomena. But to fully appreciate this we need to look more closely at what exactly the RG method does. In statistical physics we distinguish between two phases by defining an order parameter, which has a non-zero value in the ordered phase and zero in the disordered phase (high temperature). For example, in a ferromagnetic transition the order parameter is homogenous magnetisation. A nonzero value for the order parameter corresponds to symmetry breaking (here, rotational

(i.e., universal properties follow from the limiting behaviour of such iterative processes). Zinn-Justin (1998) discusses some of the connections between the use of RG in statistical physics and QFT.

symmetry).[6] In the disordered state the spin at a given point is influenced mainly by the nearby random spins on the adjacent points, so the correlation length is small. When a phase transition is approached the system becomes prepared for an ordered state, so the ordering must spread out to a larger region. In other words, in the vicinity of a phase transition a system has fluctuations that are correlated over large distances, so the correlation length ξ increases as $T \rightarrow Tc$ (provided all other parameters are fixed). If the correlation length diverges at Tc then the long-range fluctuations become completely dominant, wiping out the microscopic (small-scale) interactions. The result is that we are left without a characteristic length scale because all lengths are equally important. Reducing the number of degrees of freedom with RG amounts to establishing a correspondence between one problem with a given correlation length and another whose length is smaller by a certain factor. So we get a very concrete method (hence real-space renormalisation) for reducing degrees of freedom.

In cases of relativistic quantum field theories like QED, the theory works well for the electron because at long distances there is simply not enough energy to observe the behaviour of other charged particles; that is, they are present only at distances that are very small compared to the electron's Compton wavelength. By choosing the appropriate renormalisation scale the logarithms that appear in perturbation theory will be minimised because all the momenta will be of the order of the chosen scale. In other words, one introduces an upper limit Λ on the allowed momentum equivalent to a microscopic-length scale $h / 2\pi \Lambda c$. We can think of a change in each of these scales as analogous to a phase transition where the different phases depend on the values of the parameters, with the RG allowing us to connect each of these different scales. So, regardless of whether

---

6. In liquid-gas transition, the order parameter is defined in terms of difference in density.

you're integrating out very short wave numbers or using RG to provide an ultraviolet cutoff, the effect is the same, in that you're getting the right degrees of freedom for the problem at hand. Hence, because the *formal nature* of the problems is similar in these two domains, one can see why the RG method is so successful in dealing with different phenomena. In the momentum-space or field theory approach we can think of the high-momentum variables as corresponding to short-range fluctuations integrated out. And in the Wilson-Kadanoff version the reciprocal of a (the lattice constant representing the difference between neighbouring spins) acts as a cutoff parameter for large momenta, that is, it eliminates short wave length fluctuations with wave numbers close to the cutoff parameter.[7]

In that sense one can think of gauge theories characteristic of QFT as exhibiting different phases depending on the value of the parameters. Each phase is associated with a symmetry breaking, in the same way that phase change in statistical physics is associated with the order parameter. In statistical physics nature presents us with a microscopic-length scale. Cooperative phenomena near a critical point create a correlation length, and in the limit of the critical point the ratio of these two lengths tends to ∞. In QFT we introduce an upper limit Λ on the allowed momentum defined in terms of a microscopic length scale $h \,/\, 2\pi \Lambda c$. The real physics is recovered in the limit in which the artificial scale is small compared to the Compton wavelength of the relevant particles. In that sense all relativistic QFTs describe critical points with associated fluctuations on arbitrarily many length scales.[8] Consequently we can think of the theoretical framework in QFT and condensed matter physics as exhibiting a kind of *generic structure* for these systems; a structure that is made more explicit as a result of the application of RG techniques.

---

7. Here I follow Weinberg (1983). See his article for an excellent discussion of these issues.
8. See Weinberg (1983).

However, as we know from the philosophical debates surrounding structural realism, the notion of 'same structure' is notoriously difficult to flesh out when it comes to discussing physical theories and ontology, as is the notion of 'structure' generally.[9] Although the systems described above can be thought of as having structural similarities in the theoretical and even in the physical sense, such claims are not unproblematic, and it is sometimes claimed that RG only exposes a formal analogy between the two domains.[10] To argue in detail for a physical interpretation of the similarities in structure would require an independent chapter; moreover, it is not necessary in order to illustrate my general claim regarding the explanatory power of RG. So, in order to show that RG provides us with genuine physical information, we need to look more closely at its application in SM, expanding on some of the details mentioned above.

An important point to keep in mind when considering the issue of explanation is that although universal behaviour was observed experimentally, it lacked a theoretical foundation prior to the introduction of RG. The problem is that near critical point systems depend on two different length scales, the microscopic scale given by atoms or lattice spacing and the dynamically generated scale given by the correlation length that characterises macro phenomena. In many classical systems one can simply decouple these different scales and describe the physics by effective macroscopic parameters without reference to the microscopic degrees of freedom. In SM this approach became known as mean field theory (MFT) (Landau, 1937) and assumes that the correlations between stochastic variables at the micro scale could be treated perturbatively with the macro expectation values given by quasi-Gaussian distributions in the spirit of the central limit theorem.

9. See, for example, French and Ladyman (2003); Ladyman (2002); Psillos (2001, 2006); van Fraassen (2006, 2007).
10. Fraser, unpublished manuscript.

Mean field theory predicted a universality of the singular behaviour of thermodynamic quantities at Tc, meaning that they diverged in exactly the same way. It assumed these properties were independent of the dimension of space, the symmetry of the system, and the microphysical dynamics. However, it soon became apparent that experimental and theoretical evidence contradicted MFT (e.g. Onsanger's 1949 exact solution to the 2-Dimensional Ising model). Instead critical behaviour was found to depend not only on spatial dimensions, but on symmetries and some general features of the models. The fundamental difficulty with MFT stems from the very problem it was designed to treat—criticality. The divergences at Tc were an indication that an infinite number of stochastic degrees of freedom are in some sense relevant to what happens at the macro level, but these fluctuations on all length scales would add up to contradict the predictions of MFT.

This is unlike the typical case where physical systems have an intrinsic scale or where other relevant scales of the problem are of the same order. In these contexts phenomena occurring at different scales are almost completely suppressed, with no need for any type of renormalisation. Such is the case with planetary motion; it is possible to suppress, to a very good approximation, the existence of other stars and replace the size of the sun and planets by point-like objects. And in nonrelativistic quantum mechanics (QM) we can ignore the internal structure of the proton when calculating energy levels for the hydrogen atom. However, in MFT we have exactly the opposite situation; divergences appear when one tries to decouple different length scales. The divergence of ξ makes it impossible to assume that a system of size L is homogenous at any length scale $l \ll L$, and because ξ also represents the size of the microscopic inhomogeneities in the system, its divergence prevents the statistical fluctuations from being treated perturbatively. Hence the impossibility of using statistical averaging techniques for these types of systems.

This failure of MFT is interesting from the point of view of generic explanations. Because the statistical averaging procedures cannot accommodate the way inhomogeneities in the microscopic distributions contribute to large-scale cooperative behaviour, the task was to explain how short-range physical couplings could generate this type of behaviour at the macro level and how to predict it. What the situation seemed to imply was that it wasn't the values of specific physical quantities that were relevant but rather the features of their dependence with respect to the size N of the system and the control parameters K^{11}. In other words, the way micro features cooperated to produce universal behaviour was the object of explanation, a general feature that could be separated from more specific aspects of the microscopic dynamics. By determining, in a recursive manner, the effective interactions at a given scale and their relation to those at neighbouring scales, RG methods provided a solution to such problems.

FROM MATHEMATICS TO PHYSICAL PHENOMENA: RENORMALISATION GROUP AND STATISTICAL MECHANICS

The question of whether RG can indeed provide physical explanations involves two problematic issues. The first is the more straightforward of the two and is simply the question of whether RG is really just a calculational device, with the information it provides resulting simply from its ability to furnish values for specific parameters. The second is the more controversial of the two, one that has received a good deal of attention in the literature and an issue that I briefly

11. A control parameter is one that appears in the governing equations of a system and measures the effects of an exterior influence such as temperature, pressure, field intensity, etc.

discussed in chapter 1. It concerns the role of the thermodynamic limit when using RG to gain information about critical point behaviour.[12] As I showed in chapter 1, theory tells us that phase transitions only occur at the thermodynamic limit where the number of particles N goes to infinity, N $\rightarrow$ ∞. But of course we know that phase transitions occur in real systems where the number of particles is finite. So how can we reconcile the idealisation about N $\rightarrow$ ∞ with the fact that RG gives us concrete physical information about phase transitions? Just to clarify, the culprit here isn't RG methods but the assumption about infinite systems that forms the theoretical basis of the application. In what follows I show why RG methods do not fall prey to either difficulty and how, in fact, they clarify a substantive role for the thermodynamic limit.

In his discussion of asymptotic behaviour and its connection to universal phenomena, Batterman (2002, 38) claims that the RG arguments provide an explanation of stability by showing us *why* different phenomena can exhibit the same behaviour. The RG transformation shows us how to eliminate degrees of freedom that are irrelevant and hence provides a method for "extracting just those features. . . that are stable under perturbation of their microscopic details" (38).[13] However, Batterman goes on to claim that RG arguments are not epistemic; instead what they do provide is a *justification* for ignoring certain details and a procedure for doing it effectively. While I agree with much of Batterman's assessment, clarifying the explanatory role

---

12. Bangu (2009); Earman (2004); Callender (2001). Although one might want to argue that these two issues are related in that they are both calculational issues, the problems surrounding the thermodynamic limit itself are independent of RG. However, the use of RG in SM requires the assumption of the thermodynamic limit in order to deal with critical point phenomena.

13. In other words, the existence of structurally stable scaling solutions reflects the fact that the behaviour in the asymptotic regime has stabilised, allowing us to infer that there are genuine physical effects present and allowing us to ignore most of the micro details that are irrelevant for understanding, explaining, or predicting this behaviour.

of RG methods requires that they enjoy a more robust epistemic status. Part of their importance is not just that they show that we can focus on the energies or levels we are interested in, leaving out the rest, as we sometimes do in idealisation and model building, but also, more important, that they illustrate and explain the ontological and epistemic independence between different energy levels, something that is crucial for understanding universality.

Physics in the borderlands. Phase transitions occur in a variety of different kinds of systems/substances and under many different conditions, such as wide temperature ranges (ferromagnetic at 1000 Kelvin and Bose-Einstein condensation at 10^{-7} Kelvin). One of the interesting features of phase transitions is that thermodynamic functions become singular at the transition point and the effects of this singularity are exhibited over the entire spatial extent of the system. These singularities are required for a theoretical account of critical phenomena and give us information about the system that might not otherwise be apparent. Gitterman and Halpern (2004) describe the situation as analogous to that of observing a poor man who suddenly wins a multimillion-dollar lottery, a context that can show much more about his real character than one might deduce from his everyday behaviour.

The occurrence of a phase transition in an infinite system (infinite particles, volume, or sometimes strong interactions) involves a variation over a vast range of length scales. I have shown that from a mathematical perspective we can think of RG as a technique that allows one to investigate the changes to a physical system viewed at different distance scales. This is related to a scale invariance symmetry that enables us to see how and why the system appears the same at all scales (self-similarity). The discontinuities that often accompany phase changes in matter (i.e. magnetisation in a ferromagnet) vanish at critical point, so for temperatures above Tc the magnetisation is 0. I have also noted that a nonzero value for the order parameter is typically associated with this symmetry breaking, hence the symmetry of the phase transition is reflected in the order parameter (e.g., a vector representing rotational symmetry in the magnetic case and a complex number representing the Cooper pair wavefunction in superconductivity).[14]

One of the effects of the singular behaviour and the variation over a large range of length scales is how various physical quantities follow the changes in scale. In RG calculations these changes result from the multiplication of several small steps to produce a large change in length scale l. The physical phenomena that reflect this symmetry or scale transformation are expressed in terms of observed quantities—mathematical representations of the symmetry operation. For example, quantities that obey rotational symmetry are described by vectors, scalars, and so on, and in the case of scale transformations power laws reflect the symmetries in the multiplication operations. The physical quantities behave as powers l^x where x can be rational, irrational, positive, and so on. Behaviour near critical point is described using power laws where some critical property is written as a power of a quantity that might become very large or small.[15] The behaviour of the order parameter, the correlation length, and the correlation function are all associated with power laws, where the "power" refers to the critical exponent or index of the system. Diverse systems (liquid and magnets) with the same critical exponents exhibit the same scaling behaviour as they approach critical point. In that sense they can be shown via RG to

---

14. In other words, when symmetry is broken, one needs to introduce one or more variables to describe the state of the system.
15. A power law is essentially a functional relationship between two quantities, where one quantity varies as a power of another. Power-law relations are sometimes an indication of particular mechanisms underlying phenomena that serve to connect them with other phenomena that appear unrelated (universality). Some examples of power laws include the Gutenberg-Richter law for earthquakes, Pareto's law of income distribution, and scaling laws in biological systems.

share the same dynamical behaviour and hence belong to the same universality class.

The correlation function $\Gamma\ (r)$ measures how the value of the order parameter at one point is correlated to its value at some other point. If Γ decreases very fast with distance, then faraway points are relatively uncorrelated, and the system is dominated by its microscopic structure and short-ranged forces. A slow decrease of Γ implies that faraway points have a large degree of correlation or influence on each other and the system thus becomes organised at a macroscopic level. Usually, near the critical point $(T \rightarrow T_c)$, the correlation function can be written in the form

$$\Gamma(r) \rightarrow r^{-p} \exp(-r/\xi)$$

where ξ is the correlation length. This is a measure of the range over which fluctuations in one region of space are correlated with or influence those in another region. Two points separated by a distance larger than the correlation length will each have fluctuations that are relatively independent. Experimentally, the correlation length is found to diverge at the critical point, which means that distant points become correlated and long-wavelength fluctuations dominate. The system 'loses memory' of its microscopic structure and begins to display new long-range macroscopic correlations.

This 'memory loss' is significant for our story because it is part of the explanatory power of RG in illustrating the relation between the micro and macro levels of different systems. This is represented or achieved theoretically via the mathematics of RG. The iterative procedure associated with RG results in the system's Hamiltonian becoming more and more insensitive to what happens on smaller length scales. As the length scale changes, so do the values of the different parameters describing the system. Each transformation increases the size of the length scale so that the transformation eventually extends to information about the parts of the system that are infinitely far away. Hence, the infinite spatial extent of the system becomes part of the calculation, and this behaviour at the far reaches of the system determines the thermodynamic singularities included in the calculation. The change in the parameters is implemented by a beta function

$$\left\{\tilde{J}_k\right\} = \beta\left(\left\{J_k\right\}\right)$$

which induces what is known as an RG flow on the J-space. The values of J under the flow are called running coupling constants. The phase transition is identified as the place where the RG transformations bring the couplings to a fixed point, with further iterations producing no changes in either the couplings or the correlation length. The fixed points give the possible macroscopic states of the system at a large scale. So, although the correlation length diverges at critical point, using the RG equations reduces the degrees of freedom, which, in effect, reduces the correlation length.

The important point that distinguishes RG from previous renormalisation methods used in the 1940s to rid QED of infinities is that the number and type of relevant parameters is determined by the *outcome* of the renormalisation calculation.[16] After a sufficient number of successive renormalisations, all the irrelevant combinations have effectively disappeared, leaving a unique fixed point independent of the value of all the irrelevant couplings. Assuming that a fixed point is reached, one can find the value that defines the critical temperature, and the series expansions near the critical point provide the values of the critical indices.[17] The fixed point is identified with the critical

16. In earlier versions parameters like mass, charge, etc., were specified at the beginning, and the change in length scale simply changed the values from the bare values appearing in the basic Hamiltonian to renormalised values. The old renormalisation theory was a technique used to rid quantum electrodynamics of divergences but involved no "physics."

17. The equivalence of power laws with a particular scaling exponent can have a deeper origin in the dynamical processes that generate the power-law relation. Phase transitions in

point of a phase transition, and its properties determine the critical exponents. The latter characterise the fluctuations at the critical point, with the same fixed-point interactions describing a number of different types of systems. In that sense RG methods provide us with physical information concerning how and why different systems exhibit the same behaviour near critical point.

For full understanding of how the fixed points become the focal point for explanation, it is important to stress that the basis of the idea of universality is that the fixed points are a property of *transformations* that are not particularly sensitive to the original Hamiltonian. What the fixed points do is determine the kinds of cooperative behaviour that are possible, with each type defining a universality class. The important issue here isn't just the elimination of irrelevant degrees of freedom; rather, it is the existence of cooperative behaviour and the nature of the order parameter (associated with the symmetry breaking) that characterises the different kinds of systems or universality classes. As I have noted, the coincidence of the critical indices in very different phenomena was inexplicable prior to RG methods, so part of its success was showing that the differences were related to irrelevant observables—those that are "forgotten" as the scaling process is iterated. But the other significant feature of RG is that it showed how, in the long wavelength/large space-scale limit, the scaling process in fact *leads* to a fixed point when the system is at a critical point, with very different microscopic structures giving rise to the same long-range behaviour. What this means is that RG equations illustrate that phenomena at critical point have an underlying order. Indeed what makes the behaviour of critical point phenomena predictable,

thermodynamic systems are associated with the emergence of power-law distributions of certain quantities, whose exponents are referred to as the critical exponents of the system. Diverse systems with the same critical exponents—those that display identical scaling behaviour as they approach criticality—can be shown, via RG theory, to share the same fundamental dynamics.

even in a limited way, is the existence of certain scaling properties that exhibit 'universal' behaviour and that the different kinds of transitions, such as liquid gas, magnetic, alloy, and so on, share the same critical exponents experimentally and can be understood in terms of the same fixed-point interaction.

Understanding how the RG explains the behaviour of phenomena at critical point allows us to also see how it furnishes a *physical* understanding of the relation between the dynamics of the system and assumptions about T → ∞. It shows us how phase transitions are connected not only to symmetry operations that are part of the microscopic features of the system (as in the case of spin directions in a ferromagnet) but also to the topology of an infinite spatial region, and why the latter and its relation to the correlation of distant points is crucial for determining, within the RG calculations, that a phase transition has taken place.

In essence, then, RG methods not only provide us with physical understanding of the behaviour of certain kinds of systems insofar as they explain how the cooperative macro behaviour emerges from the micro level, they explain the foundation for universality by showing how that behaviour is related to the existence of fixed points. In connection with this, RG also illustrates the nature of the ontological relation between macro behaviour and microphysical constituents. The nature of this ontological independence is demonstrated by showing (1) how systems with completely different microstructures exhibit the same behaviour, (2) how successive transformations give you a Hamiltonian for an ensemble that contains very different couplings from those that governed the initial ensemble, and (3) the importance of the physics behind the notion of an infinite spatial extension for establishing long-range order.

Part of the physics behind an RG transformation is in the reduction of the correlation length. Mostly physical systems have an intrinsic length scale with phenomena at different scales being suppressed.

Infinities appear when one ignores length scales where relevant physical laws might be different. Prior to the introduction of RG techniques it appeared that one had to take account of infinitely many degrees of freedom. What RG showed was that of the infinitely many couplings required to encode the dynamics of infinitely many degrees of freedom, only a few are finally relevant. Summing recursively over short-distance degrees of freedom gives a sequence of Hamiltonians with the same large-distance properties.

Perhaps the most important feature of RG, and one that I mentioned at the beginning of this chapter, is that part of its explanatory power lies in the structural features associated with its implementation. An application of RG methods involves transferring the problem from a study of a particular system S to a study of scale transformations such that the results depend only on the scaling properties. What that requires is a shift away from the phase space of the system to a space of models or Hamiltonians. The transformations take place within this functional space, with each element corresponding to a physical system with some fixed value of the control parameter(s) K. Rather than studying the equilibrium state of S within a specified model (computing the value of state functions and variations with respect to variables and parameters) the focus is on the *transformation* of the model and its parameters in connection with a change in scale of the description of S. This allows for the calculation of quantitative and universal results from properties of the renormalisation flow. It enables us to see the shift away from methods used in SM that are grounded in probability theory and toward a more structurally based approach to dealing with large-scale features of phenomena.

This process also helps to highlight the deep statistical nature of critical universality, specifically the importance of distinguishing between physical couplings at the micro scale and the statistical correlations between these couplings. In other words, the essential feature in explaining the behaviour of critical phenomena is not the physical couplings themselves but the statistical coupling of these couplings (Lesne 1998). As Lesne (1998) points out, we can see how these are importantly different by considering the range λ of the direct physical couplings between elementary constituents compared with the range ξ of statistical correlations. In the Ising model λ, the lattice parameter, is the distance a separating the nearest neighbour spins on the lattice. It is a physical quantity that depends on the value and doesn't determine the critical behaviour of the system. By contrast, ξ diverges at Tc in the Ising model; it is always greater than λ and is a global statistical characteristic. In other words, a statistical organisation of the constituents and their statistical couplings is present on every scale from λ to ξ. More important, any elementary subsystems separated by any length l between λ and ξ will have correlated statistical distributions whether or not they have any physical interaction. What this means is that the only characteristic scale of the global behaviour of the system is the correlation length ξ; λ (the microscopic scale) plays no role. When a large number of degrees of freedom exhibit collective, cooperative behaviour, it is the statistical characteristics that determine the corresponding macroscopic critical behaviour.[18]

The mathematical foundation of these types of structural transformations comes from dynamical systems theory, which deals with changes under transformations and flows toward fixed points. Instead of deriving exact single solutions for a particular model, the emphasis is on the geometrical and topological structure of ensembles of solutions. A further explication of these aspects of RG methods allows us to appreciate the generic structural approach to explanation that RG provides. By focusing on large-scale structural behaviour we are

---

18. In addition to deriving the central limit theorem using RG techniques, the probabilistic approach to understanding critical behaviour involves deriving scaling properties as universal consequences of collective behaviour. The exponents are then related to the statistical properties of the configurations.

able to see how RG techniques furnish an understanding of complex behaviour that extends beyond calculating values for critical indices.[19]

EXPLANATION VERSUS CALCULATION: WHAT PHYSICAL INFORMATION IS GIVEN BY RG?

In the foregoing discussion I have tried to show how RG techniques provide us with physical information about certain kinds of systems. Whether RG is a mathematical explanation of a physical fact depends, in part, on how one categorises mathematical explanation and also what one considers 'physical' information to be. As I have noted, Steiner has a rather stringent criterion for the former; once the physics is stripped away, there must be a mathematical explanation of a mathematical truth in order for it to qualify as a mathematical explanation. Given the pervasive role of mathematics in physics and the foregoing discussion, the Steiner criterion perhaps sets the standard too high. What type of mathematical truth could be associated with the use of RG in the situations I have discussed? One possible candidate is symmetry and scale invariance, but rather than trying to argue that position, I would like to reconsider exactly what role the RG has played in statistical physics that enables it to qualify as a mathematical explanation of a physical fact. In doing so, perhaps I can relax Steiner's criterion and refine the question in the following way: how does the calculational power of RG produce physical understanding?

To answer that question, we need to ask what needed explanation in statistical physics prior to the introduction of RG methods. Earlier I briefly discussed the problems with MFT that rendered universality inexplicable. This was also especially puzzling and problematic from

19. For more on this point see Morrison, forthcoming.

an experimental perspective since there was absolutely no reason to think that systems with radically different microstructures could or should behave in a similar fashion. The calculational power of RG showed *how* the coupling constants at different length scales could be computed; *how* critical components could be estimated; and finally, that universality followed, in a sense, from the fact that the process can be iterated. In other words, universal properties follow from the limiting behaviour of such iterative processes. The RG explanation appealed not only to the fact that these systems shared the same critical indices but to the fact that when the system reached a fixed point, the microstructure was essentially washed out. This made it possible to understand how materials with radically different microstructures could behave in the same way.

In addition, RG provided a physical explanation of why decoupling of scales was unsuccessful in accounting for critical phenomena: divergences resulted from ignoring scales that had relevant physical laws. Reducing the correlation length by eliminating irrelevant degrees of freedom gives us a physical basis for explaining why only certain variables are important in accounting for universal phenomena. Finally, RG provided information about the thermodynamic limit and its role in accounting for cooperative behaviour (long-distance correlations that extend to the infinite spatial regions of the system). The thermodynamic limit was not simply a way of introducing singularities into otherwise smooth functions. Instead the RG explanation went beyond taking the thermodynamic limit as a calculational device to explain how the dynamical features of universal behaviour arise and how the micro features of the system are related to its infinite spatial extension across all length scales. It encodes the relation between the microscopic features of the system and the macroscopic in the sense that the iteration of the scaling operation represents how one moves from the very small to $N \to \infty$. Hence, RG gives us a physical understanding of how phase transitions are connected with symmetry of microscopic couplings (spin direc-tions in ferromagnetism) but also with the extended topology of the system.

At the foundation of this is the physical meaning associated with the correlation length ξ. If we force a particular spin to be aligned in some specific direction then ξ measures the distance from that spin to the other spins that tend to be aligned in that direction. In a disordered state, the spin at a given point is influenced mainly by the nearly random spins on the adjacent points, so the correlation length is small. As the system approaches a phase transition it pre-pares for an ordered state, which means that the order reflected in the correlation length must extend to farther and farther distances, that is, the correlation length has to increase. The divergence in the equation describing the free energy means that at critical point the correlation function cannot decrease exponentially with distance r but must decay as an inverse point of r. This implies that near critical point, there is no small energy parameter, because the critical tem-perature is the same order of magnitude as the interaction energy. Similarly, there is no typical length scale due to the divergence, mak-ing all length scales equally important and the problem very com-plex. Although I discussed this feature earlier in the chapter, I didn't mention the physical aspects of how one obtains long-range correla-tions from short-range interactions. Mathematically the question is how an exponentially decaying correlation can transfer the mutual influence on different atoms located far away from each other.

A nice answer to this question was given by Stanley (1999), who pointed out that although the correlations between two particles sit-uated at a long distance from each other do decay exponentially, the number of paths between them, along which the correlations occur, increase exponentially. As a result, the exponents in the two expo-nential functions (positive and negative) compensate each other at critical point, which leads to long-range power law correlations. In other words, the interdependencies give rise not to exponential functions, but rather to the power laws characteristic of critical phenomena. We can understand the infinite range propagation as arising from the multiplicity of interaction paths that connect two spins.

We can see then that the calculational power and explanatory power of RG are intimately connected. The explanations of these phenomena cannot be recovered from the framework of SM, where you start with a statistical ensemble defined by a Hamiltonian and use it to calculate an average. What is unique about RG is that we start with an ensemble and generate another ensemble. Hence it provides us with a new way not only to calculate but to understand the critical phenomena and their associated behaviour. Although the calculational and explanatory aspects of RG are intimately linked, this does not detract from my claim, since it is largely in virtue of the calculational power of RG that the physical explanations emerge.

What I hope to have illustrated in this chapter is that RG methods do indeed provide us with a mathematical explanation that furnishes physical understanding, an understanding that is not achievable using physical theory alone. Although RG allows us to derive effective laws for long-distance behaviour from the short-distance ones, the "integrating out" or the "flow" is irreversible—which is exactly why the RG operations constitute a "semigroup" rather than a "group." Hence, there are no corresponding symmetries and objects such as the 'action' associated with RG, since the action cannot be symmetric under semigroups.

The RG clearly shows what would happen if the would-be symmetry transformations were irreversible. Irreversibility always means that some information is getting lost, so the contributions to the action from the degrees of freedom whose information is lost are inevitably being suppressed; as a result, that action cannot remain constant. If one "flows" to long distances via the RG flows, the shortest distance degrees of freedom are "integrated out," which means that they cannot be excited in the new effective theory. So the operation cannot provide us with a one-to-one map for all states, a necessary condition for the existence of a symmetry. Consequently, symmetries must have groups and not just semigroups. I mention this point because as a mathematical explanation RG has a peculiar status in that its underlying structure cannot be associated with anything physical. However, as a mathematical *method* it surely yields physical explanations; and because of its independence from any specific theory, that explanatory power can only be a product of its mathematical power.

The goal in this and chapter 1 was to answer a question that has plagued a good deal of the philosophical discussion of modelling in science: how can we get physical explanatory knowledge from abstract models? The abstraction that is often referred to in this context is the result of using specific types of mathematical techniques or idealisations to represent, explain, and predict physical events or behaviours. In attempting to answer the question I have tried to show how mathematics can be physically informative. This is true not only in modelling contexts but also in the use of laws and other applications of mathematics such as RG methods. The "modelling" question is simply an instantiation of the more general issue of the role of mathematics in science. As such, the answer(s) depend not on a general feature of models but on the specific ways that mathematics is used to reconstruct and understand the physical world.

The next three chapters address three different problems that arise in the context of modelling, problems that relate specifically to how the information contained in models should be interpreted. The problems include the role of inconsistent models used in the context of a single problem, the role fictional models play in the transmission of information, and finally, how we should think about the representational features of models in the absence of a philosophical theory of representation. Representation, like explanation, is one of the problematic issues in philosophy of science. And, like explanation, it seems to defy definition. Although there are a variety of features one can associate with representation, to attempt a general theory capable of applying across a number of diverse types of models and theories seems an overly ambitious task and one that is surely destined for failure in the face of counter-examples. That said, the absence of a general theory of representation needn't prevent us from looking at specific ways that models are used to represent physical systems/phenomena. Some of those ways are the subject of chapter 5. Chapter 4, which addresses the fictional character of certain types of models is, in many ways, a continuation of the debates in chapters 1 and 2 in that it addresses how unrealistic representations—representations that don't accurately describe a physical phenomenon/entity—can yield concrete information.

PART II

WHERE MODELS MEET THE WORLD

Problems and Perspectives

3

More Than Make-Believe

Fictions, Models, and Reality

There are many ways unrealistic representations are used for modelling the physical world. In some cases we construct models that we know to be false, but not false in the sense that they involve idealisation or abstraction of real properties or situations; most models do this. Instead, they are considered false because they describe a situation that cannot, no matter how many corrections are added, accurately describe or approximate the phenomenon in question. The kind of model I have in mind here is not one that contains the type of abstraction I discussed in chapter 2 (i.e., systems consisting of an infinite number of particles). Instead it is a model that involves a concrete, physical representation but one that could never be instantiated by any physical system. James Clerk Maxwell's (1965) ether models are an obvious instance of this. No one understood or believed that the structure of the ether consisted of idle wheels located between rotating elastic solid vortices; yet models of this type formed the foundation for Maxwell's first derivation in 1861 of the electromagnetic field equations.

In chapter 1, I discussed other instances of model building involving mathematical abstractions that were also not accurate representations of physical phenomena. For example, R. A. Fisher's work on population genetics (1918, 1922) assumed an analogy between populations of genes and the way that SM models populations of molecules in a gas. These populations contained an infinite number of genes that act independently of each other. His inspiration was the velocity distribution law, which gave results about pressure (among other things) from highly idealised assumptions about the molecular structure of a gas. This kind of abstraction (assuming infinite populations of genes) was crucial in enabling Fisher to show that selection operated in Mendelian populations.[1] However, because this notion of an infinite population involved smooth as opposed to singular limits, small deviations were possible. Nonetheless, the assumption of an infinite or extremely large population was necessary for determining that a particular effect was the result of selection and not genetic drift. In situations like this, where we have mathematical abstractions that are *necessary* for arriving at a certain result, there is no question of relaxing or correcting the assumptions as we do in the deidealisation of frictionless planes and rigid rods; the abstractions are what make the model work. Instances like frictionless planes where the model is the subject of corrections and approximations that result in an increasingly realistic representation of the target are different in kind from the types of models where this process cannot be carried out.

Another type of model or modelling assumption(s) that also resists corrections is the type used to treat a specific kind of problem. For example, the typical Fisher-Wright model in modern population genetics assumes that generations are discrete—they do not overlap. However, if we want to examine changes in allele frequencies when we have overlapping generations, we don't simply add corrections or parameters to the discrete generation models; instead a different model is used (Moran model) for which parallels to the Fisher-Wright models can be drawn. As I will show in chapter 6, a similar but more

1. For an extended discussion see Morrison (2002).

extreme case of incompatible models occurs when attempting to model the nucleus. The kinds of assumptions about nuclear structure required by the liquid drop model for explaining and predicting fission are very different from those contained in the shell model for explaining magic numbers.[2] Both involve assumptions we know to be false/inaccurate of the target system, and each model contradicts the assumptions of the other. The important question here is whether these models could be considered fictional in the same sense that Maxwell's ether models are, and if not, what factors related to their structure and/or use can serve to differentiate them. Neither is open to correction or deidealisation, but that in itself seems insufficient grounds to identify them as fictional representations.

We also have the relatively straightforward cases of idealisation, mentioned earlier, where a law or a model idealises or leaves out a particular property but allows for the addition of correction factors that bring the model closer (in representational terms) to the physical system being modelled. The H-W law is a good example of a case where violations of certain conditions, like random mating, may mean that the law fails to apply, but in other situations, depending on the type and degree of deviation from idealised conditions (e.g., no mutation), the law may continue to furnish reasonably accurate predictions. In other words, the population will continue to have H-W proportions in each generation, but the allele frequencies will change with that condition. The simple pendulum is another familiar example where we know how to add correction factors that bring the model closer, in descriptive terms, to concrete phenomena. The key in each of these cases is that we know how to manipulate the idealisations to get the outcomes we want and to make the models more realistic.

---

2. For more discussion of nuclear models see Portides (2005).

Because each of the examples I just mentioned has a different structure, the important question is whether they exemplify anything *different* about the way unrealistic representations yield reliable knowledge.[3] I see this not as a logical problem of deriving true conclusions from false premises but rather an epistemic one that deals with how seemingly inaccurate representations can transmit information about concrete cases.[4] The latter is a problem that in some sense pervades many cases of knowledge acquisition to a greater or lesser extent—think of the use of both metaphors and mathematics in physical explanation; for example, the electron as a point particle and the clock metaphor used in connection with the mechanical worldview of the scientific revolution.

It is tempting to classify all of the examples just given as instances of fictional representation and then ask how fictions give us knowledge of real-world situations. Indeed, several philosophers, including Frigg (2010a and b) and Godfrey-Smith (2006), have provided accounts of why we should think of models as fictions and how that can assist us in understanding knowledge acquisition via models. Frigg, in particular, has offered an extensive treatment of how this process takes place, a treatment that is closely aligned with Walton's (1990) *Mimesis as Make Believe* theory of fiction, which stresses the role imagination plays in his 'pretense theory.' On this account, the model always involves an imagined system with imagined properties; however, this doesn't prevent us from being able to talk about 'truth

---

3. In other words, is the presence of idealised assumptions different from assumptions that are false in the sense of being deliberately false, like assuming that the ether is made up of rotating vortices of fluid or elastic solid particles? No amount of correction changes the form of these latter assumptions.

4. Although we typically say that models provide us with representations, I think we can also extend that idea to laws. By specifying the conditions under which the law holds (even if they are just straightforward ceteris paribus conditions) we have specified a scenario that defines the boundaries for the operation of the law. This specification can be understood as a representation of the context under which the law can be assumed to hold.

in a model' in the same way that we talk about truth in fiction. In that sense we are able to differentiate, within the imaginary world of the model, what is 'true' from what isn't. The game of make-believe involves certain conventions about how things are to be represented (e.g., a billiard ball represents a molecule), and the prop (the billiard ball) together with inference rules generate fictional propositions that are true in the 'imagined' context. In other words, the participants are constrained in a nonarbitrary way when it comes to what can and can't be imagined. These principles of generation, as Walton calls them, guarantee intersubjective standards that the participants must adhere to.

The idea behind the models-as-fictions view is that scientists engage in this type of make-believe when they use nonrealistic descriptions to model phenomena. These imagined fictional states of affairs enjoy the same status as props in the games of make-believe, and as in a game of make-believe, what is imagined is not arbitrary. Once the props are designated, the principles of generation specify the allowable inferences that are constrained by the model. I will have more to say about certain features of the argument later, but without going into further details there seems to be an initial and fundamental problem that besets this general picture, namely, it provides no guidance in answering the most significant question related to modelling, which is how the model system represents the target. Unless some headway can be made on that issue it isn't clear what gains are had from adopting the fictional account. Indeed, Frigg (2010b) himself in his paper on the merits of the fictional account claims that "how model systems represent their respective targets. . . is a formidable task that will have to be addressed somewhere else (267)."

One thing does seem clear, however—the notion of model systems as imaginary worlds does seem to accurately describe instances of *deliberately constructed* fictional models. However, as a 'theory' of models and modelling practice it lacks general applicability and seems unable to offer helpful answers to questions about the nature of models (i.e. different types) and how we learn from them. The reason for this, as I see it, is that the language of fictions is at once too broad and too narrow. Although it encompasses the fact that the representations are not realistic, it fails to capture specifics of the relation that certain kinds of model-representations have to real systems. I argue that this is partly because the processes involved in both abstraction and idealisation are not typically the same as those involved in constructing fictional models/representations. Introducing a mathematical abstraction that is necessary for obtaining certain results involves a different type of activity from constructing a model you know to be false in order to see whether certain analogies or similarities with real systems can be established. To simply classify all forms of nonrealistic description as fictional runs the risk of ignoring the importantly different ways that scientific representation is linked with explanation and understanding.

In this chapter I want to address the problem of unrealistic representation by introducing a finer grained distinction, one that uses the notion of fictional representation to refer only to the kind of models that fall into the category occupied by, for example, Maxwell's ether models. My aims in doing so are to reflect the motivation and practice behind the construction of these types of models. Fictional models are deliberately constructed imaginary accounts whose physical similarity to the target system is sometimes rather obscure; they are designed in order to illustrate, among other things, certain types of structural features they have in common with the target and how those features might be conceptualised within the physical system being modelled. In order to extract this type of information one needs to examine the specific details of the models themselves; only by doing this can we understand the process by which the model can be said to produce an understanding of the target. Contrast this with the use of idealisation, where we have conditions that have been deliberately omitted or idealised (e.g. frictional forces) in order to facilitate calculation or to illustrate a general principle for a simple case. Here we usually know immediately what the purported relation to the target system actually is.

In keeping with my rather narrow account of fictional representation, I want to also briefly reiterate how this differs from the account of abstraction outlined in chapter 1. Whereas idealisation distorts or omits properties that are often not necessary for the problem at hand, abstraction (typically mathematical in nature) *introduces* a specific type of representation that is not amenable to correction and is necessary for explanation/prediction of the target system. But this type of construction is different in kind from fictional modelling.[5] Characterising all these varieties of model construction as fictions is not sufficiently robust to capture the various ways that each functions in explanation and prediction.

So what is it about the structure of each of these types of representation that makes them successful in a particular context? As I mentioned earlier, the concern is with the features embedded in the model that produce knowledge. For example, what aspects of populations characterised by the H-W law account for its success in predicting genotype frequencies?[6] Similarly, what was the essential feature in Maxwell's ether model that led to the derivation of the field equations? The focus of this chapter involves two interrelated issues: (1) how do fictional representations provide reliable information, and (2) what, if anything, is essentially different about the way that fictional models, as opposed to abstraction and idealisation,

---

5. The "taking away and adding back" approach is the typical way abstraction is characterised in the literature. Cartwright (1989), in particular, describes abstraction as the taking away of properties that are part of the system under investigation. For example, when modelling a superconductor one abstracts the type of material the superconductor is made of.

6. As I will show later, it isn't really the presence of idealising conditions that is responsible for transmitting information; rather, it is what is presupposed in the binomial formula for predicting genotype frequencies.

accomplish this? My claim is that although it is possible to make some general claims about the differences between fictions, abstractions, and idealisations, the answer to (1) will be a highly context-specific affair. That is, the way a fictional model produces information will depend largely on the nature of the model itself and what we want it to do.

I begin by discussing some general issues related to fictions and falsity and then go on to examine a case of a fictional model and how it can function as the source of concrete information. My conclusion is that while fictional models can play an important role in scientific theorising, not all cases of what might be called a "false" depiction of the world should be characterised as fictional.

FABLES, FICTIONS, AND FACTS

One of the things that is especially puzzling about fictional scientific representation is the relationship it bears to, say, literary fictions. Although the latter describe worlds that we know are not real, the intention, at least in more meritorious works of fiction, is often to shed light on various aspects of our life in the real world. To that extent, we assume some kind of parallel relationship exists between the two worlds that makes the fictional one capable of "touching," in some sense, the real one. But what does this "touching" consist of? There are aspects of the fictional world that we take to be representative of the real world, but only because we can draw certain comparisons or assume that certain similarity relations hold. For example, many of the relationships described in the novels of Simone de Beauvoir can be easily assimilated to her own experiences and life with Sartre. In other words, even though the characters are not real, the dynamic that exists between them may be a more or less accurate depiction of the dynamic between real individuals.

But what about scientific fictions? There, too, we have a relationship between the real world and the world described by our models. We also want to understand certain features of those models as making some type of *realistic* claims about the world. So, although we sometimes trade in analogies or metaphors, the goal is to represent the world in as realistic a way as we are able or in as realistic a way as will facilitate calculation or understanding of some aspect of the target system. Sometimes the relation between the fictional and the real is understood in terms of the abstract and the concrete, where abstract entities or concepts are understood as fictional versions of concrete realistic entities. And, unlike the literary case, we don't always understand the model, as a whole, to be a fictional entity; sometimes there are aspects of the model that are intended as realistic representations of the system we are interested in. So the question is how the fictional aspects of these models transmit reliable information about their targets.

Cartwright (1999b) is a strong proponent of the 'model as work of fiction' view and draws on the ideas of Lessing about the relationship between fables and morals as a way of shedding light on the relation between the abstract and the concrete. Lessing sees a fable as a way of providing a graspable, intuitive content for abstract symbolic judgments (the moral). Fables are like fictions—they are stories that allegedly tell us something about the world we inhabit. The interesting thing about Lessing's fables is that they aren't allegories. That is because allegories function in terms of similarity relations; they don't have literal meaning but rather say something similar to what they seem to say. But, as Cartwright notes, for Lessing similarity is not the right relation to focus on. The relation between the moral and the fable is that of the general to the more specific; indeed, it is a misuse to say that the special bears a similarity to the general or that the individual has a similarity with its type. In more concrete terms, Lessing's account of the relation between the fable and the moral is between the abstract symbolic claim and its more concrete manifestation.

Cartwright claims that this mirrors what is going on in physics. We use abstract concepts that need "fitting out" in a particular way using more concrete models; the laws of physics are like the morals, and the models are like the fables. It is because force is an abstract concept that it can only "exist in a particular mechanical model" (1999b, 46). What she concludes is that the laws are true only of objects in the models in the way that the morals are true of their fables; so, continuing on with Lessing's analysis, we would say that the model is an instance of a scientific law. In that sense the model is less abstract than the law; but what about the relation of the model to the world? Cartwright says that even when models fit "they do not fit very exactly" (1999b, 48). This provides a context in which to understand her claim about how laws can be both false and have broad applicability. They are literally false about the world, yet the concrete models that instantiate them are what constrain their application, and it is because the models also don't have an exact fit that they can have broad applicability.

But what exactly does the 'models as fictions' view entail when we move from the model to the world? As I have noted, Frigg has a rather elaborate account of fictionalism but no answer to the model-world question. Cartwright's account suggests that we can only talk about laws in the context of the fictional world described by the model; but then how do we connect the fictional model with the real world that we are interested in explaining/predicting/describing? Because our goal is to learn how models can convey empirical information, the model-world relation must be addressed. Should we understand reality as an instance of the model in the way that the model is an instance of a law, or do we need to invoke the similarity relation as a way of understanding why the model works in the way that it does? It isn't clear to me how talking in terms of instances or appealing to the general/specific relation tells us much here. When we need to know the features of the model that are instantiated in the world, we are essentially asking how the model is similar to the world, and although the answer might be difficult, the question itself is rather uncomplicated.

Understanding the model as a concrete instantiation of a law doesn't guarantee that the model bears any similarity to the physical world. Maxwell's ether model instantiated the laws of hydrodynamics, yet it was a highly fictional representation of the ether/electromagnetic field. So, if our laws only say something about the world in virtue of the relation that the model bears to the world, the question becomes one of determining what, exactly, fictional models say about the world and how they say it. The problem, however, is that if all models are fictions then we seem forced to conclude that science provides information about the world in the same way that novels do. There are many theories of fiction that purport to explain how narratives can produce knowledge of some kind, but those are only helpful if you already think there are good reasons for casting models, generally speaking, in this mould. But if the theory of models as fictions doesn't solve any of the epistemic problems related to the model-world axis, it becomes difficult to motivate. This is especially troublesome since the goal, at least in many circumstances, is to provide a model that can depict the target system as accurately as possible.

Godfrey-Smith (2006), also a proponent of the fiction account, claims that model systems should be treated as imaginary concrete things—they are imaginary but would be concrete if they were real. The emphasis on concreteness here is intended as a contrast with models that consist of mathematical objects, where the focus of discussion is on mathematical structures like phase spaces, equations, and so on.

I have suggested that we take seriously the apparent treatment of model systems as imagined concrete things by scientists. But it would be a mistake to apply this view too strongly and uniformly. In areas where mathematical methods can be used, one part of the practice of modelers is to discuss mathematical objects and structures in their own right. In these areas, what we often see might be described as a kind of oscillation between thinking of a model system in very concrete terms, and moving to a description of purely mathematical structure. It would be a mistake to insist that one of these is "the model" and the other is not. Each kind of talk can constrain the other. A person might say: "That's the wrong equation to use if you have in mind a sexual population." But a person might also say: "If those are the equations you want to study, you should think of them as describing spatial variation in environment, not temporal variation." So the "concrete" treatment of model systems is part of the story, but it is not the only part. (736)

Of course direct reference to mathematical features of models and discussion of them "in their own right" doesn't entail that they are not also fictions. Fictionalism in mathematics is quite consistent with this type of practice (see Leng 2010). Godfrey-Smith claims that thinking about model systems in the concrete way suggested by the fictional account "seems to be a clear part of scientific practice." He maintains that a key advantage in thinking about models as the kind of imagined objects characteristic of ordinary fiction is that we have an "effortless informal facility" with the assessment of resemblance relations involving these systems. Indeed, we often assess similarities between imagined and real-world systems (Middle Earth and medieval Europe) with little effort and considerable consensus much of the time. The relation between model and target becomes very unintimidating from this perspective (2006, 737).

While much of this may be true in the assessment of literary and other types of fiction, the fact that modelling involves assumptions about imaginary systems that lack concrete features does not seem a sufficient reason for categorising them in the same way. While the initial stages of modelling sometimes involve constructing possible and in some cases imaginary systems, the end goal is always to uncover accurate information about the target, or to investigate its possibilities. In that sense focusing on the imaginary aspects seems to miss the point. And, while we can often reach consensus about the relation between imaginary fictional places or characters and the 'real' world, it is important to keep in mind that those similarities are frequently much easier to establish than those involved in scientific modelling, where the stakes are higher and the similarities much less apparent. Science is far from a game of make-believe and involves a lot more than just imagining.

The general characterisation of models as fictions seems unable to do justice to the way models are used in unearthing aspects of the world we want to understand. Put differently, we need to know the variety of ways models can represent the world if we are to have faith in those representations as sources of knowledge. To say, as Cartwright does, that force is an abstract concept that exists only in models leaves us with no insight about how to deal with physical forces that we encounter in the world. Or to say, as Frigg and Godfrey-Smith do, that modelling is a process of imagining tells us little about the power that the model has to deliver information. We need a finer grained distinction than the fictional account can provide in order to capture the various types of unrealistic representations used in model construction and how those representations function in an explanatory and predictive way. Fictional representation is just one type. But, in order to see how we might make sense of the idea that fictional models can provide us with information about the world, and how we can retrieve information directly from idealised laws/models and mathematical abstractions, let us look at some examples of how this happens.

Our first example is interesting because it provides a curious twist on Godfrey-Smith's claim that if our imaginary model were real it would be concrete. While it is certainly true that Maxwell's mechanical ether models could be concretised (i.e. built as real physical structures) they were/are still considered fictional with respect to their target, the ether. In that sense, their 'concreteness' played virtually no role in delivering them from the category of 'fiction,' nor did it enhance the ability to use them as an inferential tool. The one exception to this way of thinking was Lord Kelvin, who, as I discuss in chapter 6, placed great faith in the concrete features of mechanical models, often seeing them as a replacement for experiment. Below I outline some features of the development of Maxwell's various ether models in order to show how one can use fictional models to understand physical phenomena. What I want to stress is that the understanding and explanation gained via these models depends on how we link their specific features with the target. While the process exhibits some interesting similarities to the 'models as fictions' view, the way the models convey information requires a much richer and more context specific framework than the Walton/Frigg/ Godfrey-Smith account can deliver.

FICTIONAL MECHANISMS YIELD ACCURATE PREDICTIONS: HOW THE MODEL PROVIDES INFORMATION

In the various stages of development of the electromagnetic theory, Maxwell used a variety of tools that included different forms of a fictional ether model (which he identified as such) as well as physical analogies. Each of these played an important role in developing both mathematical and physical ideas that were crucial to the formulation and conceptual understanding of field theory. In order to appreciate exactly how a field theory emerged from these fictional representations, we need to start with Maxwell's 1856 representation of Faraday's electromagnetic theory in what he described as a mathematically precise yet visualizable form.[7] The main idea in Faraday's account was that the seat of electromagnetic phenomena was in the spaces surrounding wires and magnets, not in the objects themselves. He used iron filings to visualise the patterns of these forces in space, referring to the spatial distribution as lines of force that constituted a kind of field. Electrical charges were conceived as epiphenomena that were manifestations of the termination points of the lines of force, and as such, they had no independent existence. On this picture the field was primary, with charges and currents emerging from it.

The initial approach taken by Maxwell employed both mathematical and physical analogies between stationary fields and the motion of an incompressible fluid that flowed through tubes (where the lines of force are represented by the tubes). Using the formal equivalence between the equations of heat flow and action at a distance, Maxwell substituted the flow of the ideal fluid for the distant action. Although the pressure in the tubes varied inversely as the distance from the source, the crucial difference was that the energy of the system was in the tubes rather than being transmitted at a distance. The direction of the tubes indicated the direction of the fluid in the way that the lines of force indicated the direction and intensity of a current. Both the tubes and the lines of force satisfied the same partial differential equations (PDEs). The purpose of the analogy was to illustrate the mathematical similarity of the laws, and although the fluid was a

---

7. All the papers by Maxwell cited in this chapter are contained in the 1965 edition of his collected papers.

purely fictional entity, it provided a visual representation of this new field-theoretic approach to electromagnetism.

What Maxwell's analogy did was furnish was what he termed a physical "conception" for Faraday's lines of force; a conception that involved a fictional representation yet provided a mathematical account of electromagnetic phenomena as envisioned on this field-theoretic picture. This was important for Maxwell because his goal at this point was to provide a mathematisation of the Faraday picture. The method of physical analogy, as Maxwell referred to it, marked the beginning of what he saw as progressive stages of development in theory construction. Physical analogy was intended as a middle ground between a purely mathematical formula and a physical hypothesis. It was important as a visual representation because it enabled one to see electromagnetic phenomena in a new way. Although the analogy did provide a model (in some sense), it was merely a descriptive account of the distribution of the lines in space, with no mechanism for understanding the forces of attraction and repulsion between magnetic poles.

A physical account of how the behaviour of magnetic lines could give rise to magnetic forces was further developed in Maxwell's paper of 1861–1862 entitled "On Physical Lines of Force" (1965). The paper marked the beginnings of his famous ether model, which described the magnetic field in terms of the rotation of the ether around the lines of force. The idea of a rotating ether was first put forward by Kelvin, who explained the Faraday effect (the rotation of the plane of polarised light by magnets) as a result of the rotation of molecular vortices in a fluid ether. In order to allow for the rotation of the adjacent vortices, the forces that caused the motion of the medium and the occurrence of electric currents, the model consisted of layers of rolling particles (idle wheels) between the vortices, as indicated in figure 3.1. The forces exerted by the vortices on these particles were the cause of electromotive force, with changes

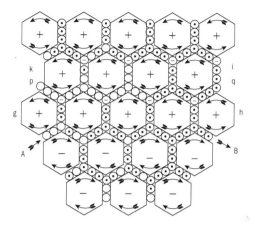

Figure 3.1: Maxwell's vortex ether model. AB is a current of electricity, with the large spaces representing the vortices and the smaller circles the idle wheels.

in their motion corresponding to electromagnetic induction. That Maxwell thought of this as a purely fictional representation is obvious from the following quotation: "The conception of a particle having its motion connected with that of a vortex by perfect rolling contact may appear somewhat awkward. I do not bring it forward as a connexion existing in nature, or even as that which one would willingly assent to as an electrical hypothesis. It is, however, a mode of connexion which is mechanically conceivable, and easily investigated" (Maxwell 1965, 1:486).

One of the problems with the original fluid vortex model was explaining how a fluid surface could exert tangential forces on the particles. In order to remedy this and extend the model to electrostatics Maxwell developed an elastic solid model made up of spherical cells endowed with elasticity, which made the medium capable of sustaining elastic waves. In addition, the wave theory of light was based on the notion of an elastic medium that could account for transverse vibrations; hence it was quite possible that the electromagnetic medium might posses the same property. The fluid vortices had uniform angular velocity and rotated as a rigid sphere, but elastic vortices would produce the deformations and displacements in the medium that were needed to account for the propagation of electromagnetic waves. With this elasticised medium in place, Maxwell now had to explain the condition of a body with respect to the surrounding medium when it is said to be charged with electricity and to account for the forces acting between electrical bodies.

According to the Faraday picture, electric lines of force were primary, and electric charge was simply a manifestation of the terminating points on the lines of force. If charge was to be identified with the accumulation of particles in some portion of the medium, then it was necessary to be able to represent that. In other words, how is it possible to represent charge as existing in a field? In the case of a charged capacitor with dielectric material between the plates, the dielectric material itself was the primary seat of the "inductive" state, and the plates served merely as bounding surfaces where the chain of polarised particles was terminated. So what is taken to be the charge on a conductor is nothing but the apparent surface charge of the adjacent dielectric medium.

The elastic vortices that constituted the ether or medium were separated by electric particles whose action on the vortex cells resulted in a type of distortion. In other words, the effect of an electromotive force (the tangential force with which the particles are pressed by the matter of the cells) is represented as a distortion of the cells caused by a change in position of the electric particles. That, in turn, gave rise to an elastic force that set off a chain reaction. Maxwell saw the cell distortion as a displacement of electricity within each molecule, with the total effect over the entire medium producing a "general displacement of electricity in a given direction" (1965 1:491). Understood literally, the notion of displacement meant that the elements of the dielectric had changed positions. And, because changes in displacement involved a motion of electricity, Maxwell argued that they should be "treated as" currents in the positive or negative direction according to whether displacement was increasing or diminishing. Displacement also served as a model for dielectric polarisation—electromotive force was responsible for distorting the cells, and its action on the dielectric produced a state of polarisation.

From this we can get some sense of just how complex the model really was and how, despite its fictional status, its various intricacies provided a representation of important features of the electromagnetic field. But most important was how this account of the displacement current(s) furnished the appropriate mathematical representation that would give rise to the field equations. In the original version of the ether model, displacement was calculated only in terms of the rotation of the vortices without any distortion, but in the elastic model displacement made an additional contribution to the electric current. In order to show how the transmission of electricity was possible in a medium, a modification of Ampere's law was required in order to generalise it to the case of open circuits. What is important here, however, is not the modification of Ampere's law per se but rather the way in which the model informed that modification. If we think for a moment about what Maxwell was trying to achieve, namely, a field-theoretic representation of electromagnetism, then it becomes obvious that some way of treating open circuits and representing charges and currents as emerging from the field rather than material sources is crucial.

To achieve that end two important elements were required. The first was the motion of idle wheels that represented electricity as governed by Ampere's law. The law related electric flux and magnetic intensity (curl $\mathbf{H} = 4\pi \mathbf{J}$, where $\mathbf{H}$ is the magnetic field and J is the electric-current density). A consequence of that law was the absence of any mechanism that could account for the accumulation of charge because it applied only in the case of closed currents. Consequently

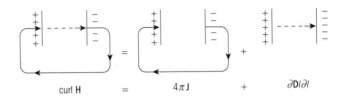

Figure 3.2: The displacement term $\partial \mathbf{D} / \partial t$ modified the original Ampere law, where $\mathbf{D} = (1 / c^2) \mathbf{E} + 4\pi \mathbf{P}$ (the polarisation vector).

a term $\partial \mathbf{D} / \partial t$ had to be added to the current so that it was no longer circuital. As I mentioned earlier, and as shown in figure 3.2, the dielectric between the coatings of a condenser fulfilled that need and was seen as the origin of the displacement current. The force of that current was seen as proportional to the rate of increase of the electric force in the dielectric and thereby produced the same magnetic effects as a true current. Hence, the charged current could be "regarded as" flowing in a dosed circuit.[8] The modified term in Ampere's law took the value zero for the case of steady currents flowing in closed circuits and nonzero values for open circuits, giving definite predictions for their magnetic effects.

As I also noted earlier, there was a second feature that concerned the account of displacement, namely, how the representation of electric current qua elastic restoring force (a crucial feature of the model) was used to represent open circuits. According to the mechanics of the model, the rotations push the small particles along giving rise to a current of magnitude $1/4\pi$ curl $\mathbf{H}$, while the elastic distortions

---

8. This is what Seigel (1991) refers to as the "standard account." He also remarks (92) that according to the standard account the motivation for introducing the displacement current was to extend Ampere's law to open circuits in a manner consistent with Coulomb's law and the continuity equation. Although I agree with Seigel that this was certainly not Maxwell's motivation, I think one can incorporate aspects of the standard account into a story that coheres with the historical evidence. My intention here is not to weigh in on the details of this debate but simply to show how various aspects of the field equations emerged from the model.

move the particles in the direction of the distortion, adding another contribution $\partial \mathbf{D} / \partial t$ to the current.[9] Maxwell had linked the equation describing displacement $(R = -4\pi E^2 h)$ with the ether's elasticity (modelled on Hooke's law) and also with an electrical equation representing the flow of charge produced by electromotive force. Hence R was interpreted as both an electromotive force in the direction of displacement and an elastic restoring force in the opposite direction. Similarly, the dielectric constant E is both an elastic coefficient and an electric constant, and h represents both charge per unit area and linear displacement. As a result, the equation served as a kind of bridge between the mechanical and electrical parts of the model. The electrical part included the introduction of the displacement current, the calculation of a numerical value for E (a coefficient that depended on the nature of the dielectric), and the derivation of the equations describing the quantity of displacement of an electric current per unit area. The mechanical part required that E represent an elastic force capable of altering the structure of the ether. The point that concerns us here, though, is exactly how the mechanical features of the model gave rise to electrical effects: that is, the relation between the mechanical distortion of the ether and the displacement current.

The answer lies in seeing how Maxwell's model represented the primacy of the field. As Seigel (1991, 99) points out, in Maxwell's equation of electric currents the curl $\mathbf{H}$ term (the magnetic field) appears on the right side with the electric current $\mathbf{J}$ on the left as the quantity to be calculated.

---

9. It is perhaps interesting to note here that in the modern version the electric current $\mathbf{J}$ appears on the right because it is regarded as the "source" of the magnetic field $\mathbf{H}$. This is because charges and currents are typically seen as the sources or causes of fields. This formulation was introduced by Lorentz, who combined the Maxwellian field theory approach with the continental charge-interaction tradition, resulting in a kind of dualistic theory where charges and currents as well as electric and magnetic fields are all fundamental, with the former being the source of the latter.

$$\mathbf{J} = 1/4\pi\left(\text{curl }\mathbf{H} - 1/c^2\ \partial\mathbf{E}/\partial t\right)$$

To illustrate how this works mechanically, consider the following example: if we take a charging capacitor there is a growing electric field pointing from positive to negative in the space between the plates. This is the current owing to the solenoidal, closed-loop curl **H** term. However, associated with this field there is a reverse polarisation (fig. 3.3) due to the elastic deformation of the vortices acting on the particles. This gives rise to a reverse current between the plates that cancels the curl **H** term. This is because it is negative and points toward the positive plate as the capacitor is charging. The solenoidal term is incapable of producing accumulations of charge, so it is the reverse polarisation that gives rise to charge on the capacitor plates and not vice versa. It is the constraint on the motion of the particles that reacts back as a constraint on the motion of the vortices that drives the elastic distortion of the vortices in the opposite direction. As a result, charge builds up through the progressive distortion of the medium. This elastic distortion is accompanied by a pattern of elastic restoring forces that correspond to the electric field **E**.

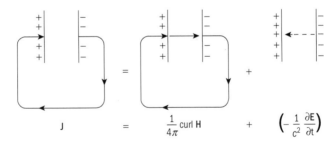

Figure 3.3: The reverse (polarisation) current term has a negative sign, which cancels the curl **H** term between the plates.

This allows us to see the relation between charge and the field: charge is the centre of elastic deformation that gives rise to a pattern of electromotive forces that constitute the field—the energy of deformation is the electric field energy. Put simply, it is the fields that give rise to charges and currents. The magnetic field gives rise to the solenoidal term in both the wire and space between the plates, and the changing electric field gives rise to a reverse current in the space between the plates. The sum of these two currents yields the conduction current **J**—an open circuit for the true current.

What this shows is how Maxwell's electrodynamics developed from a purely fictional model that provided an account of how electromagnetic forces could be produced in a mechanical ether. But, more significant is the fact that the model furnished the all important field-theoretic picture that would become the basis for the modern account we have today. Once the displacement current secured the basis for a field theory, it was in some sense a rather small step to construct the *electromechanical* theory of light. I say electromechanical because this particular model didn't identify light with electromagnetic waves; rather, it was hypothesised that both originated from the same medium or field. Instead of approaching the problem as a mathematical one and obtaining solutions for the equations for the **E** or **H** fields in the form of transverse electromagnetic waves, the model occupied centre stage, with the mathematical account emerging from the model.

To see how this culminates in an electrodynamical theory of light, we need to very briefly look at the rest of the story from the 1861–1862 paper.[10] The velocity of propagation (V) of transverse torsion waves in the medium was given by the torsion modulus m, an elastic constant that controls the strength of the electric forces, divided by the mass density of the medium ρ_μ, which controls the strength of

10. See Seigel (1991, 130–35).

magnetic forces. Maxwell set the values of these parameters through a chain of linkages between the mechanical, electrical, and magnetic aspects of the model, which resulted in $V = c$ where c is the ratio of units—a measure of the relative strengths of electrostatic forces and electromagnetic forces. This ratio of electric to magnetic units depended on a quantity that had the dimensions of a velocity. There were five different methods for determining that velocity, and using these experimental results Maxwell obtained a value for c that was very close to the velocity of light. Consequently, the velocity of waves in the magnetoelectric medium was also roughly equivalent to the velocity of light.[11] But, and this is the important point, the rationale for setting the parameters to the values Maxwell chose, together with the equivalence between V and the ratio of units, followed directly from the mechanical and electromagnetic connections that emerged from the model. In some sense the model, like an experimental novel, had played out its own story; the succession of facts or hypotheses depended on the constraints imposed by the phenomena themselves via their place or representation in the model.[12]

The problem of course was that no one, especially Maxwell, thought this model was anything but an elaborate fiction. But because the numerical relations between the optical and electromagnetic phenomena were too spectacular to ignore, he needed some way of showing that the existence of electromagnetic waves propagating with velocity c followed from electrical equations themselves, divorced from the mechanical underpinnings of the model. The

11. In addition to the agreement between the velocity of propagation of electromagnetic waves and light, there were two other connections between electromagnetic and optical phenomena that emerged from the model; one was the Faraday effect, and the other involved refractive indices of dielectric media.

12. In the end, however, there was no real explanation of the way that elastic forces produced electric lines of force. Instead, he was able to calculate the resultant electrical force without any precise specification of how it arose (i.e., there was no calculation of a stress tensor of the medium, as in the magnetic case, from which he could then derive the forces).

answer came in 1865 via a purely dynamical theory and the introduction of electromagnetic variables into the equations of dynamics.
However, with the abandonment of the mechanical model he also
needed a different justification for introducing displacement into his
equations, for without it there was literally no field theory.

A number of assumptions made this possible. On the basis of
facts about light, he assumed that space or the ether must be capable
of storing up energy, and from the form of the equations of electricity and magnetism he showed the forms that energy must have if it
is disseminated through space. If the medium is subject to dynamical principles then it will be governed by Lagrange's equations, and if
we apply dynamics to electromagnetism we can substitute magnetic
and electric energy for kinetic and potential energy. According to the
Faraday-Mossotti theory of dielectrics, when a potential difference is
applied across a dielectric it becomes polarised—molecules are positive at one end and negative at the other. This entails not only that
electric energy is stored in the dielectric but that a transient electric
current flows in it. If one assumed that space can store up energy, it
could also become polarised by a potential difference, and a changing potential difference would thereby produce a changing current
(displacement) associated with a changing magnetic field. Once the
displacement current was introduced, Maxwell was able to deduce
the properties of electromagnetic waves that accounted for light.

All of this was accomplished in his paper "A Dynamical Theory
of the Electromagnetic Field." Of course, this is not to say that the
new "dynamical theory" was without problems. Because there was
no underlying mechanical model it became difficult to conceive how
exactly displacement operated. If electricity was being displaced,
how did this occur? The problem was magnified because charge was
interpreted as a discontinuity in displacement. And although displacement appears in the fundamental equations, divorced from its
mechanical foundation, electromagnetism takes on the appearance

of a phenomenological theory.[13] The continuation of this story and the efforts to unite mechanics and electromagnetism is both long and rather complicated.[14] Although it has interesting implications for debates about the relationship between fictional representations, mathematical representations, and concrete knowledge, for the point I want to make, namely how a purely fictional model could provide the foundation for the field-theoretic view of electromagnetism, the story thus far is sufficient. I want to conclude this section by focusing on the problem I raised at the beginning: what specific features can we isolate as playing a role in the transmission of information from fictional models?

What is especially significant is that the development of the field equations did not proceed through the introduction of a new term called the displacement current as a purely mathematical modification to Ampere's law. Instead, what I showed was how the foundation for electromagnetism emerged from the molecular vortex model and was in fact determined by it, in that the structure of the model allowed for specific types of relationships among its parts. But the important issue here is not that Maxwell was capable of deriving a set of field equations from a false model, but rather, what it was about the model that underscored the applicability of the equations. Put differently, what was the conceptual or theoretical content embedded in the model that formed the basis for his electromagnetic worldview?

The answer centres, of course, on the displacement current. Maxwell knew that the ether or field did not consist of rotating vortices and idle wheels, but he also knew that in order to represent the Faraday picture of electromagnetism there had to be some account of how electricity could travel in free space and charge could build up

---

13. For an extended discussion of the differences in the two accounts of displacement see Seigel (1991, 146–47, 150–51).
14. See Morrison (2000) for a detailed account of the development of the electromagnetic theory and the unification of electromagnetism and optics.

without material bodies. Consequently, he needed a way of representing this mechanically if he was to derive a set of equations applicable to this new field-theoretic picture. The mechanical model became the focal point for an understanding of how charges and currents could be understood as field-theoretic phenomena and for the subsequent formulation of a mathematical account of those processes. Part of that account involved a modification of the relation between Ampere's law, Coulomb's law, and the equation of continuity for open circuits, something that was indicated by the structure of the model.

Once the basic mechanical features of the model were in place they constrained both the physical and mathematical descriptions of electromagnetic forces. In the same way that character development in a novel can determine, to some extent, how the story will play out, the features of the model restricted the way that certain physical relations could be represented. This is also the scenario described by Walton's theory of fiction. Once the props and principles of generation are specified, restrictions are placed on what can be imagined. However, the principles of generation in the scientific case will be given by the theoretical relations that are possible, something that is not defined solely by the model or the imaginary context but rather by the physical constraints governing the theoretical picture we want to understand. As I showed in the Maxwell case, within those constraints the model can generate new types of possibilities, and it is the latter that enable the model to enhance our understanding of the target.

By the time the *Treatise on Electricity and Magnetism* was completed in 1873, displacement had taken on the role of a primary current responsible for the transmission of electricity through space. Although the mature theory was an extension of the dynamical approach, neither would have been possible without the fictional model that provided a physical conception of how an electromagnetic field theory might be possible.

Although my story involves number of intricate details, these are necessary if one is going to show exactly how a fictional model can yield concrete information. Indeed, what this extended discussion shows is not only how certain information emerged from the fictional model but also the need for examining the model in detail in order to show exactly how that can happen. Although I have only addressed one example here, the point I want to make is a general one concerning fictional models. To say that fictional models are important sources of knowledge in virtue of a particular kind of similarity that they bear to concrete cases or systems is to say virtually nothing about *how* they do that. Instead, what is required is a careful analysis of the model itself to uncover the kind of information it yields and the ways in which that information can be used to develop physical hypotheses. There are various ways that fictional models may be able to accomplish this, but each one will do so in a way that is specific to that particular model. The situation is radically different from the case of idealisation, where an analysis of the methods employed for both the idealising process and its corrections will typically cover a variety of different cases. Consequently, what counts as an idealisation is a relatively easy category to define. Despite this, the practice of idealization presents some challenges for uncovering how idealised models relate to real systems, challenges that are not met by invoking the fictions account.

FROM THE IDEAL TO THE CONCRETE

So how exactly does the fictional case differ from an idealised law/model, where there are specific unrealistic conditions required for the law to hold, conditions that are inaccurate but nevertheless capable of approximating real physical systems? As I showed in chapter 1, the H-W law is a simple example of a fundamental law that makes assumptions not realised in any natural population. In what sense do we want to say that this law provides us with information about these populations? Should we call the law "fictional" due to the unrealistic nature of the assumptions? One of the things that renders laws explanatory, as highlighted by the deductive nomological model, is the fact that they are general enough to apply to a diverse number of phenomena. In other words, they enable us to understand specific features of phenomena as similar in certain respects; for example, universal gravitation shows that both terrestrial and celestial bodies obey an inverse square force law. Cartwright (1983) claims that this generality is a reason for thinking fundamental laws like these are false, since they are unable to accurately describe the situations they reportedly cover. The problem then is if they are false, how could they possibly provide knowledge of concrete physical systems or, in this case, populations?

If these laws apply only to objects in our models, as Cartwright suggests, and if our models are works of fiction, then it becomes difficult to see how the law could be interpreted realistically. Put differently: if the only objects governed by laws are fictional then the status of laws, as something stronger than a fiction, becomes difficult to motivate. However, as I have shown, the 'fictional' account of models, which also incorporates idealisation and abstraction, lacks the necessary tools for describing how these fictional aspects represent or 'connect with' the target system. Yet, as I showed in chapter 1, the H-W law enables us to understand fundamental features of heredity and variation by establishing a mathematical relation between allele and genotype frequencies that embodies the very gene-conserving structure that is the essential feature of Mendelism. What I also stressed there was why the unrealistic nature of the assumptions does not affect the significance of either the conclusions the law provides or the information implicit in its formulation. The reason for the stability and preservation of genetic structure could be traced directly to the absence of fusion and the discontinuous nature of the gene, which was indicative of a type of genetic structure that could conserve modification. This condition was explicitly presupposed in the way the law was formulated and how it functioned.[15] In that sense one can see the H-W law as the beginning of a completely new explanation of the role of mutation and selection and how they affect our understanding of evolution.

But what about the so-called falsity of the assumptions under which the H-W law holds. Our question here is whether it is helpful to think of these as fictional and whether doing so can bring some insight into the relation between the law and these idealising conditions. Both infinite population size and random mating are required for maintaining H-W equilibrium. Other conditions, such as the absence of selection, migration, and mutation, will not rule out H-W proportions; instead, the allele frequencies will change in accordance with the changing conditions. The latter are idealisations that may or may not hold but whose effect on the system can be straightforwardly calculated. We can think of them as external factors that isolate basic features of a Mendelian system that allow us to understand how variation could be conserved. Infinite populations are different, in that they are crucial for ruling out genetic drift, while violations of random mating can affect gene frequencies in a number of different ways. Both of these assumptions are necessary for H-W equilibrium; they cannot be relaxed if the law is to be applicable. In other words, assumptions like infinite population size are *necessary* abstractions rather than fictions describable in terms of make-believe or imaginings.

---

15. The notion of presupposition that I have in mind here is the same as the one connected to the ideal gas law—in order for the law to hold, one must presuppose that the molecules of the gas are infinitesimal in size and have no forces acting between them.

The importance of these different types of "unrealistic" constraints is to highlight the impact of different factors and the degree to which they affect the evolutionary process. Because the H-W law represents a stable stationary state for a sexually reproducing population, it enables us to judge the effects of selection, preferential mating, and so forth on the homogeneous field of allele and genotype frequencies. The fundamental underlying *assumption* required for this picture to work is that of a structure that preserves modifications. So the model of a population that exhibits H-W equilibrium contains a mixture of realistic, ideal, and abstract assumptions. Each has a role to play in producing the desired outcome. Attempting to capture this rather complex structure of relations in terms of fictionalism not only fails to capture the relevant features of these relations but gives us no understanding of how the abstract assumptions relate to the target system.

Given that abstractions like infinite populations can't be realised, concretised, or relaxed, there still may be good reasons to characterise them (rather than the entire law or model) as fictional representations. Even if we agree that they are necessary features of an explanation/prediction, we still might want to claim that this necessity doesn't automatically rule out any fictional status. Duhem, who is also concerned with abstraction in physics, claims that because physics needs to be precise, it can never fully capture the complexity that is characteristic of nature. Hence, the abstract mathematical representations used by physics do not describe reality but are better thought of as imaginary constructions—neither true nor false. Laws relate these symbols to each other and consequently are themselves symbolic. Although these symbolic laws will never touch reality, so to speak, they do involve approximations that are constantly undergoing modification due to increasing experimental knowledge (Duhem 1977, 174). In that sense, Duhem's characterisation of abstraction seems also to incorporate elements of idealisation. It is also clear from his account that the gap between symbolic laws and reality is due, essentially, to an epistemic problem that besets us in the quest for scientific knowledge. Laws are constantly being revised and rejected; consequently, we can never claim that they are true or false. In addition, because of the precise nature of physics we must represent reality in a simple and incomplete way in order to facilitate calculation. This describes both idealisation and abstraction, depending on how one chooses to simplify.

What Duhem's view captures is a philosophical problem that focuses on the gap between reality and our representation of it. His account of abstraction is part of a more general account of the epistemic problems that beset physics, especially a realist interpretation of theories, laws, and models. Although those issues have some bearing on my point, my overall concern stems from the way that we are *required* to represent certain kinds of systems in a mathematically abstract way if we are to understand how they behave, and why characterising that as fictional representation is inadequate. This was particularly evident in the examples of mathematical explanation discussed in chapter 2. As I showed there, the issues related to mathematical abstraction go well beyond problems of calculation to include explanation and prediction. To that extent, we need to think differently about the role of abstraction in physics; a role that involves more than simply the 'subtraction' and 'adding back' of properties or constructing imaginary representations of the phenomena we are interested in.

We can see how the processes of idealisation and abstraction differ significantly from the way fictional models are used to convey information. Although fictional models may constrain the physical possibilities once the model structure is in place, there is typically a choice about how to construct the model and how to represent the system/phenomenon. While the background physical theory and the target system impose certain structural constraints on model construction (Maxwell's ether model had to account for the flow of electricity through space) there are many different ways this process could have been modelled. There is less freedom of movement with idealisation, in that specific kinds of approximation techniques inform and determine how the system is represented. Although there is sometimes a choice about which parameters we can leave out or idealise, that choice is also limited by the problem at hand. In cases of mathematical abstraction, as I have defined it, we are completely constrained as to how the system is represented, with the abstraction functioning as a necessary feature of our theoretical account. This necessity marks a sharp contrast with 'fictional' representation. The lack of 'choice' regarding how to model the system and the fact that the abstraction requires a theoretical foundation (e.g., results that depend on infinite populations are grounded in aspects of the central limit theorem) undermines the notion of 'make-believe' that accompanies the models-as-fictions account.

One of my goals in this chapter has been to introduce distinctions among the processes involved in constructing a fictional model, an idealisation, and a mathematical abstraction. Each of these categories transmits knowledge, despite the presence of highly unrealistic assumptions. Although there is a temptation to categorise any type of unrealistic representation as a "fiction," I have argued that this would be a mistake, primarily because it tells us very little about the role those representations play in producing knowledge. That said, fictional models do have an important role to play in science and can function in significant ways at various stages of theory development. But in order to uncover the way these models produce information, we need to pay particular attention to the specific structure given by the model itself. There is no general method that captures how fictional models function or transmit knowledge; each will do so in a different way, depending on the nature of the problem. By separating these models from other cases of unrealistic representation, we can recognise what is distinctive about each and how they deliver concrete information about the physical world.

4

Mediated Knowledge

Representation and the Theory-Model Axis

MEDIATORS AND MEDIATION: A QUICK OVERVIEW

So far we have been discussing various perspectives on the question of how models can deliver information and how mathematics in general assists in that task. I want to begin, in this chapter, by fleshing out some aspects of the relation between a model that represents a physical system (a representative or representational model) and its role as a mediator. Since the publication of *Models as Mediators* in 1999 there has been extensive discussion of how models can mediate and what mediation consists in. The general theme articulated in some of my earlier papers (1998, 1999) involved two different senses of mediation. In the first case, we model a physical system in a particular way in order to see which laws/concepts of a theory can be applied for the purposes of explanation and prediction. Here the starting point is some physical system about which we have insufficient knowledge; so we construct a model in an attempt to learn more about its hypothetical features. In the second case, the model also functions as a way to apply theory, but the starting point is the theory itself. In order to apply highly idealised and abstract laws to phenomena, one first needs to construct models that represent specific features of the system to which the theory can be applied. An example of the first type would be models that describe physics beyond the standard model, what the role of SUSY is, and so on. Models of the second type would simply be the finite and infinite potential well or the particle in a box model used for particular applications of QM.

As I showed in earlier chapters (particularly in the discussion of Maxwell) a model can also function as a mediator in its role as the 'object' of inquiry. In other words, the model itself, rather than the physical system, is the thing being investigated. In that context it serves as a source of 'mediated' knowledge, either because our knowledge of the physical system is limited, or the system is inaccessible. Hence we know only how the model behaves in certain circumstances. Various kinds of cosmological models or astrophysical models are examples of this sort.

There are also a variety of ways that models can represent their target system. In fact, the philosophical question that is often posed in this context concerns the characteristics of a model that license it as a representation in the first place. One might be tempted to think that in order to answer this question it is first necessary to determine what, exactly, a model is. In other words, we need to have a 'theory' of models before we can say anything about their representational powers. This is a project that I think is neither necessary nor possible. In the same way that understanding defies codification, so, too, with models. They are simply too numerous and diverse to think that we can somehow capture their basic features in a general way. I will have more to say about this and the relation between models and representation below, but for now let me be clear about what exactly my aims are in this chapter and where I stand on the issue of representation.

As I have mentioned, my primary goal is to illustrate the importance of the representational function of models and how it relates to their role as a mediator. For several reasons, I have chosen to focus the discussion on models related to the Bardeen, Cooper, and Schrieffer

(BCS) theory of superconductivity. First, as an example it is particularly rich in detail and exposes the various intricacies involved in model construction. But it has also been discussed in the literature by several philosophers, including Cartwright (1999c) and Cartwright et al. (1995), as well as French and Ladyman (1997). Because my views on representational models are mostly at odds with those in the literature, the BCS theory is a particularly useful focal point for highlighting those differences and thereby illustrating what I take to be the important aspects of representation.

I should, however, explain at the outset that although my focus is the role of representation in the context of modelling, my intention is not to address specific arguments related to the larger issue of scientific representation. The latter is a widely discussed topic in the literature, so much so that an adequate treatment would require a book-length treatise. Moreover, my own views on scientific representation, and indeed representation generally, are best characterised as 'deflationary,' in the sense that I am sceptical about the ability to formulate a theory of scientific representation that will adequately cover the diverse ways that theories and models can be said to represent target systems. That is not to say, of course, that there are not philosophically interesting things to be said about representation where the focus is specific models or theories; rather, my view is that what is illuminating from the representational perspective of a particular model or model type may not be so for others. I should add here that I am also not a proponent of the view that "anything can represent anything as long as the stipulation has been made explicit by the users" (Callendar and Cohen 2006 [hereafter C&C], 15). While this claim is, in some sense, uncontroversially true, I don't think it helps us to shed light on the way more specific features of scientific representation provide information.

In the preface I said that my focus in this book concerns the various philosophical issues related to the practice of modelling, issues that will enable us to better understand the role models play in knowledge acquisition. To that extent I see this chapter as providing some insight into how representation can be understood within the modelling context without an accompanying theory that constrains its boundaries. Put differently, in attempting to highlight the details of the representational features of models I hope to also show also that the reasons we don't require a theory of models apply, mutatis mutandis, to scientific representation. Not only do we not need a sophisticated theory of representation to illustrate the representational power of models, but any such theory is likely to be too general to capture its many nuances.

REPRESENTATION: A QUICK OVERVIEW

As I have noted, in the context of modelling it is tempting to link representation with an account of what a model is. The motivation behind this is somewhat intuitive: if one is going to locate representational power in the model then it makes sense to answer the question of what a model might be before we can determine what enables it to fulfill this representational role. Regardless of how one interprets the relation between models and representation, perhaps the most important feature of a model is that it contains a certain degree of representational inaccuracy.[1] In other words, it is a model because it fails to accurately represent nature. Sometimes we know specifically the type of inaccuracy the model contains because we have constructed it precisely in this way for a particular reason. Alternatively, we may be simply unsure of the kind and degree of inaccuracy because we do

---

1. I should mention here that the notion of representation used by the semanticists—isomorphism—does not really incorporate this notion of inaccuracy. I will say more about isomorphism later.

not have access to the system that is being modelled and thus have no basis for comparison. However, we also expect that our models will deliver some kind of accurate information about the physical world, so how do these two features come together and do they rely on different senses of representation?

One way of thinking about the representational features of a model is to think of it as incorporating a type of picture or likeness of the phenomena in question, a notion that has had a long and distinguished history in the development of the physical sciences. But the idea of likeness here can be construed in a variety of ways. For example, some scale models of the solar system constructed before and after Copernicus were designed in an attempt to demonstrate that a planetary conjunction would not result in a planetary collision. One can think of these as representing, in the physical sense, both the orbits and the relation of the planets to each other in the way that a scale model of a building represents certain relevant features of the building itself.

In keeping with the more logically oriented definition of a model, semanticists have another way of thinking about representation, one grounded in the notion of a structural mapping (e.g. an isomorphism). The semantic view defines models as nonlinguistic entities and, on certain formulations, interprets the empirical substructures of the model as candidates for "the *direct representation* of the observable phenomena" (van Fraassen, 1980, 64, italics added). This representation is achieved via isomorphism between the empirical substructures and data models. Giere (1999), also a proponent of the semantic view, sees representation rather differently, defining it in terms of a similarity relation that is expressed via a theoretical hypothesis. The hypothesis specifies the way in which the model captures features of or is similar to the empirical system under investigation.

Others such as Suarez (2003) and Frigg (2006, 2010b) argue against isomorphism and similarity as capable of determining what is required for a representation relation but put forward completely different accounts of what constitutes representation in the context of modelling. Frigg claims that one can only analyse how representation works once we understand the intrinsic character of the vehicle that does the representing. In chapter 3 I discussed Frigg's 'fictional' view of models, which takes them to be similar to the places and characters in works of literary fiction.[2] He suggests that theories of fiction that enable us to appreciate the way fictions transmit information can also play an essential role in explaining the nature of model systems. The core of the fiction view is the claim that model systems that are likened to characters in literary fiction should, like their counterparts, be regarded as props because they prompt the reader or user in this case to imagine certain things. By doing so a fiction generates its own game of make-believe, which is entered into by the model user. In that sense the fictional model will serve also as a representational vehicle once the various constraints have been agreed on by the users.

Suarez argues for what he calls an "inferential conception" of scientific representation, which, unlike linguistic reference, is not a matter of stipulation by an agent. Instead, it requires the correct application of functional cognitive powers (valid reasoning) by means that are objectively appropriate for the tasks at hand. In other words agents engage in surrogate reasoning using models that are inferentially suited to their targets.

My goal here is not to comment in detail on these various accounts of representation, each of which has merits and difficulties (see Morrison 2007 for an extended discussion). Part of the worry regarding attempts to define the nature of both representation and models is that it presupposes that one account can capture all the different facets of what it means for a model to represent an empirical

---

2. Cartwright also claims that that "a model is a work of fiction" (1983, 153) and, as I discussed in chapter 3 has even suggested an analysis of models considered as fables.

system. Without articulating a specific theory of representation we can nevertheless appeal to some general ideas about what it means for models to represent phenomena or systems, especially in the context of their mediating function. The representational function of models is extremely important in their ability to transmit information; but, given the multidimensional ways this can be accomplished, why think the process can be described in a single theory? The development of the BCS model presents an interesting example of how these representational features are crucial not only for the informational goals but for integrating the model into the larger theoretical context.

Despite my deflationary attitude toward representation, I should also remark that my sympathies align with some of what van Fraassen (2008) has recently claimed about the nature of representation. In addition to pointing out that representation can happen with physical or mathematical artifacts, with pictures and diagrams, he stresses that, most important, representation requires an agent because it requires that the objects mentioned above are used in a certain way or taken to represent things in a specific way. In that sense there is no notion of a representation that exists in nature without some accompanying cognitive activity (24). Because many different phenomena can be represented using the same mathematical structures or models, it seems obvious that the representation relation must involve the kind of indexical element van Fraassen suggests. And, once this indexical element becomes part of the representational relation, it becomes difficult, if not impossible, to define representation in anything but a pragmatic way. Consequently, in order to appreciate the various aspects of representation, the best approach is to look at contexts where it plays a vital role in the development and use of a particular model. As van Fraassen remarks, "place it in a context where we know our way around" (7), which is exactly my goal in this chapter.

Callender and Cohen (C&C 2006) also argue for a minimalist view of scientific representation, claiming that it is simply a special case of a more general notion of representation, and that the relatively well worked-out and plausible theories of the latter are directly applicable to the scientific case. The theory they have in mind is the General Gricean approach to representation, which advocates that all types of representation (artistic, linguistic, and in C&C's case, scientific) can be explained in terms of more fundamental types of representations, typically mental states. While this view requires an independently constituted theory of representation for the fundamental entities, once that is in place any further problems related to specific types of representation disappear. The representational powers of mental states are so wide-ranging that they can bring about other representational relations between arbitrary relata simply by stipulation. Anything can be used to represent anything else.

One of the examples they discuss is the geometric similarity between the upturned human right hands and the geography of Michigan, a similarity that can make the former a particularly useful way of representing relative locations in Michigan. But, they claim, it would normally be foolish (but not impossible) to use an upturned left hand for this purpose since a more easily interpreted representational vehicle is typically available. What this account stresses is the pragmatic and permissive features of representation. Because stipulation is what connects a representational vehicle with a representational target, it follows that the representational features cannot lie in the vehicle used to represent but rather needs to lie in the needs of the users. In that sense resemblance, isomorphism, partial isomorphism, and so on are unnecessary for scientific representation, but they can serve as pragmatic aids to communication about one's choice of representational vehicle. All one needs to do it make the representational stipulations clear. "The behavior of billiard balls may prove a useful choice of model for the behavior of elastic particle interactions in a gas because there is a salient similarity/isomorphism between the dynamics of the vehicle's objects (billiard balls) and the target's objects (gas particles). This is not to say that the very same target could not be represented by an upturned left hand, or anything else" (C&C 2006, 16).

Of course one might simply object that while anything can, in principle, represent anything, not all representations will be useful; so surely we need some constraints on scientific representation in order to account for this. C&C claim that questions about the utility of representational vehicles are just questions about the pragmatics of things that are representational vehicles, not questions about their representational status per se. If the upturned hand doesn't rank highly as a useful representation, that is a different issue from whether it *is* a representational vehicle. They see the distinction between the two as the result of running together the constitution question (what constitutes representation?) with the normative question (what makes a representation a good one?). But this, they think, is simply to confuse the matter, since an answer to the latter question will depend on specific assumptions about pragmatic purposes. What this means is that while there may be outstanding issues about *representation* and the metaphysics of mental states as the basis of representation, there is no special problem about *scientific* representation. And if all that is required is mere stipulation, then there is "nothing to distinguish a stipulation connecting a vehicle to electrons, on the one hand, from a stipulation connecting a vehicle to phlogiston, on the other" (C&C, 19).

While I find myself in agreement with much of what Callender and Cohen say about the pragmatics of representation, I am reluctant to embrace the consequences of the view. Although their account is motivated by what they see as the "nonproblem" of scientific representation, the solution overlooks what is significant about scientific representation, namely the larger role that representation plays in generating scientific knowledge. In other words, while the agent or interested parties play a crucial role in assessing the merits of a representation, what it is required for x to represent y in a scientific context requires certain constraints such as the influence of background theory and the nature of the system itself. In other words, if we expect a representation to communicate information, it will need to take account of certain features such as the physical possibilities dictated by the theoretical context. This is not necessarily reducible to the normative question about what makes a good representation, nor is it simply the descriptive issue addressed by C&C. A view that places no constraints on what makes something a representation and claims that what makes a good scientific representation depends on the users and what they want ignores theoretical aspects that determine crucial features of scientific representation.

For example, Maxwell's ether model was a useful representation, not because it was true or approximately true but because it could be used to generate hypotheses about how electromagnetic waves were propagated through space. But that model needed to represent the ether as a mechanical system if it was to yield any useful results. Similarly, if we want to model the helium atom there are a number of possibilities, but the important thing to know is that there is no closed-form solution to the Schrödinger equation for the helium atom. One possibility is to use density functional theory, which describes the particle density $\rho(\vec{r}), r \in \mathbb{R}^3$ and the ground state energy $E(N)$, where N is the number of electrons in the atom. The Thomas-Fermi model gives a very good representation of what is happening in the ground states of atoms and molecules with N electrons. The point here is that we can't use just anything to represent the helium atom if the goal is to understand its structure; nor is the decision based on purely pragmatic considerations. There may be no representation without users, but that doesn't mean that users determine what s required for something to represent something else.

In scientific modelling the goal is typically to find out or communicate information about physical phenomena, and for that we want the best possible representation. Given that much of our concern in debating the nature of representation centres on theories and models, it seems unhelpful to separate the normative and the descriptive in the way suggested by C&C. To reiterate the point above: while there can be no representation without stipulation, stipulation doesn't mean that in science it's reasonable to represent anything with anything. Links with theory, explanation, and prediction are crucial aspects of the process of representation; to simply say that we can represent anything with anything trivialises the problem.

But perhaps I've been too quick in my criticism of the C&C approach. One might argue that the normative claim that a good representation depends on the users will automatically involve embedding the representation in the appropriate theoretical context, for only then will they reap the desired benefits. But what are the determining factors here? The users want information about x, but the decision about which representation to use is not determined by them but largely by the theoretical constraints on the modelling problem. Theory determines what is the right or best way to model/represent the system in question, not the users of theory. The latter determine what they want from the representation, but which representation will deliver on that request is not a decision that rests solely with them.

That is not to say that you need to embrace some form of realism; clearly you don't, because fictional representation can be an enormously fruitful way of modelling phenomena. What you do need is a representation that will enable you to extend the problem in interesting ways. In that sense, scientific representation is about conceptualising something in a way that makes it amenable to a theoretical or mathematical formulation, exactly in the way Maxwell's ether model did. Moreover, we don't need a metaphysics of representation to understand how specific examples of representational models can convey information about their target.

Now that I have provided a basic picture of how I see models and representation aligned with each other I want to turn to a discussion of a distinction introduced by Cartwright (1999c) between representative and interpretive models. Not only does she have rather definite views about the inability of theories to represent, she also seems to suggest that there is a category of models (interpretive) whose character is nonrepresentational. Because I want to argue that all models have some kind of representational quality, the contrast with Cartwright can prove helpful in showing why and how this is the case.

CARTWRIGHT ON HOW MODELS REPRESENT

Cartwright's account of the differences between representational and interpretive models is presented in her paper "Models and the Limits of Theory: Quantum Hamiltonians and the BCS Model of Superconductivity" (1999c). As I have noted, my disagreements focus on the role of representation, both the lack of it, in the case of interpretive models, and the absence of what she terms "representative models" in the development of the BCS account of superconductivity.[3] Since it is sometimes said that the devil is in the details, it is

---

3. Cartwright uses the terms 'interpretive' and 'representative' models, so in the spirit of consistency I will do so as well. I see no difference between her use of representative models and what some people call representational models. Both allegedly represent, to a greater or lesser extent, some aspect of the world. I would extend that use and say that models can also represent theory insofar as they provide a concrete instantiation of some formal aspects of a theory, as in the case of the pendulum model representing laws of motion. This is the role Cartwright assigns to interpretive models, and I assume this is what she means when she says that interpretive models can also represent. I understand function here to mean, literally, what the model 'does' rather than the role it plays in developing the theory. Cartwright's account seems to imply that interpretive models are the crucial ones for the development of the BCS account. I want to claim that while their role is important in filling out the theoretical story, it is secondary and depends, ultimately, on having a representative model in place before the interpretive models can be put to work in the appropriate way. While I am not

important to point out how the details buried in the BCS paper can be put to work to highlight the significance of representative models for the process of theory construction.[4] Hence, the particulars of the case will be used to reveal methodological issues about the role and importance of different kinds of models. I want to claim that before interpretive models, of the sort characterised by Cartwright, can do their job there first needs to be a representative model in place that provides a physical/causal account of the phenomenon in question.[5] In this case such an account would tell us something about the causal aspects of superconductivity, what the important mechanisms are in its production, and so on.

Cartwright maintains that theories in physics do not generally represent what happens in the world; only models represent in this way, and the models that do so are not already part of any theory.[6] The reason fundamental principles associated with physical theories do not represent is because theories give purely abstract relations between abstract concepts (e.g. force), and they tell us the capacities of systems that fall under these concepts. Those systems need to be

prepared to say that this is universally the case, it certainly is so in the case of BCS and, I suspect, in the development of a number of theories.

4. I was reminded of this phrase by Robert Batterman's (2003) book.

5. Just as a point of clarification, I am not making any metaphysical claims here about the nature of causation or that the story must have some kind of truth/necessity attached to it. Instead the notion of 'cause' is meant only to indicate that the model depicts what we should/can typically identify as a causal process.

6. This depends on what one takes to be a theory or a part of a theory and what one takes to be a model. This is a complicated issue and one that requires more than a few lines to clarify the differences. In Morrison and Morgan (1999) we focused on various aspects of models and modelling practices in an attempt to lay some groundwork for what models do and how they function. We did this specifically because it wasn't clear to us that one could give a straight-forward definition of what constitutes a model (leaving aside the way model is defined in model theory or by the semantic view, a view we wanted to distance ourselves from). That said, I, at least, think it is possible to differentiate a model from a theory in specific contexts, but I am still not convinced that there are general criteria for doing so that are applicable across the board. To that extent I want to here resist the temptation, so irresistible to many philosophers, to 'define' what a model is.

"located in very specific kinds of situations" (1999c, 242) in order for their behaviour to be fixed; and when we want to represent what happens in these situations we need to go beyond theory and construct a representative model.[7] However, many theories (e.g. QM, QED) require more than this; the abstract concepts need "fitting out" in more concrete form before representative models can be built in a principled or systematic way. This fitting out is done by interpretive models that are laid out via the theory's bridge principles. An example of such an interpretive model for classical mechanics is 'two compact masses separated by a distance r' (243). It is the job of these models to ensure that abstract concepts like force have a precise content.

I claim that the correct story with respect to theory, models, and representation is exactly the reverse. While it is true that interpretive models are prior in the sense of being already part of a background theoretical framework (e.g., the infinite potential well in QM), one needs a representative model before we can determine how the abstract concepts/theory are going to be applied in a specific situation. In other words, we need a representation of the physical system to which we can then apply the abstract concepts via the interpretive models. My justification for this story will emerge in the discussion of the BCS theory, but first, in order to fully understand the implications of Cartwright's distinction between representative and interpretive models, we need to look at her characterisation of models and theory.

Many characterisations of model construction (e.g. Giere 1988; McMullin 1985) describe the process as involving the addition of refinements and corrections to the laws of the theory that we use to represent, in an idealised way, certain aspects of a physical system. In the well-worn case of the pendulum we can add, among other things,

---

7. I will have more to say about these representative models, but for now I will just focus on the schematic picture.

frictional forces in order to incorporate more details about the behaviour of real pendulums. Moreover, many view the addition of corrections as involving a cumulative process, with the model coming closer and closer to an accurate representation of the real system. By contrast, Cartwright claims that the corrections needed to turn models provided by theory into models that accurately represent physical systems are rarely, if ever, consistent with theory, let alone suggested by it (1999c, 251). For example, she claims that only pendulums in really nice environments will satisfy Galileo's law even approximately; real pendulums are subject to all types of perturbing influences that do not appear to fit the models available in Newtonian theory.[8]

The problem, as Cartwright sees it, appears to be the following: while theory gives us interpretive models that can be applied to concrete systems, this applicability often does not extend very far. In most cases there are factors relevant to the real-world situations that cannot be had from theory via its interpretive models, so we need to go beyond them to get more precise descriptions and predictions. In other words, the interpretive models provide concrete descriptions for more abstract concepts, but their domain of application with respect to realistic situations is limited; more concrete details are needed if the situation is to be described in a reasonably accurate way. At this point the representative model takes over and furnishes those details. This lack of representational power in the case of interpretive models is clearly a consequence of their relation to theory, which, as one will recall, has no representational function whatsoever.

However, if the interpretive models provide concrete descriptions for theoretical laws, then surely they must also be seen as having at least a limited representational role; they represent some aspects of a physical system, but only up to a point and in a rather abstract

---

8. For a discussion of how we can, in fact, add these various corrections to the models see Morrison (1999).

way (e.g., inextensible springs and incompressible fluids). But what about the representative models themselves; how do we take account of their function, except to say that they provide a more realistic and inclusive picture of the phenomenon? Cartwright herself claims that she has little to say about how representative models represent, except that we should not think in terms of analogy with structural isomorphism. Again, Cartwright takes us to the domain of the interpretive model as a way of illustrating what the notion of representation *isn't*. She warns against thinking of the models linked to Hamiltonians as picturing individually isolatable physical mechanisms associated with the kinetic energy term plus the Coulomb interaction; in other words, we don't explain Hamiltonians by citing physical mechanisms that supposedly give rise to them. Instead Hamiltonians are assigned via quantum bridge principles for each of the concrete interpretive models available in quantum theory, such as the central potential and the harmonic oscillator. These bridge principles are ways of making abstract terms more concrete. For example, in the case of a body falling in a uniform gravitational field we can set $F = -mg$, which enables us to go on to define more specific models. In that sense the theory extends to all and only those situations that can be described by the interpretive models/bridge principles.[9]

It is important to note that the issue of representation here is not simply one of picturing. In the case of QFT, we model the field as a collection of harmonic oscillators in order to get Hamiltonians that give the correct structure to the allowed energies. But, Cartwright points out, this does not commit us to the existence of a set of objects behaving like springs. Nevertheless, she appeals to a loose notion of resemblance, claiming that models resemble the situations they represent where the idea of a correct representation is not defined

---

9. In some cases ad hoc Hamiltonians are used, but these are not assigned in a principled way from the theory, hence the theory receives no confirmation from the derived predictions.

simply in terms of successful prediction but requires independent ways of identifying the representation as correct.

But surely this is not sufficient; more needs to be said if we are to have some understanding of how the representational function of models aids in the production of scientific knowledge. The crux of the problem of representation is the following: in virtue of *what* do models represent and how do we identify what constitutes a correct or informative representation? In order to sketch an answer, I think we need to first look at some different *ways* in which models can represent. As I mentioned at the outset, what I mean when I say that models function as mediators between theory and the world is that part of their task is to represent each domain. In other words, sometimes models represent theory by providing a more or less concrete instantiation of one of its laws. For example, in QM we have the example of particle in a one-dimensional ring, where the Schrödinger equation for a free particle whose configuration space the circle S^1 is

$$-\frac{\hbar^\circ}{2m}\nabla^2\psi = E\psi$$

We also use models to represent physical situations that we are uncertain about or have no access to, as is the case with models of stellar structure.

As a way of illustrating some aspects of this representational feature of models, let me now turn to the example of the BCS theory of superconductivity. I draw particular attention to what I take to be the representative model[s] that were prominent in the construction and development of the BCS theory, particularly the model of electrons as Cooper pairs. I say 'models' here instead of 'model' because I want to show how the development of the BCS account of superconductivity relied on a variety of representational models, culminating in the model that represents the electrons as Cooper pairs. The historical evolution of that representation makes use of many different representational models along the way, but the physical account of Cooper pairs is what functions as *the* representative model that forms the foundation for the BCS account of superconductivity. It does this by providing an account of how electrons need to be *represented or conceptualised* in order for superconductivity to be understood.[10]

My argument that representative models are prior is based partly on the view that in their role as mediator between the theory and the world they function as the source of "mediated" knowledge. That is to say, representative models typically supplant the physical system as the object treated by the theory's interpretive models. Hence, our knowledge in this context is "mediated" because it comes via the representation we have constructed; it gives us a physical picture of how the system might be constituted. Only then can we see whether the interpretive models of the theory can be applied in the appropriate kinds of ways. The types of interpretive models that Cartwright mentions (harmonic oscillator, Coulomb potential, etc.) function across all contexts where QM is applied. In that sense there is nothing specific about their application in particular instances, except in the construction of the appropriate Hamiltonian. Although this is a significant feature of how interpretive models function, I want to claim that even this is highly dependent on the kind of representative model we have constructed.

ON THE PRIORITY OF REPRESENTATIVE MODELS

Cartwright begins her discussion of the BCS paper (Bardeen et al. 1957) by highlighting two important steps in its development. The

---

10. Some ideas associated with pairing come from QM while others are motivated in a more indirect way.

first is the attractive potential due to electron interactions via lattice vibrations, and the second is the notion of Cooper pairs. Together these ideas suggested that there was a state of lower energy at absolute zero (lower than the one where all the levels in the Fermi sea are filled) that could be identified as the superconducting state. Cartwright claims that the first job of the BCS paper was to produce a Hamiltonian for which such a state will be the solution of lowest energy and then to calculate the state. The important derivations in the BCS paper were based on a reduced Hamiltonian with only three terms, two for the energies of the electrons moving in a distorted periodic potential and one for a simple scattering interaction. The longer Hamiltonian introduced earlier in the paper also uses only the basic models referred to earlier (kinetic energy of moving particles, the harmonic oscillator, the Coulomb interaction and scattering between electrons) plus one more, the 'Bloch' Hamiltonian for particles in a periodic potential (which is closely related to the basic model of the central potential). Cartwright claims that "superconductivity is a quantum phenomenon precisely because superconducting materials can be represented by the special models that quantum theory supplies" (1999c, 266).

But what exactly is being represented here and what kind of representation is it? From her description it would seem that the answer is relatively straightforward; we use the quantum models as a way of representing the processes responsible for superconductivity. While I agree with this as a minimal claim, it leaves out an important part of the story about how superconductivity is represented. The situation Cartwright describes is a quantum-theoretical representation that involves an application of theoretical (for her, interpretive) models to a particular kind of process. What licenses this kind of representation is theory (QM); but my point is that in order to apply these models we first need some fundamental idea about how the phenomenon of superconductivity can occur. This we obtain from a representative model that describes the causal process(es) required for producing superconductivity. In other words, we need an initial representation that explains how the electrons in the metal can give rise to the energy gap characteristic of superconductivity, and how their behaviour can be accounted for within the constraints imposed by QM, specifically the exclusion principle. Only when this representation is in place can we then go on to give a full theoretical representation that includes the appropriate Hamiltonian and so on. Very briefly, representative models are necessary before interpretive models can even be applied. Cartwright is suggesting that the interpretive models are where one ought to locate the crux of the BCS account; but I think this is incorrect, for reasons I will discuss. However, before doing that I need to briefly mention the problem of constructing the BCS Hamiltonian, an important example for illustrating the role of representational models.

Crucial to the construction of the Hamiltonian is an assumption involving restrictions on which states will interact with each other. As Cartwright points out, the choice here is motivated by physical ideas associated with Cooper's notion of paired electrons (1999c, 269). BCS assumed that scattering interactions are dramatically more significant for pairs of electrons with equal and opposite momenta. Consequently, the assumptions about what states will interact significantly are imposed as an ansatz, "motivated but not justified and ultimately judged by the success of the theory at accounting for the peculiar features associated with superconductivity" (269). In relation to this Cartwright claims that because of these ad hoc features it makes sense to talk of both the BCS theory and separately of the BCS model. This is because the assumptions made in the theory go beyond what can be justified using "acceptable quantum principles from the model that BCS offer to represent superconducting phenomena" (269). Indeed she maintains that the principled/ad hoc distinction "depends on having an established bridge principle that links a given Hamiltonian with a specific model that licenses the use of that Hamiltonian" (271).

My disagreement with this interpretation rests mainly with the characterisation of the principled/ad hoc distinction; in particular with the role assigned to the "physical ideas" related to Cooper pairing. What the foregoing quote suggests is that the only principled constraints placed on the construction of the Hamiltonian are those that come directly from theory (QM), while the ideas that appeal to Cooper pairing are ad hoc in the sense that they lack this 'theoretical' justification.[11] As I will show, the fact that assumptions about Cooper pairing and interacting states are not derived directly from quantum theory does not, in itself, make them ad hoc, unless of course one classifies the construction of representative models as itself an ad hoc process. Had BCS been unable to provide a quantum-theoretical treatment for the pairing hypothesis/model, then one could legitimately claim ad hocness. However, it was firmly established as a quantum phenomenon and as such played a vital and systematic role in the BCS paper. Indeed, the success of the BCS paper lay in its ability to demonstrate that the basic interaction responsible for superconductivity was electron pairing by means of an interchange of virtual phonons; a demonstration made possible in virtue of a representative model.[12]

---

11. The 1957 paper is sometimes referred to in connection with the BCS model, with certain assumptions retained in the later and more comprehensive BCS theory. Distinguishing between the two is not important for my purposes here, so I will simply refer to the BCS theory/model. Ultimately I would want to distinguish between the BCS theory as a *generic* theory, in which Cooper pairs are formed, and the BCS model as including *specific* assumptions made in the 1957 paper about the form of the attractive potential and so on. See Morrison (2007).

12. Essentially the lattice is distorted by a moving electron, and this distortion gives rise to a phonon. A second distant electron is in turn affected when it is reached by the propagating fluctuation in the lattice charge distribution. The nature of the resulting electron-electron interaction depends on the relative magnitudes of the electronic energy change and the phonon energy. When the latter exceeds the former the interaction is attractive.

THE EVOLUTION OF AN IDEA

In order to demonstrate exactly how the notion of pairing developed by Cooper can be considered a representative model and not just an ad hoc assumption, one must first show how it provides a framework for incorporating several of the ideas about superconductivity that were in place at the time. By 1953 phenomenological approaches grounded in experiment had provided an impressive account of many of the phenomena associated with superconductivity. The Londons assumed that the superconducting state could be modelled by representing the superconductor as a giant atom made up of individual atoms, with electrons whirling around its periphery and producing the shielding currents responsible for the Meissner effect. In other words, the superconductor behaved as a single object rather than as a collection of atoms. In order to produce currents, there needed to be some order or correlation among all the electrons throughout the 'atom,' an order that could be described by a wavefunction.

The succeeded in showing that if there was a 'rigidity' of the wave function, then their equation could be derived. This rigidity, required to explain the Meissner effect, meant that the wavefunction was essentially unchanged by the presence of an eternally applied magnetic field. In the case of atoms, rigidity arises due to the energy required for the excitations of the system, which causes a large diamagnetism in a magnetic field. This led the Londons to suggest that the rigidity of the wavefunction may be due to a separation between the ground state and the excited states; in other words, an energy gap may be present. The idea that a macroscopic piece of matter could have a macroscopic wavefunction was certainly controversial, since the application of quantum mechanical ideas of this sort typically involved microscopic objects. No correlation among atoms of the type supposed by the Londons seemed applicable in the macroscopic domain. However, the quantum mechanical picture imposed on their representational model (which presented a hypothetical picture of a superconductor) enabled them to account for the coherent behaviour required for supercurrents. In fact, Fritz London (1950) suggested that a superconductor is a quantum structure on a macroscopic scale, a kind of solidification or condensation of the average momentum distribution of the electrons.

Even in this early stage in the development of superconductivity we have a representative model of the superconducting state that involves interaction between electrons in a giant atom. And it was the attempt to account for this interaction that led to ideas about the rigidity of the wavefunction and a connection with QM. As Schrieffer (1973, 24) notes, the momentum-space condensation associated with the quantum macroscopic idea was crucial to the BCS paper; indeed "many of the important general concepts were correctly conceived before the microscopic theory was developed." But, and perhaps most important, the Londons' representative model spawned the idea of an energy gap that would eventually prove crucial in the development of the microscopic theory. My point, however, is not to delve into the many different lines of thought that went into the early representation of a superconductor; instead I simply want to call attention to the main ideas and how they became incorporated into the notion of Cooper pairing, *the* fundamental feature of the representative model from which the BCS account arises. In order to see how these ideas fit together we need to briefly explain how the energy gap functions in the larger theoretical picture.

Several theorists, including Ginzburg, Frolich, and Bardeen himself, had all developed models incorporating an energy gap to describe thermal properties. It now became the task of a microscopic theory to explain this gap. That was the problem that stimulated the work of Cooper, who investigated whether one could explain, in the context of general theories of QM, why an energy gap arises. In ordinary metals one of the basic mechanisms of electrical resistance is the interaction between moving electrons (i.e. electric current) and vibrations of the crystal lattice. However, if there is a gap in the energy spectrum, quantum transitions in the electron fluid will not always be possible; the electrons will not be excited when they are moving slowly. What this implies is the possibility of movement without friction.[13] Work by Frohlich (1950) and Bardeen (1951) pointed out that an electron moving through a crystal lattice has a self-energy by being 'clothed' in virtual phonons. This distorts the lattice, which then acts on the electron by virtue of the electrostatic forces between them. Because the oscillatory distortion of the lattice is quantised in terms of phonons, one can think of the interaction between the lattice and electron as the constant emission and reabsorption of phonons by the latter. The problem, however, is that the phonon-induced interaction must be strong enough to overcome the repulsive Coulomb interaction; otherwise the former will be swamped, and superconductivity would be impossible.[14] The problem then was how to account for the strength of the phonon-induced interaction.[15] The solution was Cooper pairs.

We can see here how the representative model initially suggested by the Londons gradually evolved into a more complex account of

13. However, at temperatures near absolute zero the interaction between the electrons and the lattice is very weak, hence there is not sufficient inter-electron attraction to overcome the Coulomb repulsion. Consequently, there is no transition into the superconducting state.

14. This is what happens in the case of semiconductors, i.e., solids that also have an energy band gap but yet don't show superconducting properties. The key difference between these two types of metals is of course the presence of Cooper pairs.

15. I should mention here that the discovery of the isotope effect was crucial to both the development (in Bardeen's case) and the confirmation (in Frohlich's case) of the account of electron-phonon interactions. This discovery in 1950 confirmed that the critical temperature varies inversely with the square root of the isotopic mass. Bardeen took this to suggest that the energy gap might arise from dynamic interactions with the lattice vibrations or phonons rather than from static lattice distortions. Both had concluded that the amount of self-energy was proportional to the square of the average phonon energy. In turn this was inversely proportional to the lattice mass, so that a condensation energy equal to this self-energy would have the correct mass dependence mediated by the isotope effect. (The isotope effect showed that the critical temperature is related to the mass of the atoms of the solid.) Unfortunately, the size turns out to be three to four orders of magnitude too large.

how one might describe, in qualitative terms, the superconducting state. Although there were many twists and turns along the way, the basic ideas remained intact (i.e., the energy gap, electron interaction, and the connection with QM); only the details about how they might be implemented varied. It was another representative model describing Cooper pairs that provided the foundation from which the quantitative microscopic account could then be developed.

Cooper's (1956) paper involves an attempt to determine whether the electron-phonon interactions could give rise to a gap in the one-electron energy spectrum and in particular how one could show this primarily as a result of the exclusion principle. His approach consisted of adding two electrons to the system of electrons filling the Fermi sea. He further assumed that the electrons in the sea are held rigidly in their states so that these states are forbidden by the exclusion principle to the two extra electrons. The problem is somewhat artificial, since the electrons in the sea would be scattered above the Fermi surface; however, if this possibility was allowed, then one would immediately have to solve a many-body rather than just a two-body problem.

Cooper's wavefunction was essentially a solution to a problem that neglected all terms involving operators referring to states within the sea.[16] He worked out the problem of two electrons interacting via an attractive potential V above a quiescent Fermi sea, that is, the electrons in the sea were not influenced by V, and the extra pair was restricted to states within an energy $\hbar\omega$ above the Fermi surface.[17] He found that two electrons with the same velocity moving in opposite directions with opposite spins had an attractive part that was stronger

16. For a technical discussion of the construction of the wave equation see Schrieffer (1973) and, of course, Cooper (1956) and Bardeen et al. (1957).
17. The concept of a Fermi sphere or sea refers to the idea that all the particles (nucleons or electrons) are distributed mostly into the lowest energy states, which (in the simplest case) form a spherical shape in k-space.

143

than the normal Coulomb repulsion. It was this net attractive interaction, resulting in a pairing process of the two electrons, that came to be known as Cooper pairing. As long as the net force is attractive, no matter how weak, the two electrons will form a bound state separated by an energy gap below the continuum states.

The qualitative physical picture now seemed to be in place; the phonon-induced interaction gives rise to Cooper pairing, which is responsible for the energy gap. These ideas formed the basis for the representative model of electron-electron interactions, and Cooper had shown that the relevant part of the Hamiltonian was that which coupled together the pairs.[18] Even at this point we can see that, far from being ad hoc, the pairing hypothesis had a firm quantum mechanical foundation and explained many of the features required for superconductivity. In the remaining part of this chapter I want to look at the ways in which this representative model influenced the quantitative account presented in the BCS paper, specifically the construction of the ground state wave equation. I conclude with

18. However, the conceptual centre-piece of the model of a superconductor, the notion of Cooper pairs, was not without its problems. As I have noted, Cooper's model for pairing was essentially a two-body problem; a more realistic account of the superconducting state required that one be able to write down a many-body wavefunction taking the pairing into account. But in order to do that, some fundamental problems needed to be resolved. One such problem was that if all the electrons near the Fermi surface were paired in the way that Cooper described, the pairs would strongly overlap. This results from the determination of the binding energy, which in turn determines the size of the pair wavefunction at 10^{-4} cm. However, if all the electrons take part in pairing, the average spacing between pairs would be only about 10^{-6} cm, a distance much smaller than the size of the pair. The other difficulty concerned the subtlety of the energy change in the transition from the normal to the superconducting state, which was of the order of 10^{-8} eV per electron, far smaller than the accuracy with which one could hope to calculate the energy of either the normal or the superconducting state. The root of these problems was the fact that the situation described by the model was highly artificial. More specifically, the two electrons whose interaction was considered were treated differently from the others whose role was only to occupy the Fermi sea and prevent certain states within from being occupied by the principle actors. A satisfactory account would require that all electrons be treated equally, especially with respect to the Fermi statistics. In other words, the many-body wavefunction must be anti-symmetric under interchange of the coordinates and spin indices of any two electrons.

some remarks about the importance of representation in the assessment of models.

FROM REPRESENTATIVE MODEL TO QUANTITATIVE THEORY: CONSTRUCTING THE BCS GROUND STATE

Recall that the reduced Hamiltonian expressed only terms for interactions among pairs; the question was: what kind of wavefunction composed of pairs would solve the Hamiltonian? Although the idea that led to the formulation of the wave equation came primarily from Shreiffer, Bardeen also played a significant role. He had been strongly influenced by London's notion of a macroscopic quantum state and by the idea that there would be a type of condensation in momentum space, that is, a "kind of solidification or condensation of the average momentum distribution" (1973a, 41).[19] However, because of the thermodynamic properties of the transition between the normal and superconducting state, Bardeen was also convinced that the condensation was not of the Bose-Einstein type. The strategy was to focus on the states near the Fermi surface (since those were the ones important for the superconducting transition) and set up a linear combination of those that would give the lowest energy. In doing that, certain considerations about the nature of Cooper pairs figured prominently.

The electrons that form the bound state lie in a thin shell of width $\approx \hbar\omega_q$, where $\hbar\omega_q$ is of the order of the average phonon energy of the metal. The matrix elements that take a pair of electrons from any two k values in a shell to any two others, alternate in sign due to Fermi statistics. One can, however, impose a restriction on matrix elements of a single sign by associating all possible k values in pairs (k_1 and k_2) and requiring that either none or both of the members of the pair

19. For a discussion of the influence of these ideas see Bardeen's own articles (1973a and b).

be occupied. Because the lowest energy is obtained by having the largest number of transitions, it is desirable to choose the pairs such that from any one set of values $(\mathbf{k}_1, \mathbf{k}_2)$ transitions are possible into all other pairs $(\mathbf{k'}_1, \mathbf{k'}_2)$. In addition, because the Hamiltonian conserves momentum, it would connect only those pairs that had the same total momentum $\mathbf{K}$. In other words, $\mathbf{k}_1 + \mathbf{k}_2 = \mathbf{k'}_1 + \mathbf{k'}_2 = \mathbf{K}$.

The largest number of possible transitions yielding the most appreciable lowering of energy is obtained by pairing all possible states such that their total momentum vanishes.[20] It is also energetically most favourable to restrict the pairs to those of opposite spin. In other words, BCS made the assumption that bound Cooper pairs would still result when all the electrons interacted with each other. We can understand the situation as follows: *At 0°K the superconducting ground state is a highly correlated one where in momentum space the normal electron states in a thin shell near the Fermi surface are, to the fullest extent possible, occupied by pairs of opposite spin and momentum.* Hence BCS's focus on the 'reduced' problem involving only those single electron states that had paired states filled.[21]

The 'reduced' Hamiltonian has the following form:

$$H_{red} = \Sigma_{ks} \varepsilon_k n_{ks} - \Sigma_{kk'} V_{k'k} b_{k'} b_k^+$$

The first term gives the unperturbed energy of the quasiparticles forming the pairs, while the second term is the pairing interaction in which a pair of quasiparticles in $(\mathbf{k}\uparrow, -\mathbf{k}\downarrow)$ scatter to $(\mathbf{k'}\uparrow,$

---

20. This is because resonance between each two pairs would lower the energy, so some of the possible energy lowering would be lost if all the pairs did not have the same momentum.
21. Moreover, it produced an intuitive explanation of the energy gap—each pair was interacting with many others, hence breaking one of the pairs meant losing all the negative energy that had been derived through those many interactions.

$-\mathbf{k'}\downarrow$).[22] An important feature of the Hamiltonian is that the operators $b_k^+ = c_k\uparrow^+ c_{-k}\downarrow^+$, being a product of two fermion (quasiparticle) creation operators, do not satisfy Bose statistics, since $b_k^{+2} = 0$.[23] The ground state is actually a linear superposition of the pair states, but the question is which one.

In addition to assuming that superconducting ground state energy is due uniquely to the correlation between Cooper pairs, BCS also presuppose that all interactions, except for the crucial ones, are the same for the superconducting as for the normal ground state at 0°K. The main problem in constructing the ground state wave equation is that one could not use a wavefunction where each pair state is definitely occupied or definitely empty because this would prevent the pairs from scattering and thus lowering the energy. In other words, there had to be an amplitude, say v_k, where $(\mathbf{k}\uparrow, -\mathbf{k}\downarrow)$ is occupied in ψ_0 and consequently an amplitude $u_k = (1 - v_k^2)^{\frac{1}{2}}$ where the pair state is empty. Because a large number, roughly 10^{19} pair states ($\mathbf{k'}\uparrow$, $-\mathbf{k'}\downarrow$), are involved in scattering, how the pairs interact couldn't be important; instead what was important was some kind of statistical average. Hence, the wavefunction was a kind of statistical ensemble where pairs were allowed to interact but weren't strongly correlated.

As I mentioned earlier, one of the novel features of the BCS ground state was that it did not have a definite number of electrons; a rather odd situation since there clearly could be no creation processes going on in a superconductor. What made this novel was not the notion of an indefinite number of particles itself but that this constraint was used to describe Fermi as opposed to Bose particles;

---

22. This is actually a truncated version of the three-term Hamiltonian that appears in Bardeen et al. (1957). The interaction terms are defined with a negative sign so that $V_{kk'}$ will be predominately positive for a superconductor.

23. This point is essential to the theory and leads to the energy gap being present not only for dissociating a pair but for making a pair move with a total momentum different from the common momentum of the rest of the pairs.

that the creation and annihilation operators referred to electrons. The *form* of the wavefunction was not novel; others, including Pines and Frolich, had used it in conjunction with Bose particles since these (e.g., phonons, photons, and mesons) clearly could be created. Similarly, in other high-energy contexts involving scattering phenomena it was common to write down wavefunctions that had an indefinite number of particles. However, this was not the case for the low-energy phenomena, where it was assumed that the number of particles should be definite.

How did BCS justify this rather bold step? Essentially they appealed to a fundamental idea from SM. Given that there were so many pairs spread over such a large volume, it made sense to think of them as not being completely correlated with one another but correlated only in a statistical sense.[24] In other words the wavefunction represented a kind of statistical ensemble where the pairs were partly independent, constituting a superposition of states with different numbers of particles. A Hartree type approximation (which does not conserve the number of particles) was used where the probability distribution of a particular state does not depend (at the level of description that is given) on the distribution of the others, something that had never been applied to electrons. This was justified by arguing that the occupancy of any one state was basically independent of whether other states were occupied.[25]

24. Bardeen later pointed out, however, that the form of the wavefunction, with the all-important common momentum for paired states, is determined by energetic rather than purely statistical considerations. See his 1957 reply to Dyson, quoted in Bardeen (1973b).

25. This particular aspect of the model definitely had the appearance of an ad hoc assumption, and despite its apparent efficacy BCS were not happy with the idea of an indefinite number of states. They attempted to downplay the idea by claiming that the spread of particle number in their state would be small, or by claiming that the superconducting wavefunction could be taken to be the projection of the state that they had introduced onto the space that did have a definite number of particles. Later developments in the theory would reveal that this indefiniteness was an essential feature of the superconducting state since it

The basic picture, then, that constitutes the representative model can be summarised in the following way. The foundation of super-conductivity is the attractive interaction (Cooper pairing) between electrons that results from their coupling to phonons. Once this physical picture was in place, BCS then focused on providing a full quantum mechanical treatment that involved solving the "pairing Hamiltonian." While this required the use of the type of interpretive models Cartwright discusses, those models would be required for any application of QM. In this case much more was needed to flesh out the complete picture, specifically how the details of electron pair-ing described by the representative model could be embedded into the larger theoretical framework of QM.

The representative model tells us that in the presence of the electron interaction the system forms a coherent superconducting ground state characterised by occupation of the individual particle states in pairs such that if one member of the pair is occupied the other is also. Then BCS went on to calculate the energy difference between the normal and the superconducting phase at zero tem-perature and found it to be proportional to the square of the num-ber of electrons (n_c) virtually excited in coherent pairs above the Fermi surface. They also showed that the electron-hole spectrum contains a gap proportional to n_c. We can see then that the entire theoretical picture on which the BCS account developed was pro-vided by the representative model. The model itself underwent an evolution during the development of the theory, but it remained the focal point from which the various other aspects of the account emerged.

allowed for the introduction of the quantum phase defined over the whole of the macro-scopic superconductor. However, it was still not possible to think of electrons being created or destroyed, since we were dealing with low-temperature, solid-state phenomena. To that extent BCS emphasised that their system really did have a definite number of electrons despite the form of the wavefunction.

SOME PHILOSOPHICAL CONCLUSIONS

The foregoing discussion was intended to illustrate two points: (1) the role of the representative model in the development of the quantitative theory of BCS, and (2) some general features of representational nature of models. With respect to (1) we can see that many of the fundamental ideas present in the original model developed in the Londons' work find a place, albeit in a different form, in the BCS theory. By transforming the way these ideas were understood, BCS incorporated many of Fritz London's suggestions into the context of modern field theory. But perhaps the most important issue is the focus on the reduced or pairing Hamiltonian, which is a direct consequence of how the causal role of Cooper pairing was understood. Rather than being ad hoc, this emphasis on the reduced Hamiltonian emerges naturally from the representative model used to describe what BCS took to be the essential features of the superconducting state.

However, once it came to finding a solution for the pairing Hamiltonian, a seemingly ad hoc strategy emerged. The fact that the occupation of one state was independent of the occupation of another was the essence of the Hartree approximation. In order to avoid the specific *physical* assumption of an indefinite number of particles, BCS took as the ground state wavefunction the projection of ψ onto the space of exactly N pairs—a projection onto a space that had a definite number of pairs. In other words, it was possible to distinguish particular ad hoc assumptions from those that resulted from a systematic development of earlier work, or those that were simply idealising, such as the neglect of anisotropic effects that result in superconducting properties being dependent only on gross features rather than details of the band structure.

While some of these details, like the indefiniteness assumption, seemed ad hoc at the time, the latter soon emerged as an essential feature of superconductivity relating to the phase of the wavefunction and the Josephson effect. Although many different accounts of electron pairing have been put forward, accounts that differ from the one provided by BCS, the basic fact of pairing, which constituted the core of the representative model, was and remains the fundamental mechanism at the foundation of superconductivity. Indeed, measurements on superconductors are now used to derive detailed quantitative information about electron-phonon interaction and its energy dependence.

Quite simply, the representative model furnished the fundamental causal mechanism responsible for superconductivity and provided the justification for focusing on the reduced Hamiltonian, as well as informing the specific constraints imposed on the BCS wavefunction.[26] The notion of representation present in the BCS model is straightforward in that it provides an account of how a superconducting system might be constituted. The model served as the source of mediated knowledge, in the sense that one does not have direct

26. Cartwright of course discusses some of these ideas regarding representation in what she calls the 'full underlying model' (275). She describes it in the following way: "there is a sea of loose electrons of well-defined momenta moving through a periodic lattice of positive ions whose natural behaviour, discounting interactions with the electron sea, is represented as a lattice of coupled harmonic oscillators, subject to Born-Karman boundary conditions" (275). But her point is that this is *not* a literal presentation but rather a representation of the structure of some given sample of superconducting material. It is itself a model and not the "real thing" truncated (276). A primary model of this kind aims to be explanatory not only by representing the essential features of superconductivity but also by bringing these elements under the umbrella of the theory (276). Cartwright's description of the underlying model involves a number of QM assumptions: (1) the particles in the model called 'electrons' are fermions and hence obey the exclusion principle; (2) those referred to as positive ions are bosons; and (3) the particles in the model affect each other through Coulomb interactions. She goes on to claim that the only kind of Hamiltonian used to describe this underlying model is the one for the Coulomb potential. Moreover, it is impossible to solve the equation for the ground state of a Hamiltonian like this. Instead, BCS substitute the new interpretive models (like the harmonic model) with their corresponding Hamiltonians, together with other constraints that one hopes will result in the full underlying model agreeing with the results from the BCS model (276).
    I am unclear as to what exactly this full underlying model is, but, it certainly isn't what I have called the "representative model." Moreover, the steps in Cartwright's story seem to present an account that differs significantly from the development of Bardeen et al. (1957).

access to the pairing process itself; in other words, the model was the focus of investigation and provided the foundation for the development of the theoretical account. Other aspects of the system were neglected, in that they dealt only with a reduced Hamiltonian. For example, there are many terms in the complete interaction that connect pairs with total momentum $q \neq 0$. These have little effect on the energy and can be treated as a perturbation. The justification for this stems from the way the representative model describes the system; in other words, it is representative of the processes responsible for superconductivity, and the theory is then applied accordingly.

This kind of mediated knowledge furnished by representative models is, I think, characteristic of a good deal of scientific modelling, with differences across contexts dependent on the specific nature of the representation required in each case. In the BCS example the representative model provided a causal account of the mechanisms responsible for superconductivity, but this isn't necessary; one could simply have a hypothetical representation of the sort described by Maxwell's ether model. There the representation involved a number of fictional components employed for the purposes of developing a quantitative account of field-theoretic phenomena. In other words, representative models can 'represent' in a variety of ways, and the adequacy of the representation will depend, to a great extent, on what we want the model to do for us and how well it can fit into extant theoretical frameworks. These pragmatic features related to

As I understand it, once the representative model was in place BCS could then focus on the reduced or pairing Hamiltonian, which connects the pairs with zero net momentum and supplies the interaction terms. While the representative model embodies some of the ideas outlined in Cartwright's underlying model, the construction of the wave equation involves the extension of the model to include conditions specific to the. pairing mechanism. As she presents it, Cartwright's "full underlying model" doesn't really tell us much about how we get an account of superconductivity within a quantum framework. Her reconstruction does tell us about the importance of "Bloch states" and the "Coulomb potential," but we need much more than this to properly understand how the qualitative and quantitative aspects of superconductivity are brought together in the BCS account.

use is in complete agreement with C&C. My disagreement with their account is that it tells only part of the story and does so in a way that is somewhat misleading about how scientific models represent physical systems.

In Morrison (1998) and (1999) I discussed various kinds of representation, ranging from the attempts to accurately depict the pendulum in its use as a measuring instrument to the structural dependencies that exist in the model used for the construction of boundary layer theory in hydrodynamics. In each case the legitimacy of the representation is a function of the model's intended domain and use, but none of that can be determined independently of theoretical constraints that guide the process of representation at one level or another. Once we decide what needs to be modelled, these constraints determine, to some extent, how to do it. They function like rules in a game. In some contexts we may only need a partial description of the system in order to use the model for prediction and/or explanation of some specific phenomenon. In other contexts, such as superconductivity, we want to know how (possibly) the superconducting state arises, and for that we need a reasonably well worked-out model of the basic processes that go on in superconducting metals generally. That function is fulfilled by the representative model described earlier: a model that provides an explanation of the fundamental features that give rise to superconductivity. The model, by nature, leaves out certain elements deemed to be inessential parts of the real system and in doing so offers us a 'mediated' account of how the system is constituted. Again, I use the term 'mediated' here to indicate that the model functions as a kind of 'stand-in' or replacement for the system under investigation and that it furnishes only a partial representation; it is, in essence, one step removed from the real system.

Because scientific modelling typically embodies this kind of partial representation, the natural question to ask concerns when there is sufficient detail for the model to count as a credible source of knowledge. This, however, cannot be answered in advance, nor is there an algorithm for determining the appropriate methods for model construction and legitimation. This fact is perhaps best illustrated in Bohr's response to BCS, where he claims that while they had the essential answer, the understanding of what the pairs *really were* and why the other terms were unimportant was completely obscure. Bohr claimed it was an interesting idea, but nature just wasn't that simple. Clearly, for Bohr more explanatory principles or facts were necessary to justify the BCS account. For others, the model was sufficient as an explanation of superconductivity, but the lack of gauge invariance spoke against its status as a general theory. But these kinds of debates are not indicative of epistemological difficulties; rather they are simply a part of the practice of model construction and acceptance, as well as a general feature of scientific investigation.

Let me end with a remark, or perhaps a question, about representation. Has our understanding of the role of representational models in BCS been hindered by not having a "theory" of representation? In other words, what questions concerning how the model informed theory construction that haven't been answered here would be answered if a theory of representation were in place; and what would such a theory look like? van Fraassen (2008) claims that there are no representations in nature; there can't be any representations without agents. But I don't take this to mean that representation is completely open-ended. However, attempting to articulate a theory of scientific representation seems like a hopeless endeavour, not only because of the pragmatic features of an agent-based relation but also because of the variety of different contexts in which models function in a representational role. As I have noted, none of this suggests that the representational features of models are arbitrary, that BCS could have represented superconductivity in a variety of different ways. But any further explanation of what constitutes a representation will most likely fall under the domain of cognitive psychology.

In chapter 5, I continue with the 'representation' theme by examining the role played by inconsistent models in representing a physical system. As I will show, inconsistency is a peculiar problem where modelling is concerned; in some cases it prevents us from drawing any conclusions about the relationship between the model and its target system, while in others it seems necessary for capturing the diversity of the system/phenomenon under investigation. In chapter 3, I showed how fictional representation allows us to draw empirical conclusions about concrete phenomena and examined the differences between fictional representation and more common forms of idealisation and abstraction. In each of these contexts the model's ability to represent the target is crucial, but in each case the nature of the representation is different, further illustrating why a theory of representation seems unnecessary.

5

Making the Best of It

Inconsistent versus Complementary Models

INCONSISTENCY AND PERSPECTIVISM

Inconsistency has always been seen as perhaps the most worrisome problem for human reasoning. Elementary logic tells us that everything follows from a contradiction; hence, if one holds inconsistent beliefs, absurdities ensue. One way of attempting to deal with this problem has been the development of paraconsistent logic (Priest 2002 and Brown 2002, among others), which simply denies the idea that everything follows from a contradiction (the principle of explosion), a conclusion arrived at by rejecting, for example, disjunctive syllogism or other inference rules such as double negation and transitivity. Regardless of which approach one favours, what paraconsistent logic purports to do is facilitate reasoning with inconsistent information and allow us to apply that information in practical contexts. While many of the motivations for paraconsistency come from logic and mathematics (attempts to solve the liar paradox, inconsistent models of arithmetic, etc.), there are also more practical ones, such as cases of automated reasoning where a computer has a large information store, not all of which is consistent.

A related worry stems from the problem of inconsistent theories and models in science. These, too, are sometimes seen as motivations for the application of paraconsistent logic and some authors, including Brown (1992), have attempted to deal with the problem in exactly that way. Other discussions of inconsistency have focused on problems with allegedly inconsistent theories like electrodynamics and Newtonian cosmology.[1] My concern here is not to uncover the logical structure of reasoning with inconsistent theories/models but rather to inquire as to whether, and under what circumstances, the use of many different models to describe the same system actually results in inconsistency, and if so, whether that inconsistency undermines the epistemic status of the information we receive via those models.

If we take models as providing information about physical systems, then inconsistency presents a problem for how we should understand the models themselves (should they be interpreted realistically, instrumentally, etc.) as well as the accuracy/reliability of the information they provide. In some sense the problem of idealisation and how to understand the information supplied by idealised models is a variation on the problem of inconsistency, since the idealisations present in models and theories are typically inconsistent with realistic descriptions of the phenomena. However, these cases are often seen as unproblematic since the alleged gap between the model and reality can be closed by the addition of parameters and the use of approximation techniques when applying the model to concrete systems. If this is achieved in a non–ad hoc way, then it is typically taken as evidence for a realistic interpretation of the model. In cases of genuine inconsistency these options are often limited, resulting

---

1. Although there is an ongoing debate in the literature about the status of internally inconsistent theories, particularly electrodynamics, my concern here is about models and other types of inconsistency. For discussion of the former see Meheus (2002), Frisch (2005), Belot (2007), Muller (2007), and Vickers (2008).

in radically different models of the system being proposed, each of which describes it in ways that contradict the assumptions of the original model. In other words, the problem of inconsistent models often arises because of the limited capacity of the models to account for and explain a system's behaviour.

In these contexts we usually have no way to determine which of the many contradictory models is the more faithful representation, especially if each is able to generate accurate predictions for a certain features of the phenomena. Hence the issue of how to interpret the model—as a work of fiction, a tool with instrumental value, or a more or less literal description of the system—raises philosophical as well as scientific concerns.[2] For example, there is currently no coherent account of the structure of the atomic nucleus. Although QM is the theory that best describes protons and neutrons and their many properties, there is no established account of how these particles interact with each other inside nuclei. Consequently, the epistemic status of nuclear models is highly questionable.

Due to the difficulties motivating a realist account of idealised and inconsistent models (and theories), many weakened versions of realism have evolved, including different varieties of structuralism.[3] A more promising approach seems to be the form of perspectival realism recently put forward by Giere (2006). The position is intended as

2. A common view is that inconsistent models present no more of an epistemic problem than other types of "false" models. This doesn't seem right to me, if only for the simple reason that all models are false in that they embody idealisations, but in most cases we can add correction factors to refine the model and thereby make it a more realistic representation of a physical system. If we think that process enhances the epistemic status of the model, then we have no corresponding way to achieve that if the system in question admits of several (in the case of the nucleus, 32) inconsistent models that make fundamentally different claims about theoretical structure. One or several models of the same system that are not fundamentally inconsistent presents a completely different epistemic challenge from several models that are.
3. The epistemic version emphasises a commitment to only the structural and/or mathematical features of theories/models, while the ontic version stresses the existence of only these structures, as opposed to scientific entities and properties. While this seems to accord well

a middle ground between strong realism and strong constructivism with respect to model/theory interpretation. One of his main claims about perspectivism is that laws of nature should be understood as general principles that define a perspective but make no claims about the world. Models constructed in accordance with a perspective (e.g. quantum theory) make specific claims about specific parts of the world, which are then tested against various other instrumental perspectives. We should reject the search for absolute "complete" models in favour of contingency and "good fit" to some specific aspect of a system. Representational models are designed so that "elements of the model can be identified or coordinated with features of the world" (63). What this means is that c is a fundamental constant of nature relative to the perspectives in which it appears. Consequently, it would seem that from different perspectives phenomena will have different characteristics; hence we needn't assume there is only one correct model for a physical system. We can use quantum models in some contexts and classical models in others, even if we're dealing with the same phenomena. Very briefly, perspectivism is the view that: from the perspective of theory T, model M represents system S in a particular way.

While this sounds like an appealing way to address the problem of inconsistent models, some nagging worries remain; in particular, how we should answer the general question "Is model M an accurate representation of system S?" What perspectivism seems to imply is that the question itself has no meaning unless a perspective has been specified. There is one obvious sense in which this is true—we are always working within the confines of our current theories, and it is they that form the backdrop against which such questions are

---

with the increasing mathematisation of science, it also seems clear that empirical science is about objects, hence we expect our theories/models to incorporate that information in a meaningful way.

asked. But epistemically it isn't clear that anything significant follows from this, or whether perspectivism can help us solve the problem of interpreting the information that inconsistent models provide. For example, there is only one nucleus, but if we say that from perspective x it looks like y, and from perspective a it looks like b, we are no further ahead in finding out its real nature. We know the nucleus is a quantum phenomenon, yet we use classical models to represent fission. Despite the success of the model, no one is prepared to claim that there is any sense in which the liquid drop model could be an accurate representation of the nucleus. So adopting a particular perspective doesn't help in these contexts. In other words, it doesn't help us to say that from the classical perspective the nucleus behaves like a liquid drop if we know that the particles inside the nucleus are quantum mechanical. If we take perspectivism seriously, then we are forced to say that the nucleus has no nature in itself and we can only answer questions about it once a particular perspective is specified.

Giere sees this situation as unproblematic, claiming that perspectivism provides "an account of science that brings observation and theory, perception and cognition, closer together than they have seemed in objective accounts" (2006, 15). Moreover, despite the legitimacy of the different perspectives used to evaluate the epistemic status of theoretical claims, perspectivism does not "degenerate into a silly relativism" (13). But it isn't at all clear why not. Although we needn't assume there is only one correct model for a system or that there is anything like a "complete" model, it shouldn't follow from this that we can have contradictory accounts of how a system is constituted. Perspectivism allows this, or at the very least doesn't seem to rule it out. But if we insist on denying the seeming relativistic consequences of perspectivism, we must at least acknowledge that it commits us to a nontrivial version of instrumentalism, particularly since we have no obvious way of eliminating the less profitable or useful perspectives.

While scientific perspectivism may not be able to aid us in reconciling theoretical inconsistencies, other forms of perspectivism may be more promising. Epistemic perspectivism, which is essentially the claim that there is "no view from nowhere," has had a long and distinguished history in addressing epistemological problems more generally. The most established account of perspectivism is probably Kantian constructivism, but many attribute the articulation of perspectivism as a philosophical view to Nietzsche. Although its roots likely go back to Plato's Protagoras, other philosophers, including Wittgenstein and Leibniz, all adopted some form of perspectivism in dealing with problems of knowledge. More recently, van Fraassen (2008) has embraced perspectivism in connection with his views on representation—that there can be no representation other than the way things are used, taken, and so on. While I am certainly sympathetic to the idea that there is always some general perspective, whether it is cognitive, sensory, or another form, that we as human agents use to engage with the world, nothing follows from this about the more restrictive account that utilises particular theories as the perspective from which we should make ontological claims. While there may not be a "view from nowhere," it doesn't follow that there has to be a "view from everywhere," which is, in a sense, what scientific perspectivism prescribes, or at least allows.

In the remainder of this chapter I look at some examples from scientific modelling where perspectivism seems to play a prominent role. However, despite the appearance of success, perspectivism is of no help in resolving the problem of conflicting models. It is only appropriate in cases where there is no real inconsistency among the different models or where it is already embedded in the theory or framework being applied. In other words, the scientific context itself embodies a form of perspectivism. Hence, philosophically speaking, perspectivism is completely idle as a position from which to interpret or shed light on inconsistent or incompatible scientific claims.

The examples I discuss involve two distinct approaches for using diverse models for the same system. I show why in some cases this seems relatively unproblematic (models of turbulence), while others represent genuine difficulties when attempting to interpret the information that models provide (nuclear models). What the examples show is that while complementary models needn't be a hindrance to knowledge acquisition, the kind of inconsistency present in nuclear cases *is*, since it is indicative of a lack of genuine theoretical understanding. It is important to note here that the differences in modelling are not a direct consequence of the status of our knowledge of turbulent flows, as opposed to nuclear dynamics; both face fundamental theoretical problems in the construction and application of models. However, as I will show, the 'problem context(s)' in which the modelling takes place plays a decisive role in evaluating the epistemic merit of the models themselves. The theoretical difficulties that give rise to inconsistent, as opposed to complementary, models impose epistemic and methodological burdens that cannot be overcome by invoking philosophical strategies like perspectivism, paraconsistency, or partial structures.

MODELS AND METHODS: THE CASE OF TURBULENT FLOWS

As I mentioned, the problem of inconsistent models can be understood as a variant on the problem of idealisation—albeit one that adds a layer of complexity to what to what many already see as a philosophical quandary. This quandary involves the question mentioned in some of the previous chapters: how is it possible to extract information from idealised models and how we should determine the epistemic value of that information? Put differently, how do we get reliable information from models that depict the world in nonrealistic ways? In chapter 4, I discussed various strategies for bridging the gap between the description offered by the model and the reality it is meant to depict. In some cases this can be done very effectively by adding various parameters to the model to make it more realistic. In others, gaps remain because we don't know the nature of the physical system being modelled and are unaware of its properties, or we are unable to use approximation techniques in an effective way.

In the case of inconsistent models, however, there is a further difficulty to overcome, namely, determining which of a variety of different, contradictory descriptions actually provides us with correct information about what the target system is like. So not only are there problems bridging the gap between the model description and the physical system itself, but there is often no way to determine the status of the information the model(s) provide because each one gives a different account of how the physical system is constituted. The addition of parameters doesn't help, because we have a number of different models that cannot be reconciled with each other. Consequently, no increase in coherence accompanies successful deidealisation of any particular model. In other words, we have a case of under determination in the extreme. And, as I will show, this is enhanced in cases where the successes of one model rest on exactly the assumptions that are contradicted by others.

The problem of inconsistent models typically involves either those that are inconsistent with each other or those that are inconsistent with background theory, or both. In some contexts the problem is easily dealt with and poses no significant difficulties. This is especially true for cases where inconsistent models are implemented for different *parts* of a physical system, rather than having inconsistent models for one and the same system taken as a whole. In the former case some features can be modelled in isolation from others, making the different model assumptions relatively independent in that they have no impact on the assumptions relevant to the other features.

Models of fluid flows provide an especially clear illustration of this type of practice, and in that sense, even though the models themselves involve different and incompatible ways of representing the flows, when taken together they are better understood as complementary rather than contradictory. The discussion that follows highlights the reasons why these models are best understood as complementary and how the context of application facilitates that interpretation. Ironically it was modelling different parts of a fluid in two different ways that provided the solution to a glaring inconsistency that existed between theory and experiment in early twentieth-century fluid dynamics—the problem of frictional flows.[4]

Different representations ≠ inconsistency. Fluid dynamics and turbulent flows constitute some of the least understood areas of modern physics. Because of the complex nature of certain types of flows, together with the mathematical intractability associated with the N-S equations, several different types of models are used; in fact there are several groups of models each of which contains different submodels that are employed in different circumstances. The important issues for the present purpose are how this kind of multifaceted approach to modelling in fluid dynamics differs in important ways from the proliferation of models in nuclear physics, and what the philosophical implications of those differences are, especially with respect to perspectivism. To argue that case we need to see how what I have called the 'problem context' determines various aspects of model construction and application and why models that might appear inconsistent may not actually be so.

4. In Morrison (1999) I discussed the development of the boundary layer theory based on a model constructed by Ludwig Prandtl in the early 1900s in an effort to show how model construction and development often progressed independently of an overarching theory. In other words, the equations governing fluid dynamics provided no insight into how one might solve the problem of frictional flows. Here I want to use the example of turbulent flows to show not only how we can use incompatible models in a consistent way but also why perspectivalism lacks the resources to solve the problem.

The first real example of multiple modelling for fluids was the development of the boundary layer by Ludwig Prandtl in 1904. This concept allowed for a simplification of the equations of fluid flow by dividing the flow field into two areas: inside the boundary layer, where viscosity is dominant, creating the drag on a body, and outside the boundary layer, where viscosity can be neglected. At the time it was thought that in most cases, like water and air, there are very small coefficients of viscosity resulting in small shearing stresses. As a result, the theory of perfect fluids (derived from Euler's equations) neglected viscosity, thereby allowing for far-reaching simplification of the equations of motion. The problem, however, is that even in cases of very small viscosity (air and water) there is an adherence to a solid boundary (no-slip), which creates a large discrepancy between the value of drag in a real and perfect fluid. The N-S equations incorporated frictional forces but were too complicated to allow a full solution.

Once the fluid is divided conceptually, a mathematical model was able to facilitate a number of approximations to the N-S equations that apply in the boundary layer. One then obtains a set of solvable equations for that area while treating the rest of the fluid as ideal, thereby allowing for a different set of solvable equations for the remainder of the fluid. What is particularly interesting in this case is that the approximations used in the solutions come not from a direct simplification of the mathematics of the theory but from the phenomenology of the fluid flow. In other words, it was impossible to reconcile the physical differences between real and ideal fluids simply by retaining the no-slip condition in the mathematical analysis of inviscid fluids. The importance of this fact is that it illustrates, in a very pointed way, how theoretical modelling differs from what might be termed 'mathematical manipulation.' In the latter context the goal is to massage the mathematics to coincide with empirical data. Theoretical modelling on the other hand involves representing the system in such a way that empirical data can be predicted or explained from those assumptions. The boundary layer case provides a clear example of the difference.

In the model of the fluid containing a boundary layer, if we assume that the layer is very thin, the N-S equation can be simplified into a solvable form. Provided that certain boundary conditions are satisfied, an analytical continuation of the solution in the boundary layer to the region of ideal flow can be given. A very simple example is the case of steady flow of a fluid over a flat plate, where we choose the x axis in the direction of flow and the origin so that the plate occupies the plane $y = 0$, $x \geq 0$. (Assume the system is infinite in the z direction so that velocity is independent of z.) The N-S and continuity equations are:

$$\partial v_x / \partial x + \partial v_y / \partial y = 0 \qquad (1)$$

$$v_x \partial v_x / \partial x + v_y \partial v_x / \partial y = \left(-1/\rho\right) / \partial p / \partial x$$
$$+ \left(\eta/\rho\right)(\partial^2 v_x / \partial x^2 + \partial^2 v_x / \partial y^2) \ (2)$$

$$v_x \partial v_y / \partial x + v_y \partial v_y / \partial y = \left(-1/\rho\right) / \partial p / \partial y$$
$$+ \left(\eta/\rho\right)(\partial^2 v_y / \partial x^2 + \partial^2 v_y / \partial y^2) \ (3)$$

The thinness δ of the boundary layer compared with the linear dimensions of the boundary (l) allows for the possibility of certain approximations in the equations of motion, thereby enabling one to determine the flow in the boundary layer. In that area $\partial / \partial x$ will be of the order $1 / l$ and hence much smaller than $\partial / \partial y$, which is of the order $1 / \delta$. This allows us to replace (2) with the simpler boundary layer equation

$$v_x \partial v_x / \partial x + v_y \partial v_x / \partial y = \left(\eta/\rho\right)(\partial^2 v_x / \partial y^2 \qquad (4)$$

which is solved in conjunction with (5). For this system of equations we have boundary conditions at the surface of the plate

$$V_x = V_y = 0, \text{ for } y = 0 \text{ and } x \geq 0 \qquad (5)$$

while at large distances from the plate the velocity is the same as in the main area of the fluid. These equations can be solved by defining a stream function φ (x,y) that allows us to solve the continuity equation. By changing to dimensionless variables, we can then define a function that satisfies a nonlinear ordinary differential equation (the Blausius equation), which can be solved numerically.

The boundary layer concept allowed for a reduction of the N-S equations to a simpler form that was applicable only to the layer, with the rest of the fluid modelled in the usual way. The boundary layer equations are similar to N-S in that they consist of coupled, nonlinear PDEs but behave in a completely different way mathematically. The N-S equations have elliptical behaviour which requires that the complete flow field be solved simultaneously in accordance with specific boundary conditions defined along the entire boundary of the flow. The boundary layer equations have parabolic behaviour, which can be solved in a step-by-step fashion from the point where the flow encounters a body and is subject to certain inflow conditions and boundary conditions at the edge of the boundary layer. The systematic calculation yields the flow variables in the boundary layer, including the velocity gradient at the surface of the wall. The shear stress at the wall and the skin-friction drag on the surface is obtained directly from the velocity gradients.[5]

5. Although Prandtl only offered some solution approaches to the boundary layer equations, he nevertheless gave rough calculations of friction drag on a flat plate and discussed aspects of boundary layer separation under the influence of an adverse pressure gradient. The equations themselves were solved by Blausius, who showed that for certain types of pressure gradients in the flow, the boundary layer equations reduce from coupled nonlinear partial differentials to a single ordinary differential equation. Prandtl's work clarified the conceptual

Prandtl's solution involved using different descriptions for different areas of the fluid that exhibit different properties.[6] What this means is that we cannot have a single model of the fluid that represents the way it flows around a boundary. Despite the two different models, they needn't be interpreted as inconsistent, since they apply to different types of behaviour in different parts of the fluid. This is exactly the type of situation for which perspectivism is ideally suited; depending on the perspective one takes, one will choose to model the fluid in different ways. But, and this is the important point, scientific perspectivism is already implicit in the scientific context; any appeal to philosophy as the interpretive vehicle is redundant. Scientific perspectivism is simply part of the problem solving technique.

The subsequent history of fluid dynamics is replete with the use of different models used for treating different features of fluids, especially cases of turbulent flows. Because turbulent motions contribute to the transport of momentum, heat, and mass in most fluids, they exert an important influence on such things as velocity and temperature over the flow, and in that sense are part of the fundamentals of fluid mechanics. As I will show, the different types of modelling display very different approaches from those used in the Prandtl boundary layer example. While they may appear to give conflicting interpretations about the nature of fluids, a closer examination reveals that they involve different approaches for idealising the nature of turbulent flows rather than different fundamental assumptions about the

confusion surrounding the role of viscosity in fluid flow, including the physical mechanisms responsible for flow separation from a surface, and in doing so enabled the calculation of skin-friction drag.

6. Rueger (2005) provides very nice discussion of this case with an eye to showing how one can give a unified treatment of the fluid by employing two different perspectives. While his account is interesting, approaching the problem in this way would not have facilitated the result arrived at using Prandtl's methodology. Moreover, it tends to gloss over the fact that the fluid itself behaves differently in different regions—the physical fact that motivated and underlies the mathematical treatment.

dynamics of the flows. Here again perspectivism plays a role, but that role is defined by the scientific context of the problem, not a philosophical interpretation of apparent incompatibilities associated with modelling assumptions.

DIFFERENT MODELS–DIFFERENT METHODS

The N-S equations together with the continuity equation provide a closed set that give a valid description of laminar and turbulent flows. In principle these can be simulated by solving the exact equations with appropriate boundary conditions using direct numerical simulation. In practice, however, this is rarely done, since it requires that the time-step for the simulations be small enough to resolve the fastest fluctuations, making the computing time and memory prohibitive.

Until recently, these problems were dealt with using empirical methods, which did little more than correlate experimental results using dimensional analysis. These were used only for very simple problems and provided no generality or theoretical insight into the nature of turbulence. Consequently, different methods were established that were based on conservation laws for mass, momentum, and energy. These were exact equations that expressed the details of fluid motion, but because they could not be solved, a statistical approach was developed that averaged over a long time scale relative to that of the turbulent motion. This created a new problem in that the averaged equations no longer constituted a closed system and contained unknown terms representing the transport of mean momentum, heat, and mass by the turbulent motion. Their closure required empirical input which could be introduced in two different ways: (1) integral methods (suitable for thin shears or boundary layer flows) that make use of empirical shapes so that PDEs can be reduced to ordinary ones, and (2) field methods that employ PDEs and require the specification, determined by a model, of the turbulent transport terms appearing in the equations at each point in the flow. In summary, because transport processes cannot be calculated using exact methods, they must be approximated using models that relate the transport quantities to the mean flow field.

In most cases one needn't be concerned with all the details of the turbulent motion, only with its effects on the gross properties of the flow. Consequently, there is no need to solve for the instantaneous variables if averaged variables can be used instead. Because the statistical-averaging process introduces unknown turbulent correlations into the mean-flow equations, the turbulence model involves a set of relations and equations needed to determine the unknown turbulent correlations that have arisen from the averaging process. Although there are a variety of different models with different complexity, they can be generally classified as eddy-viscosity or Reynolds stress models. The former deals with transport and dissipation of energy, and the unknown correlations are assumed to be proportional to the spatial gradients of the quantity they are meant to transport. In the Reynolds stress models, the unknown correlations are determined directly from the solution of differential transport equations in which they are the dependent variables, but there are several different methods for doing so.

The major difficulty is that in all cases the averaging implies more unknowns than equations, and various modelling assumptions are required to close the set. A consequence of this is that solutions of equations closed with turbulence models are no longer exact representations of physical problems implied by the boundary conditions. This requires that the uncertainties be subject to some type of appraisal, usually a comparison with experiment if possible. The extent to which a turbulent model is able to represent a flow depends on the complexity, making assessments difficult and lacking in objective constraints regarding the legitimacy of the model.

The use of Reynolds averaged equations means that certain information has been lost and further approximations are required to represent the fluctuating quantities known as Reynolds stresses. This has the advantage of reducing the number of unknowns to equal the number of equations. Many turbulence models use the eddy-viscosity concept to determine the Reynolds stresses from

$$-\rho \overline{u_i u_j} = \mu_T \left(\frac{\partial U_i}{\partial x_j} + \frac{\partial U_j}{\partial x_i} \right) - \rho \times KE \frac{2d_{ij}}{3}$$

where $-u_i u_j$ are Reynolds stress components, μ_T is the eddy viscosity and KE is the turbulent kinetic energy; μ_T is not a fluid property but depends on the state of turbulence and hence must be determined by the turbulence model. It can vary significantly from one point to another in the flow and from flow to flow.[7] The eddies are conceived as lumps of fluid that, like molecules, collide and exchange momentum. Like molecular viscosity, which is proportional to the average velocity and mean free path of the molecules, the eddy viscosity is considered proportional to a velocity characterising the fluctuating motion and to a typical length of that motion (the Prandtl mixing length). There are of course several places where the analogy breaks down: turbulent eddies are not rigid bodies that retain their identity, and large eddies responsible for momentum transfer, as well as their mean free paths, are not small compared with the flow domain as required by the kinetic theory. Still, models employing this notion work well, primarily because the eddy viscosity V_t is defined in such a way that it can be determined to a good approximation. This is due

7. See Cebeci (2004).

to the fact that the velocity and length scales can be approximated reasonably well in many flows.

The simplest turbulence models are the "zero-equation" models, named so because they do not solve an additional transport equation in order to predict the contributions of the turbulence. The simplest of these uses a constant value for the eddy viscosity. These are often used for hydraulics problems but are not proper turbulence models, since they are too coarse to describe the flow behaviour. Mixing length models, originally developed by Prandtl, are more realistic in relating eddy viscosity to the mean-velocity gradient but contain an unknown parameter l_m. They are, however, of little use in complex flows because of the difficulty in specifying l_m, which can be determined empirically in simple shear-layer flows. But for turbulent shear flows other than wall boundary layers, the models require different expressions for mixing lengths and eddy viscosity.

Some of these limitations are overcome by using what are called one-equation models, which account for the transport of turbulence quantities. There are many such models, most of which involve a modelled form of the k-equation, where k is the kinetic energy of the turbulent motion and is a direct measure of the intensity of the turbulent fluctuations. Many of these models are complex and involve different parameters, such as wall distance calculations; but the overall difficulty is in specifying L—the length scale distribution. The specification of L depends on the different ways that different models introduce assumptions for diffusion and dissipation terms, resulting in different formulations of the k-equation.

These problems have led to the development of two equation models where L is determined from a transport equation in a manner similar to k. The types of models in this category are too numerous to mention, but what distinguishes the two-equation models generally is their success in cases where the length scale of the flow cannot be measured in an empirically easy way (e.g., recirculating flows and complex shear layers). The final example I want to mention is the two-layer method, which employs a simple model near the wall (a mixing length or one equation model valid only near the wall region) and a transport equation model in the outer region of the boundary layer. The two solutions are then matched at a certain point in the boundary layer. Although these models give a more realistic representation of turbulent processes, they are sometimes unstable and actually give poor predictions for complex flows. The effects of streamline curvature are not naturally reproduced, and empirical 'fixes' have been unreliable. Hence, despite their unrealistic nature, the more idealised eddy-viscosity models are often preferred.

What the discussion (and table 5.1) illustrate is that although the eddy-viscosity concept models the eddies in a way that is highly unrealistic, most of the differences among the various models relate to different ways of specifying parameters or taking account of aspects of the flow that other models have neglected. An important feature of these models is how they illustrate the problem-dependent nature of turbulent transport processes. In other words, they depend on geometrical conditions of large and small scale, such as wall shape and texture, buoyancy, and viscous effects. The models can only ever give an approximate description and with a particular set of empirical constants are valid only for certain flows or ranges of flows. A similar situation occurs with the Reynolds averaged models listed in table 5.2. The goal is to have the predictive power of the model extendable with a specific set of empirical constraints, but adjusting the constraints to match specific flows is more properly characterised as the interpolation of data rather than an example of modelling per se.[8]

8. See Cebeci and Cousteix (2005).

TABLE 5.1 LARGE EDDY MODELS

Isochoric LES Turbulence Models
Smagorinsky model
Smagorinsky model with 3-D filter
Dynamic Smagorinsky
Homogeneous dynamic Smagorinsky model
Lagrangian two equation eddy-viscosity model
Scale similarity model
Mixed Smagorinsky/scale similarity model
Dynamic mixed Smagorinsky/scale similarity model
k–ω-SST scale adaptive simulation (SAS) model
k-equation eddy-viscosity model
Dynamic k-equation eddy-viscosity model
Localised dynamic k-equation eddy-viscosity model
Spectral eddy viscosity model
LRR differential stress model
Deardorff differential stress model
Spalart-Allmaras model
Spalart-Allmaras delayed detached eddy simulation (DDES) model
Spalart-Allmaras improved DDES (IDDES) model

Anisochoric LES Turbulence Models
Smagorinsky model
k-equation eddy-viscosity model
Dynamic k-equation eddy-viscosity model
Low-Re k-equation eddy-viscosity model
Deardorff differential stress model
Spalart-Allmaras 1-eqn mixing-length model

LES Deltas
PrandtlDelta
cubeRootVolDelta

TABLE 5.1 (CONTINUED)

maxDeltaxyz
smoothDelta

LES Filters
laplaceFilter
simpleFilter
anisotropicFilter

The point of introducing some of the details of turbulence modelling is to draw attention to the fact that although each of these models embodies different ways of describing flows with different parameters, they are best seen as complementary rather than contradictory. In this context the neglect of certain features should be understood as simply a case of idealisation where properties are either omitted or idealised, depending on the nature of the problem. As I have shown, the complex nature of calculating effects of turbulent flows often requires giving up more realistic model representations in favour of simplified ones. Due to the complex nature (both computational and physical) of turbulent flows, models are often chosen for their combination of complexity and solvability. Although the models describe the fluid differently, the process is one of adjusting constraints and parameters to match specific types of flows, different boundary conditions, and so on. There is no contradiction with the basic underlying structure of fluid dynamics.

We can understand this situation in terms of perspectivism in that it encompasses a unified approach to understanding how the models relate to each and to fundamental theory. The principles

TABLE 5.2 REYNOLDS-AVERAGED MODELS

RAS Turbulence Models for Incompressible Fluids
Dummy turbulence model for laminar flow
Standard high-Re $k - \varepsilon$ model
Standard high-Re $k - \omega$ model
$k - \omega$-SST model
RNG $k - \varepsilon$ model
Non-linear Shih $k - \varepsilon$ model
Lien cubic $k - \varepsilon$ model
$q - \varsigma$ model
Launder-Sharma low-Re $k - \varepsilon$ model
Lam-Bremhorst low-Re $k - \varepsilon$ model
Lien cubic low-Re $k - \varepsilon$ model
Lien-Leschziner low-Re $k - \varepsilon$ model
Launder-Reece-Rodi RSTM
Launder-Gibson RSTM with wall-reflection terms
Realizable $k - \varepsilon$ model
Spalart-Allmaras 1-eqn mixing-length model

RAS Turbulence Models for Compressible Fluids
Dummy turbulence model for laminar flow
Standard $k - \varepsilon_l$ model
$k - \omega - SST$ model
RNG $k - \varepsilon$ model
Launder-Sharma low-Re $k - \varepsilon$ model
Launder-Reece-Rodi RSTM
Launder-Gibson RSTM
Realizable $k - \varepsilon$ model
Spalart-Allmaras 1-eqn mixing-length model

that constitute the theoretical basis of fluid dynamics provide the backdrop from which we can utilise different models for different purposes. But here again the legitimacy of perspectivism (or any specific perspective) is grounded in the theoretical aspects of the problem solving context rather than in an appeal to philosophy for an interpretation of the modelling practices. The consistency of the models with fundamental theory means that adopting different perspectives needn't imply a form of relativism or instrumentalism. As I will show, the situation is markedly different in the case of nuclear models, where radically different assumptions about the nature of the nucleus and its theoretical underpinnings are required in order to account for different experimental data.

NUCLEAR MODELS: INCONSISTENCY AND IRRECONCILABLE PROBLEMS

Nuclear physics provides us with models that are also successful within a particular domain but where the *falsity* of the assumptions seems directly related to their predictive success. What I have in mind here is not simply the use of idealisations like point particles to describe nucleons, or assumptions like those associated with the eddy viscosity concept, but assumptions, such as the one contained in the liquid drop model (that the nucleus is a classical object), that are necessary not for calculational expediency but for generating accurate predictions. It is important to distinguish between the use of nonrealistic assumptions of the type found in idealisations and the use of 'false' assumptions in the sense that you know they are not, and cannot, be true. Fictional models fall into the latter category. The nuclear case presents a slightly different example of the use of false assumptions because the models employ descriptions that are not fictional in the typical sense but nevertheless cannot be true of the phenomena given what we know about their nature. This results in fundamental inconsistencies in the way that models depict the nuclear structure.

The word 'fundamental' here refers to claims about the structure of the nucleus responsible for determining specific types of behaviour. Some models assume that nucleons move approximately independently in the nucleus, where the latter is regarded as a simple potential well or a nonspherical potential and so forth, while others characterise the nucleons as strongly coupled due to their strong short-range interactions. According to these models, the nucleus itself seems to exhibit different types of behaviour, both classical—as in the liquid drop case—and quantum mechanical, where it shows a shell structure similar to that of atoms. Although the models are largely phenomenological, in that they were constructed to explain experimental evidence, they also embody important theoretical assumptions, especially in cases where quantum mechanical effects are built in.[9] And these assumptions play an important role in the predictive and explanatory successes of the different models.

The accepted theoretical view is that nuclei are typically described as bound together by the residual strong force that is a minor residuum of the strong interaction that binds quarks together to form protons and neutrons. One of the central problems of nuclear structure is to construct a model that explains how much energy is needed to bind nucleons (protons and neutrons) together into stable nuclei. Although the liquid drop model provides an approximate solution, a larger problem exists. Specifically, the quantitative description of the nuclear force that emerges from nucleon-nucleon reaction studies is incompatible with what is known about nuclei; in addition, the short-range strong interaction known from experimental work

9. On the phenomenological character of nuclear shell models, see also Demetris Portides (2011).

cannot be used to derive properties of nuclei. As a result, theorists speak of an effective nuclear force that is the sum of effects that arise from complex many body systems. Experimentalists on the other hand tend to focus on what they refer to as a realistic force that is known with great precision from experiments on two-body nucleon interactions.

Although this is a fundamental problem, the difficulties run much deeper and pervade the entire science of nuclear physics. There are over 30 different nuclear models based on very different assumptions, each of which provides some "insight" into nuclear structure and dynamics. However, none offers more than partial "truths," and each is in conflict with claims made by the others. While each model has its particular successes, and together they are sometimes taken as complementary insofar as each contributes to an overall explanation of much of the available experimental data, many basic questions are left unanswered precisely due to the lack of a comprehensive account. One is the nature of nucleons themselves—are they probability waves, point particles, or space-occupying objects? Another problem concerns the phase state of nuclear matter, as well as the specific nature of the nuclear force and whether it is strong, extending only to nearest neighbour nucleons, or weak and extending long range to all nucleons in the nucleus. Each of the models uses very different parameters that assume the nucleus, nucleon, and nuclear forces have specific characteristics and not others.

In order to show just how these models conflict with each other, why they shouldn't be viewed as complementary, and the extent to which they can or cannot be said to provide information, we need to look at some of the more basic models and their relation to both theory and experimental data. Unlike the case of turbulence models, whose use is dictated by specific problem conditions that relate mostly to computational issues, the application of different types of nuclear models depends on assumptions about the nature of nuclear structure that are required for furnishing accurate predictions. In other words, each makes very different assumptions about exactly the same thing. Although there are a few different ways that one can classify or group nuclear models together, this doesn't help to resolve the inconsistencies.

One approach is to group them according to the supposed phase state of nuclear matter—liquid, gas, or semisolid (cluster models), with a fourth based on quarks. The gaseous phase models are also known as the shell or independent particle models, while the liquid phase corresponds to the liquid drop or collective models. The latter are sometimes classified as strong interaction models based on the assumption of a short-range strong interaction among nuclei, while the independent particle models are identified with the weak nuclear force. The nucleon clustering models constitute a separate category, while the quark models are associated with a very strong nuclear force. I will have more to say about these particular classifications and how they relate to each other, but before moving on there is one further method of distinguishing nuclear models that should be mentioned, a classification presented by Greiner and Maruhn (1996) that focuses on degrees of freedom. Within this scheme there are three types of models: microscopic, collective, and mixed which are somewhere in between.

This latter way of characterising models is important because it focuses on degrees of freedom for both individual nucleons (microscopic models) and those that indicate some bulk property of the nucleus as a whole (collective models). In the former case, because one cannot derive the nucleon-nucleon interaction from theory, various parameterisations are employed for different purposes in an effort to reproduce experimental data. Collective coordinates, such as the centre of mass vector for the nucleus, can, in principle, be expressed in terms of microscopic models, but in practice coordinates are often introduced without any reference to microscopic physics. As one might expect, the basic idea behind this classification structure is an attempt to unify the two types. While the collective models could be used to classify spectra and explain their structure, the microscopic models could, in principle, explain why collective coordinates of a particular type would lead to a viable model. This would produce a kind of conceptual unity in the approach to nuclear structure without producing a unification of the models themselves. In other words, there would be a single conceptual framework within which many different models could be used to explain different types of phenomena. This is roughly the situation with turbulence models: there are basic principles of fluid dynamics that govern the many different models that are employed for various types of flows.

However, even this modest goal seems largely unattainable in the case of nuclear structure. To see why, it is important to examine the types of assumptions that are included in the different kinds of models to determine whether they can be said to provide some reasonably accurate information despite their inconsistency with each other. Figures 5.1 and 5.2 represent different classifications for the nuclear models mentioned above. Figure 5.1 shows the "conceptual" ordering of Greiner and Maruhn (1996); table 5.3 is arranged according to forces and the types of evidence that each explains. One of the problems I will address is the fact that the number, complexity, and sophistication of these various models makes it extremely difficult to determine whether any given one has provided an "explanation""" of the empirical data or it has simply been manipulated via its adjustable parameters to agree with the data.

It is tempting to understand the inconsistency among these models as simply involving different types of idealised assumptions in different experimental contexts, much like the turbulence case. However, as I will show in the brief discussion that follows, the

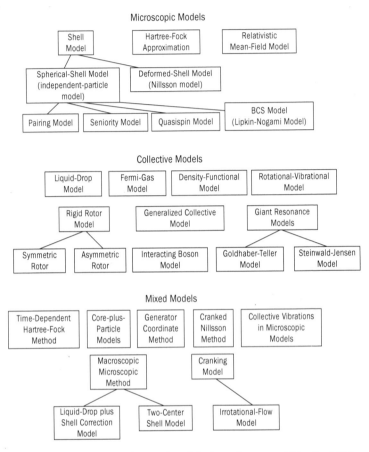

Figure 5.1: Three general classes of models From Greiner and Maruhn 1996.

problem is different in kind and more serious from the perspective of theoretical coherence. Perhaps one of the most famous of all nuclear models is the liquid drop mentioned earlier. It is a collective model in that it was formulated to explain gross properties of medium-sized and large collections of nucleons. It describes the nucleus as a classical fluid consisting of protons and neutrons that strongly interact with an internal repulsive force proportional to the number of protons.

TABLE 5.3 NUCLEAR MODELS

THEORY	SUPPORTING DATA
Weak Nuclear Force:	
Shell Model	Magic Nuclei
Independent Particle Model	Systematics of Nucleon Quantum Numbers
Fermi Gas Model	Nuclear Angular Momentum and Parities
	Nuclear Magnetic moments
Strong Force:	
Liquid Drop Model	Constant Nuclear Density
Compound Nucleus	Saturation of Nuclear Force
Collective Model	Nuclear Surface Tension Effects
Lattice Model	Fragmentation of nuclei due to nuclear projectiles.
Nucleon Clustering:	
Alpha Cluster Model	Alpha Particle Radiation
Spheron Model	Unusual Stability/Abundance of 4n nuclei
2D Ising Model	4n Clusters in Nuclear Fragmentation
Interacting Boson Model	Nucleon Pairing Effects
Very Strong Nuclear Force:	
Quark Models	Known Properties of Nuclear Force

This table shows nuclear models grouped together according to theory and empirical support. Most of this information is taken from Cook (2006).

The nucleons move randomly and bump into each other frequently. Despite its essentially classical structure, the quantum nature of the particles appears via the exclusion principle, where no two nucleons of the same kind can be at the same state.

But even at this point difficulties emerge in relation to the classical-quantum nature of the nucleons as governed by the exclusion principle itself. Most nucleons in the nuclear core have no available, unoccupied low-energy states to which they can move, because all are filled. Hence, if a nucleon moves to a state above a certain energy level, it would be ejected from the nucleus, since high-energy states are not available for low-energy interactions. However, at low-energy excitations the nucleon is not ejected, but all the low-energy states are filled—so if we interpret the exclusion principle as having a dynamic role, then we have no way to explain the energy change because the interacting nucleons have no place to go. Consequently, we have no way to explain the collision.[10]

Although the liquid drop model is extremely successful in accounting for fission, experimental data on binding energies, and general features of nuclei such as radius, no firm conclusions about nuclear force can be ascertained, and the model is unable to account for nuclei with protons and neutrons close to magic numbers. Evidence that the nuclei have a constant density (a liquid drop–type texture) comes from experimental data on comparison with atomic radii which show significant substructure within each shell, but this phenomenon is not observed in nuclei. Similarly, the near-linear correlation between the radius and number of nucleons suggests that each nucleon occupies a constant volume, as predicted by the liquid drop model.

10. For a longer discussion of the difficulties with the exclusion principle see Cook (2006, 108–22). My discussion of many of the general problems with nuclear models borrows heavily from his work.

But, as noted, the successes of any given model are limited in number and significantly circumscribed. Measurements on binding energies for certain nuclei deviate significantly from those predicted by the liquid drop model, a fact that led to the development of a model with a shell structure of nucleons similar to that of electrons within atoms. This shell structure consists of a set of energy levels separated by a gap. The nucleons are assumed to be point particles free to orbit within the nucleus, due to the net attractive force that acts between them and produces a net potential well drawing all the nucleons toward the centre rather than toward other nucleons. Each nucleon has a set of quantum numbers that defines its state of motion and they obey the exclusion principle which explains the relative stability of their states. The lowest energy state of the nucleus is one where nucleons fill all energy levels from the bottom up to some level, with a nucleus having full shells being exceptionally stable. The basic assumptions that give a more or less precise theoretical framework for the shell model are (1) the atomic nucleus is a quantum n-body system; (2) it is not a relativistic object, and its equation of motion (the system wavefunction) is the Schrödinger equation; (3) the nucleons interact only via a two-body interaction, which is, in effect, a practical consequence of the exclusion principle. The mean free path of a nucleon is large with respect to the size of the nucleus, and the probability that three nucleons would interact simultaneously is considered so small as to be negligible; and finally (4) for simplicity reasons, nucleons are considered point like.

As we can see, the properties of the shell model directly contradict those of the liquid drop model, and it, too, is vulnerable to problems with the exclusion principle. Moreover, in order to account for properties of nuclei away from closed shells, it is necessary to introduce a different model with a distortion of the potential well from spherical to various ellipsoidal shapes. However, the complexity of nuclear states speaks to both the strengths and weaknesses of the central potential well approach to nuclear structure. Deformations of the well allow for a post hoc explanation of almost any experimentally detected sequence of energy states that differs from the predictions of the spherical shell model. But the flexibility of the allowed manipulations creates difficulties in evaluating its epistemic status. In other words, it is difficult to determine whether manipulations of the potential well correspond, in any sense, to spatial deformations in real nuclei. While this latter issue is a problem internal to the potential well approach, it nevertheless illustrates the variety of different and ad hoc assumptions various models bring to bear in attempting to determine or account for features of nuclear structure.

This kind of ad hoc approach characteristic of the potential well has led theorists to develop models and methods that promise similar predictive power while insisting on firmer constraints on the underlying nuclear force. One such model is the quark model, which is based on a methodology of two- or three-body nuclear force effects that form the building blocks of the nucleus. Instead of manipulating a potential well, we have the interaction of nucleons dominated by the exchange of quarks. But here again several problems arise. Quark-quark interaction is much more complicated at lower energies (due to colour confinement and asymptotic freedom), and the standard model does not allow for the deduction of nucleon interaction from quark interaction. Even if this problem were solved, it isn't clear that it would allow one to derive interactions for nucleons interacting in matter (as opposed to in vacuo). This type of model requires the concept of an effective interaction, which involves several arbitrary parameters adjusted to agree with experimental data. Hence, with respect to the ad hoc quality of the model, it fares little better that the deformed shell approach.

The collective and/or unified model is an extension of some of the ideas from both the liquid drop and shell models giving a type of unified account of nuclear structure and is sometimes taken to represent a truly unified picture (see Portides, 2006). Here the nucleons move nearly independently in a common, slowly changing, nonspherical potential. It is used in both excitations of individual nucleons and collective motions involving the nucleus as a whole. One reason for the success of the unified model is that a great number of high-energy states can only be understood as statistical effects of many nucleons in motion together; hence collective vibrations, oscillations, and rotations are extremely important. Although it is probably the most successful model to date, it is by no means able to account for all the properties necessary for a coherent account of the nucleus. Nor is the so-called unification the result of bringing the various assumptions together in a single conceptual framework. Instead it represents more of a patching together of liquid drop features with a distorted potential well.

Depending on the type of model we are interested in, some pairs of models can provide a consistent body of assumptions. For example, if the focus is the independence of protons and neutrons, then some of the independent particle models can provide a coherent framework within which to understand specific problems. Although there are several different individual models I haven't mentioned, it is important to draw attention to another generic type—cluster models—which are based on the assumption that the nucleus consists of aggregates or small clusters of nucleons. These models are important because one of these clusters is the alpha particle, which is released from many large radioactive nuclei. Given this fact, it is crucial that some way of accounting for these types of emissions is part of the modelling of nuclear structure and dynamics.

SCIENTIFIC PROBLEMS AND PHILOSOPHICAL WORRIES

What this discussion shows is that nuclear spin, size, binding energy, fission, and several other properties of stable nuclei are all accounted for using models that describe one and the same entity (the nucleus) in different and contradictory ways. Although much of the work currently being done is at the level of particles (i.e. sub-nuclear) in the area of nuclear force, many of the unresolved problems that directly relate to nuclear structure remain. At this point one might be tempted to ask why these problems can't be handled by quantum chromodynamics, the theory of the strong force that governs the nucleus. Some of the difficulties can be traced to the fact that nuclei are too complex and contain too many constituents to be accounted for in a precise way by formal theories. In addition, they are too small and idiosyncratic to be handled with rigorous statistical methods that require large numbers to justify stochastic assumptions. Because nuclei contain fewer than 300 constituents, they fall into a kind of no-man's-land between theory and reliable statistics. So what should the strategy be if we want to claim that nuclear models give us information about the world (i.e. nuclei)?

One option is to adopt the kind of perspectivism suggested by Giere that I discussed earlier in the chapter. This amounts to endorsing a claim of the form: taken as a classical system (or as a liquid etc.) the nucleus looks like x; as a quantum system it looks like Y, and so on for any given model we choose. But surely this isn't a satisfactory option, because none of these perspectives can be claimed to "represent" the nucleus in even a quasi-realistic way, since they all contradict each other on fundamental assumptions about dynamics and structure.[11] In this case, perspectivism is simply a rebranded version of instrumentalism. Given that we assume there is an object called "the atomic nucleus" that has a particular structure and dynamics, it becomes difficult to see how to interpret any of these models realistically. Each is successful in

---

11. It is important to clarify there that this isn't the problem where we have two different theories that are both successful with respect to the same phenomena. See Saatsi and Vickers (2011). In the case of the atomic nucleus we have over 30 (!) different models telling us very different things about the structure of the nucleus and the behaviour of nucleons.

accounting only for particular kinds of experimental evidence and provides very little in the way of theoretical understanding. In other words, the inference from predictive success to realism is blocked due not only to the extensive underdetermination but also to the internal problems that beset each of the individual models.

For example, the mean free path of nucleons in stable nuclei is a central concept in nuclear theory, but neither theory nor experiment has been wholly successful in answering basic questions about it.[12] The independent particle model demands a lengthy mean free path to justify its main assumption of the collisionless orbiting of nucleons inside the nucleus. However, experimental measurement and most theoretical estimates give a significantly shorter MFP of about 3 fm. Although the independent particle model explains a great variety of data, including nuclear spins, parities, and other properties, the independent orbiting of nucleons inside a dense nuclear interior is clearly a fiction. In that sense its predictive success rests on an assumption that cannot possibly be correct, making any increase in epistemic value via predictive power illusory. Other models face similar problems, so not only do we have inconsistency among the models but no single one emerges as having greater predictive power with fewer internal difficulties and contradictions with experimental findings. Hence, even if we wanted to we couldn't successfully motivate an inference to the best explanation argument because each of the models is problematic in a different, yet significant, way.

Despite this fact, and the piecemeal nature of nuclear models, they have been tremendously successful in mapping onto sophisticated experimental and engineering technologies that have, in turn, generated information about nuclear phenomena that can be used in practical contexts. But unfortunately, and perhaps surprisingly, this practical success has not translated into increased theoretical

12. For a discussion of these issues see Cook (2006, ch. 5).

knowledge. Attempts to harness the kinetic energy released in fission requires both a qualitative and quantitative knowledge of certain aspects of the process. The liquid drop model has provided a reasonably successful account of fission, but significant problems prevent it (and other models) from providing a coherent theoretical understanding.

Because one of the features of the liquid drop model is a parameterisation of the binding energy of nuclei, one can perform a calculation to analyse the stability of a liquid drop under perturbation. Hence, on the basis of the model it is possible to provide an account of why thermal neutrons induce fission in U235 while only higher energy neutrons produce fission in U238. In that sense the model furnishes a framework that extends its use as a predictive device to an explanatory foundation for understanding certain processes (why some nuclei are stable and some undergo fission) and performing energy calculations associated with certain aspects of nuclear power and technology. But that explanatory framework emerges from the model's mathematical features rather than a theoretical underpinning and consequently is severely limited in its application. Moreover, there is no real hope of explaining this using the resources of the liquid drop model because its very nature does not allow for nuclear substructure.[13]

What this illustrates is that the prevalence of contradictory models has indeed prevented us from gaining important knowledge about fundamental aspects of nuclear structure and dynamics. Notably, the difficulties resulting in the proliferation of models are not simply the result of calculational problems. The question that naturally arises is whether these difficulties are related to the inconsistent nature of the

---

13. Because it is an amorphous, structureless object, the random distribution of positive changes within the drop inevitably lead to symmetric fission. It is possible to introduce an adjustable parameter into the model, but the strategy of choice is to explain the asymmetry using shell structure effects.

models or are simply the result of more general theoretical challenges in attempting to understand the elusive nature of the nucleus—problems that would result regardless of whether the models were complementary rather than inconsistent. In some sense these two issues are closely related, but the additional challenges presented by the inconsistencies among the models themselves are made clearly evident simply by summarising a few of the details discussed above.

For instance, the short mean free path of nucleons inside the nucleus is accounted for by the liquid drop model, but if that represents the approximate texture of the nucleus, then the experimental data showing a distinct shell and subshell of orbiting nucleons are left unexplained. The liquid drop model also accounts well for nuclear binding energies, but experimental evidence for magic numbers indicates variations in nuclear stability that the amorphous drop cannot account for. Cluster models explain the structure and vibrational states of some small nuclei, but a rigid cluster geometry is inconsistent with the structureless texture of the liquid drop and Fermi gas models. Radial values of nuclei are consistent with the liquid drop model, but other phenomena are more suggestive of a diffuse gas than a liquid. And if the asymmetry of fission is explained using the shell model (to the extent that it can be), then that clearly undermines the energetic successes of the liquid drop model. Part of the difficulty is the internal theoretical contradiction concerning the nature of the nuclear force; that is, the effective force that is allegedly weak and long-range and the realistic force that is strong and short-range. Until that discrepancy is resolved any hope for a coherent account of nuclear phenomena seems impossible.

So we are left in an epistemic quandary when trying to evaluate the realistic status of these nuclear models and the information they provide. We can't simply conclude that all the information extracted from the models is dubious, since some provides the very foundation on which a good deal of technological knowledge (and some theoretical knowledge) is based. However, and unfortunately, in some cases the successes of the models are directly connected with highly questionable, and sometimes explicitly false, assumptions. Add to that the fact that the models' sheer number and diversity prevents us formulating any clear picture of how they might converge in a coherent account, and we are left with little reason to give credence to any particular model or group of models. What is significant for philosophical purposes is that this is not a situation that is resolvable using strategies like partial structures, paraconsistent logic, or perspectivism. No amount of philosophical wizardry can solve what is essentially a scientific problem of theoretical consistency and coherence.

What this reveals is an interesting disconnect between philosophical views about inconsistency and scientific approaches to the problem. The nuclear models are extremely successful in their particular domains, and although a coherent theoretical account would certainly be preferable, the inconsistency does not prevent research and refinement of the models themselves or further investigation into the nature of nuclear structure. But what is interesting from a philosophical perspective is that in some sense the question of 'realism' becomes a moot point in evaluating these models. Put differently: it isn't obvious how it applies. While Giere's perspectivism goes some way toward accounting for how these models are actually used, its stated alliance with realism makes it less plausible; instead, the instrumentalism to which it seems more intimately connected better reflects that problematic context of nuclear models. From a philosophical angle it is simply not possible to be 'realists' about the nuclear structure outlined in these models; the inconsistency prevents the legitimacy of any such epistemic attitude. So should philosophers of science worry about the problem of inconsistent models? Only to the extent that there may be interesting philosophical questions and conceptual clarification about specific ways that these models actually deliver information. Beyond that, questions about their ontological foundations and epistemic status require, first and foremost, scientific answers. Only then can philosophical analysis have something informative to add.

SUMMING UP

Both nuclear physics and turbulent flows are among the most challenging and difficult areas of modern physics, yet I have shown here that despite the problems in each domain we are faced with very different strategies for the construction and employment of models in each field. Nuclear models and turbulence models differ significantly with respect to the way they are employed. In the latter case having different models for different features of a phenomenon needn't involve inconsistency. Even in the case of the boundary layer, we have distinct aspects of the fluid modelled in different ways rather than the same structure being treated with significantly different models. Different turbulent models are employed to treat different types of flows, sometimes for calculational expediency and other times because the specific nature of the problem can be addressed by either leaving out certain features of the fluid or adding back ones that have been ignored in other models. The complexity of the phenomena requires the use of many different types of models, but in none of these cases is there a problem of inconsistency. Instead the models function in a complementary way, representing the different behaviour of the fluid as well as different boundary conditions. The emphasis is on using different approaches that are appropriate for different idealisations when treating features of turbulent flows. In that sense the different models do not embody different fundamental theoretical claims about the nature of fluids. Here perspectivism plays an important role in understanding both model construction and use, but it is motivated solely by scientific concerns related to calculational and other modelling issues.

The nuclear case exhibits a radically different approach. Here we have exactly the same phenomenon (the atomic nucleus and its constituents) modelled in entirely different ways depending on the data that need explanation. However, in most cases these models go beyond mere data fitting to provide some type of dynamical account of how and why the phenomena are produced. But because there are over 30 fundamentally different models that incorporate different and contradictory assumptions about structure and dynamics, there is no way to determine which of the models can even be said to even approximate the true nature of the nucleus. In other words, there is no reasonable interpretation of "approximate" that would make sense of even a minimally realist claim. Perspectivism clearly has a role to play here but one whose motivation is grounded in the scientific circumstances. However, given those circumstances, perspectivism becomes identified with instrumentalism—the only legitimate philosophical attitude given the data.

Each of the nuclear models is both predictively and, in some cases, explanatorily successful in its particular domain, but there is no way to build on and extend the models in a cumulative way. Consequently, we have no way of assessing the epistemic status of that information over and above its success in predicting certain types of nuclear phenomena. In that sense paraconsistent logic offers no solution either, since its stated goals are to facilitate reasoning with inconsistent information and allow us to apply that information in practical contexts. Both of those aims are already fulfilled in the case of nuclear models and motivated from within a purely scientific context.

There are a number of lessons we can take away from this discussion, but perhaps the most important relates to the impact of perspectivism on the evaluation of scientific models. Each modelling context (turbulence models and nuclear models) illustrates a use of perspectivism, but one that has radically different implications in each case. Turbulence models form a coherent group consistent with the fundamental principles of fluid dynamics, with nuclear models presenting a very different picture. But in both cases the perspectivism is grounded in the theoretical relations and models that are used for treating the phenomena in question. Neither requires an additional appeal to philosophical argument for its legitimation. In the case of nuclear models, perspectivism is implicit in the way the models are used, yet that use entails a thoroughgoing instrumentalism rather than the "realism" to which philosophical perspectivism aligns itself. The goal of scientific perspectivism as a philosophical position is to facilitate a better understanding of the way scientific investigation and validation is carried out. Yet, in the cases I have discussed, where perspectivism is important, it either adds nothing that is not already implicit in the modelling context or it fails to provide a solution to the problems of inconsistency.

I have also discussed the different approaches to the use of multiple models for representing the same system. In some cases this proves unproblematic, while in others it results in deep theoretical problems. In that sense it isn't the use of multiple models that proves problematic but rather the reasons why they are used and the epistemic consequences of their use. It is perhaps important to reiterate that the theoretical difficulties accompanying the use of inconsistent models are not philosophical problems of interpretation, solvable by invoking perspectivism or paraconsistent logic. These are a scientific problems that pervade the very foundations of nuclear physics and as examples of fundamental inconsistency require scientific rather than philosophical strategies for their solution.

PART III

COMPUTER SIMULATION

The New Reality

6

Why Materiality Is Not Enough

Models, Measurement, and Computer Simulation

DEFINING THE PROBLEM

The epistemic problems that arise in the context of modelling are often magnified when evaluating the status of CS. Not only does one have to worry about whether the theoretical model accurately represents the target system but the discretisation process required for making the theoretical model amenable to numerical solution can involve significant changes to the informational content of the original model. So in addition to worries about whether the model has actually been solved correctly, there is the problem of determining to what extent the solved simulation model represents the target system. There are several other epistemological problems that arise in dealing with simulation itself, and those will be addressed in chapter 7. But before we get to those problems, I want to begin here by arguing that we should take simulations seriously as a method for providing experimental knowledge. I use the word "experimental" here to indicate that in some cases and under certain conditions it is legitimate to claim that simulations can measure theoretical quantities.[1] While this may sound like a rather extravagant and counterintuitive claim,

1. I don't mean to imply here that all experiment involves measurement but only that some

it appears less so when we examine what is actually involved in some cases of experimental measurement. Once those practices are properly analysed, we can see that in under the right circumstances simulation functions in ways that are sufficiently similar to experimental measurement to render the results epistemically comparable.

Part of the argument for the "simulation as measurement" thesis requires showing that the practices involving experimental measurement reveal a methodology that is far from straightforward. The extensive use of modelling in both contexts shows why the similarities are much closer than we might otherwise think. I begin with a discussion of how models function as "measuring instruments" and go on to examine the ways in which simulation can be said to constitute an experimental activity. Establishing the connections between simulation and particular types of modelling strategies and highlighting how those strategies are also essential features of experimentation allows us to clarify the contexts in which we can legitimately call CS a form of experimental measurement. In other words, simulation shares features in common with modelling and experiment, but it is connections between the latter two that are important for clarifying aspects of simulation. Finally, I provide a reply to the claim that simulations are simply measurement substitutes and hence fail to have the epistemic status I ascribe to them.

SETTING THE CONTEXT—SOME HISTORICAL PECULIARITIES

Lord Kelvin is well known for his emphasis on the role of models in producing scientific knowledge. "I never satisfy myself until I can make a mechanical model of a thing. If I can make a mechanical

cases of experiment involve measuring a value for theoretical quantities.

model I can understand it. As long as I cannot make a mechanical model all the way through I cannot understand; and that is why I cannot get the electromagnetic theory. I firmly believe in an electro-magnetic theory of light, and that when we understand electricity and magnetism and light we shall see them all together as parts of a whole" (6, 132, 270–71).

In this remark Kelvin is criticising Maxwell's Lagrangian formulation of electrodynamics and the lack of a suitable mechanical model that would show how electromagnetic waves could be propagated through space. However, in addition to these famous remarks on models he had this to say about measurement: "I often say that when you can measure what you are speaking about and express it in numbers, you know something about it; but when you cannot express it in numbers your knowledge is of a meagre and unsatisfactory kind; it may be the beginning of knowledge, but you have scarcely, in your thoughts, advanced to the stage of science whatever the matter may be" (Thomson 1891, 80–81). On closer inspection these passages suggest a connection between models and measurement that is linked with scientific understanding. Kelvin claims he cannot understand a phenomenon unless he has a mechanical model that illustrates how it is constructed and how it can be integrated into a broader theoretical context. An important part of that task is the ability to quantify various aspects of the model in a way that is related to the measurement of different values and parameters. Kelvin does not elaborate, specifically, on this connection, but it is an important one, not just for him but also for contemporary aspects of modelling and measurement.

As I will show, determining the possible connections between models and measurement is important for distinguishing between measurement and calculation and also for thinking about the relation between experiment and simulation. Initially these distinctions might seem relatively straightforward. Measurement is typically thought to involve some type of causal interaction with the material world via instruments, something that is also characteristic of experiment. Calculation on the other hand is a mathematical activity involving abstract reasoning often carried out with pencil and paper or computers. Because simulations are frequently associated with computers, their status as experiments is linked to the notion of 'numerical experiments' that involve using numerical methods to find approximate solutions to mathematical models/equations that cannot be solved analytically.[2] This is sometimes referred to as 'experimenting on a model.' But, on reflection, these distinctions are less than straightforward. In recent years CSs have evolved from the kinds of number crunching activities suggested by the label 'numerical experiments' to tools for investigative research in areas such as climate science and astrophysics.[3] The issue is complicated by, among other things, the question of whether these activities establish links between simulation and experiment and whether the outputs and data produced by simulations can be characterised as measurements.

What, exactly, would it mean to characterise the product of a simulation as a measurement and the simulation itself as an experiment? I should point out that my concern here is not with theory of measurement discussed by Krantz et al. (1971, 1989) but rather with the activity of measuring—what is involved in the *process* of measurement. My goal here, however, is not to provide a full account of measurement practices, nor do I try to embed my account of simulation in existing views of measurement; instead I simply want to point out that as a feature of experimental practice, measurement (however you want to interpret it) is heavily reliant on models and modelling assumptions.[4] The issues related to measurement in many

2. For a discussion of what is meant by a 'numerical experiment' see Parker (2008).
3. For an excellent paper on modelling in climate science see Norton and Suppe (2001).
4. For an extended account of the model-based view of measurement see Eran Tal(2012) *The Epistemology of Measurement: A Model-Based Account*. Ph.D Dissertation, University of Toronto.

sciences focus primarily on the technical features of instrumentation, specifically the development of the appropriate type of techniques to precisely and accurately measure a property or feature of a phenomenon, as well as methods for the interpretation of results. Current accounts of CS can easily be accommodated in this picture: the computer functions as the apparatus, and the act of running the simulation is regarded as a numerical experiment. But this doesn't really tell us much about whether or why we can classify simulation outputs as measurements. I claim that we can answer that question by looking at the role models play in the context of both traditional experiment and simulation. Not only do models allow us to interpret measurement outputs, but the models themselves can function as measuring instruments, and it is this latter role that figures importantly in the analysis of simulation as measurement/experiment.[5]

This idea of models as measuring instruments is particularly important in the context of nineteenth-century British field theory, where the manipulation of different types of physical models was used to determine features or quantities associated with the electromagnetic field, which were in turn used to modify Maxwell's original equations. In this case the model operated as a device that was, at least in the hands of Kelvin, able to 'measure' certain quantities supposedly associated with the ether. The status of these measurements was highly questionable but a less problematic example is the use the physical plane pendulum to measure local gravitational acceleration. While this seems to involve a more direct notion of measurement, it is important to note that even in this case there is an extensive reliance on theoretical models and

5. A model can be based on some theoretical belief about the world that is suggested by the data, or it can sometimes be understood as simply a statistical summary of a data set. Data assimilation is an example that extends beyond straightforward issues of description; here observations are incorporated into computer models of the data and are used to fill in gaps in observational data as well as to translate noisy observations into a collection of initial model-states. In that sense data assimilation is a tool for generating data.

approximation techniques that are necessary to guarantee the accuracy of the measuring process/outcome. The connection between models and measurement in this case extends beyond the theoretical interpretation of outputs to an understanding of the apparatus itself and how the representation of physical phenomena 'embedded' in the model/instrument enables us to use it as a measuring device.[6] Although the sophistication of the apparatus (the physical pendulum) determines the precision of the measurement of g, the accuracy of the measurement depends on the analysis of all the incidental factors that are part of the 'experimental' setup.[7] Indeed the ability of the physical pendulum to function as a measuring instrument is completely dependent on the presence of these models. That is the sense in which models themselves also play the role of measuring instruments.

In what follows I explore some of these issues in greater detail in order to illustrate how models function both in measurement contexts and as measuring instruments, and I discuss the implications of this for assessing the epistemic status of CSs.[8] Drawing attention to the mediating role of models in measurement contexts helps to clarify how models themselves are often the focus of investigation. They

6. This notion of 'embedding' will be discussed in more detail later.
7. Consequently, we need very sophisticated models in order to represent the apparatus in the appropriate way. Because the knowledge associated with the measurement comes via the model, the apparatus and the model function, in many respects, as a single system.
8. What is less clear is the connection between models, measurement, and representation when we are dealing with statistical models. Statistics, in particular structural equation modelling, makes use of measurement models that specify the relationships among latent variables and determines how these variables will be measured. This is sometimes referred to as model specification and is probably the most important and difficult step in the process, since if the model is incorrectly specified or the wrong measured variables are chosen to reflect the latent ones, there is little hope the model will give any kind of useful information. Here the model takes centre stage in defining the object of study, and it is the model itself that is investigated. Again, the question of whether this kind of activity is best described as measurement or calculation will determine, at least to some extent, the kind of results we take the model to provide. Space does not permit me to address issues related to this type of modelling in this chapter. I mention it simply to highlight the pervasiveness of the connection between models and measurement.

mediate between us and the world and between us and our theories by acting as objects of inquiry and as the source of mediated knowledge of physical phenomena. This mediated knowledge is characteristic of the type of knowledge we acquire in measurement contexts.

Let me begin with a brief discussion of the relation between models, experiment, and measurement in Kelvin's work. His emphasis on models and measurement provides an interesting context for seeing how the debate over abstract methods versus materiality has developed historically. It also highlights the way models were seen as experimental tools for bridging the gap between measurement and calculation. From there I will explore questions concerning the status of simulation as an experimental activity and connect features of simulation with the characterisation of models as measuring instruments. Ultimately, I claim that the connection between models and measurement is what provides the basis for treating certain types of simulation outputs as epistemically on a par with experimental measurements, or indeed as measurements themselves.

MODELS AND MANIPULATION

In Galileo's *Dialogue Concerning the Two Chief World Systems* Simplicio is urged to put forward arguments and demonstrations rather than just texts; his debate with Salviati must engage the sensible world and not just the world on paper. This distinction nicely captures many of our intuitions regarding the distinction between experiment and simulation. The former is thought to directly engage the physical world, while the latter is seen as a more abstract type of activity. This distinction between abstract theorising and more material-based investigation was also important in the development of nineteenth-century electrodynamics. In formulating his field-theoretic account Maxwell relied heavily on mechanical models of the ether, models that consisted of mechanical depictions drawn on paper whose functions were described in detail using mathematical equations. Realising that they were merely fictional entities used as heuristic devices for deriving a set of field equations, Maxwell jettisoned them in later formulations of the theory in favour of the abstract analytical mechanics of Lagrange. This enabled him to ignore difficult questions about hidden mechanisms or material causes that might be responsible for the production of electromagnetic phenomena in the ether.[9]

Maxwell's contemporary Lord Kelvin was extremely critical of this approach to modelling. He saw models as tactile structures that could be manipulated manually, thereby allowing one to know the target system or phenomenon as a "real" thing. In fact, it was a common theme throughout his *Baltimore Lectures* that theoretical expressions were acceptable only to the degree that they could be observed or felt; and because mechanical models could deliver this kind of tangible knowledge they provided convincing evidence for the properties and objects they represented. For example, when demonstrating the model of a molecule interacting with the ether Kelvin used a ball in a bowl of jelly and produced vibrations by moving the ball back and forth. For him this provided a more realistic account of the relation between matter and the ether because one could see how vibrations were produced and travelled through the medium. Kelvin claimed these models were demonstrative in a way that Maxwell's "paper" models were not. In fact, he claimed that one could predict

---

9. Despite this "paper" approach to theorising, Maxwell claimed that his field equations were deduced from experimental facts with the aid of general dynamical principles about matter in motion. This allowed him to treat the field variables as generalised mechanical variables that contained terms corresponding only to observables. Once a physical phenomenon can be completely described as a change in the configuration and motion of a material system, the dynamical explanation is complete. Until that time, however, we must rely on mechanical images, analogies, and models that furnish visual conceptions of the phenomena, conceptions whose sole function is heuristic. For more on Maxwell's claims about deduction from phenomena see Morrison (1992).

features of the molecule based on model manipulation alone, without recourse to traditional experimental methods.[10]

This emphasis on the power of models was especially prominent in cases where the phenomena in question were difficult to access—like the structure of molecules and the ether. By contrast, the mathematical formulas and imaginary constructions characteristic of Maxwell's electromagnetic theory had no basis in reality and gave rise to what Kelvin called nihilism—a system comprised of only words and symbols. But what exactly was the basis for this link between manipulation and reality? In other words, why did Kelvin think that manipulating mechanical models was akin to experimental demonstrations?

Part of the answer is that, for Kelvin, the debate about models was a debate not only about the methodology of modelling but also the justification of certain theoretical features of the new electrodynamics—features at odds with his brand of model-based empiricism. According to Kelvin, the elastic solid ether model, which was the basis for the wave theory of light, provided the only viable account of electromagnetic wave propagation. The foundation of Maxwell's field theory was the introduction of the displacement current, which was responsible for the dissemination of electricity in the spaces surrounding magnets and conductors. In chapter 3 I discussed some of the details of Maxwell's account of displacement, and although these are not important for my story here, what is important is the fact that once Maxwell abandoned the mechanical ether model there was no way to explain how charge or electricity in general was produced.[11] Instead it was the displacement current, as the source of the magnetic field, together with Faraday's law of electromagnetic induction that provided the description of the so-called physical basis for the

10. See Thomson (1987, 282–83).
11. For a more extensive account see chapter 3.

interaction between the **E** and **H** fields that constituted electromagnetic waves. This enabled Maxwell to derive a wave equation with solutions in the form of propagating waves with magnetic and electrical disturbances transverse to the direction of propagation. But here displacement was merely a term in the equations; so in what sense could it/they furnish a "physical" foundation for a theory, especially if there was no accompanying causal-mechanical explanation of how displacement was produced?

This was exactly the problem that vexed Kelvin. The derivation of these transverse waves involved no mechanical hypotheses, only electromagnetic equations.[12] According to his elastic solid model the ether had the structure of a jelly-like substance with light waves described as bodily vibrations in the jelly. Neither it nor any modifications of it were capable of supporting transverse waves. Moreover, this elastic solid ether model formed the foundation for a good deal of his work on the transatlantic telegraph cable. The telegraph theory entailed the existence of longitudinal waves—they were simply telegraph signals in wires with their propagation beyond the wire supported by an elastic solid ether. For Maxwell, of course, not only were electromagnetic waves transverse but they travelled in the space surrounding the wire, not in the wire itself. In that sense there was complete conceptual dissonance between the two accounts. According to Kelvin, any account of displacement could not be separated from matter, but matter and motion required a mechanical model in order to understand its nature and effects. Hence the displacement current was not only methodologically suspect but it defied the very physical

---

12. Kelvin complained that even the so-called measurement of c involved a purely electromagnetic procedure. The only use made of light was to see the instruments; c was determined by measuring the electromotive force used to charge a condenser of a known capacity, which was then discharged through a galvanometer. This would give an electromagnetic measure of the quantity of electricity in the galvanometer.

foundations of electromagnetism as understood by Kelvin. Theory and method were deeply intertwined!

As I mentioned at the outset, Kelvin saw mechanical models as intimately connected to measurement and experiment. He considered numerical calculation to be measurement, as long as it was performed in the context of model construction, testing, and manipulation. All of these features enabled one to know an object "directly" rather than simply becoming acquainted with a mere representation. This combination of a mechanical model and its practical application in the success of the Atlantic cable stood as a bold challenge to the kind of paper models and abstract mathematics found in Maxwell's work. The cable required a number of precise measurements that simply were not possible without a mechanical model. Displacement, understood as a field process, could not be measured because he was unable to build a model that could replicate it. Because the manipulation of these models often took the place of direct experiment, the ether, although inaccessible in many respects, was considered real by Kelvin insofar as he was able to experiment on it using models. As we can see, it was largely the model that came to define and constrain reality, and not vice versa. What was physically realisable was what could be mechanically constructed, and what was mechanically constructed could be measured. This constituted the experimental basis for theoretical beliefs and ontological commitments, and in that sense the model-based unity of theory, method, and ontology created a very powerful web of belief.[13]

From the foregoing discussion one can see how the calculation versus measurement distinction is important here. Kelvin's liberal attitude toward what counted as measurement resulted in a notion

---

13. Even after the experimental proof of the existence of electromagnetic waves by Hertz in 1888, Kelvin remained critical of Maxwell's theory and its postulation of the displacement current. For more on Kelvin's views about measurement and models see Smith and Wise (1989).

of experiment that extended much further than what one would normally allow as the basis for inference.[14] Maxwell was clearly able to calculate the velocity of wave propagation and values associated with the displacement current, but there was no "physical" basis for these calculations. However, the materiality Kelvin associated with mechanical models was not really a sufficient foundation for ontological claims about measurement. Neither mechanical models nor the success of the telegraph could ground a methodology that simply assumed a connection between physical reality and the ability to manipulate mechanical models that supposedly represented it.

Yet, if we look to modern science, we often find extensive reliance on models as the source of knowledge of physical systems, especially when these systems are largely inaccessible, as the ether was for Kelvin. In disciplines like astrophysics and cosmology, modelling has given way to CS, enabling researchers to investigate the formation of stars, galaxies, and the large-scale structure of the universe. Even in biological contexts like population genetics, highly abstract mathematical models and CSs, rather than the evolution of natural populations, are often the focus of inquiry. Although models and modelling techniques play an important role in these types of exploration, they are also crucial in more traditional forms of experimentation.

The interesting question is whether the prevalence of models and simulations in these contexts indicates a narrowing of the gap between measurement and calculation, particularly in cases where the model/simulation functions as the object of investigation—as a stand-in for the physical system. To answer that question we need to evaluate the epistemic role and limits of model-based inference in both experiment and CS. A crucial part of the answer will involve an

14. To that extent, it is more than a little ironic that the empiricism that motivated Kelvin's use of mechanical models evolved into a form of methodological and theoretical dogmatism that prevented him from understanding and accepting the fundamental components of the most successful theory of his time.

assessment of the status of simulation as experiment. Several philosophers have drawn attention to connections between modelling and simulation, as well as the similarities and differences between simulation and experimental inquiry.[15] Opinion is divided about whether simulation can be properly classified as experimental inquiry, with some citing the lack of materiality as crucial in the epistemic evaluation of CS. The materiality condition rests on the idea that experimental inquiry typically involves not only a concrete physical system but typically one that is made of the "same stuff" as the target. Hence, inferences from the experimental context to the target system are more epistemically reliable due to the ontological features and the similarities they exhibit (Guala 2002; Morgan 2005). Others argue that materiality is not epistemically important when associating simulations with experiment—that formal similarity should be of greater concern (cf. Parker 2008; Winsberg 2008).[16]

While I agree with the latter view, nagging questions about materiality arise when the object of investigation is to establish the existence of a specific phenomenon or effect. Although this seems to suggest an important role for materiality, I will argue that the situation is less straightforward than might appear, and as I will show in the final chapter, materiality in and of itself doesn't really tell us much, if anything, in experiments like the Higgs search. The role of models and simulation in the experimental process calls into question

---

15. Humphreys (1990) was one of the first to draw our attention to the importance of simulation in understanding features of mathematically oriented theorising and their connection to mathematical models and modelling practices more generally. That discussion continues in Humphreys (2004). Hartmann (1995) has also emphasised several important features of simulation, including their dynamical aspects. For a discussion of issues surrounding the materiality of simulations see excellent papers by Winsberg (2008) and Parker (2008) as well as Morgan (2003a and b). Hughes (1999) has an interesting discussion of CS and the Ising model.

16. The notion of experiment I am interested in here is one that goes beyond numerical experiment intended as a kind of mathematical number crunching.

appeals to materiality that are allegedly responsible for grounding ontological claims.

In the next section I discuss why I think there is sometimes very little basis on which to epistemically differentiate the activities involved in certain types of simulation and experimentation. What I argue is that in some instances this notion of 'being in causal contact with the system' has no relevant epistemic or ontological implications for the way the outcomes are evaluated. As a consequence, any sharp distinction between the outputs of simulation and experimental measurement is called into question. In order to establish my claim and show how models and simulation are linked with measurement and experiment, let me first look at some of the philosophical issues associated with simulation.

COMPUTER SIMULATIONS AND EXPERIMENT: HIGHLIGHTING THE DIFFERENCES

The straightforward notion of simulation is used in a variety of scientific contexts where one type of system is used to represent or mimic the behaviour of another. An example is the use of wind tunnels to simulate certain aerodynamic features of flight. Computer simulation builds on this notion not just through the calculational power of computers but in the actual processes that are involved in the simulation itself. While we can capture a good deal of the straightforward aspects of the wind tunnel simulation in the traditional framework of modelling, CS extends modelling practices in a variety of ways. Its use in condensed matter physics provides a clear example.

When presented with some initial microscopic arrangement for the system being investigated, one uses an algorithm or set of instructions that generates a different microscopic arrangement. The earliest arrangements in the sequence generated by repeated applications of the algorithm reflect the specific choice of the initial arrangement. However, the algorithm is designed such that irrespective of the initial arrangement, the arrangements appearing later in the sequence do so with a frequency defined by an equation from statistical physics that gives the probability that a physical system at a particular temperature will have a particular microscopic arrangement of energy. In other words, the simulation tracks the dynamical evolution of the system. The desired properties can then be determined by computer "measuring" the average value of the property in question over a suitably large number of arrangements. This type of simulation involves renormalisation group methods and is used to investigate systems at critical point where the system is forced to choose, as it were, among a number of macroscopically different sets of microscopic arrangements. The CS illustrates the way the ordering process takes place. The basic ingredients of the algorithm take the form of a set of probabilities that an s-variable in a given state with its immediate neighbours (with which it interacts) in a given arrangement will, in unit time, jump to a different state.

From this example we can see that the CS not only enables us to represent the evolution of the system but also to "measure" the values of specific properties as it approaches critical point. The question of whether this so-called measurement is properly characterised as such or is better described as calculation depends, to a great extent, on whether simulation can be labelled as a type of experiment. As is typically the case in these kinds of debates, there are persuasive arguments on both sides. If simulations enjoy the same epistemic status as experiments then why spend money building large colliders designed to test the results produced by Monte Carlo simulations of particle interactions. On the other hand there are a variety of contexts where CSs do take centre stage as the source of experimental knowledge simply because the systems we are interested in are inaccessible to us. An example is the evolution of spiral structure in galaxies. Because the typical time and distance scales are so vast, the only way experiments can be performed is by simulating the system on a computer and experimenting on the simulation. In the case of stellar evolution, what this involves is solving PDEs for heat transfer within a star simultaneously with equations determining the burning of nuclear fuel. This type of study has been so successful that the life histories of most types of stars, from birth to death and all the stages in between, are thought to be well understood, with no suggestion that the knowledge we gain in these contexts is in any way inferior.

In the astrophysics case we may want to say that simulation is an acceptable source of experimental knowledge simply because we are unable to conduct materially based experiments the way we can with other types of systems. But in cases where both simulations and material experiments are utilised, are there good reasons to give priority to the latter? In other words, is there anything that justifies an appeal to materiality in motivating an epistemic distinction between simulation and experiment, and is there something significant about the access to material systems that renders experiments epistemically privileged?

Winsberg (2008) cites Gilbert and Troitzsch (1999, 13), who discuss simulation in the social sciences and claim that the major difference between simulation and experiment is that in the latter case one is controlling the actual object of interest, while in a simulation one is experimenting with a model rather than the phenomenon itself. In a similar vein Morgan (2002, 2003a and b) claims that what differentiates simulation from experiment is the materiality of the latter, which is an important feature in establishing the external validity of the experiment. Because simulations bear only a formal or abstract similarity to the target system their validity is much more difficult to assess.

Both Winsberg (2003, 2008) and Parker (2008) have also drawn attention to ways of distinguishing experiment and simulation.

Parker defines a CS as a time-ordered sequence of events that serves as a representation of some other time-ordered sequence of events where the simulating system has certain properties that represent the properties of the target system. Experiment on the other hand involves intervening on a system and observing how certain properties change in light of the intervention. The former do not qualify as experiments, but "computer simulation studies" do, because they involve intervening on a system (the digital computer) to see how properties of interest change. In that sense it is the activity, the intervening, that renders something an experiment.

But this is not an experiment in the ordinary sense of the word since the intervention is directed toward the computer and not the physical system we are interested in studying, which is typically the case with experimentation. However, as Winsberg (2008, 4) points out, if we fixate on the experimental qualities of simulations we can classify them as numerical experiments that produce certain kinds of data. As a way of methodologically distinguishing experiment and CS I take this latter claim to be relatively unproblematic. But if our goal is a comparison of the data produced by experiment and CS, then we need to move beyond a methodological distinction to an epistemological analysis.

Winsberg attempts to address this issue by distinguishing two kinds of simulation: SR is a type of representational entity, and SA is an activity on a methodological par with experiment but is distinct from ordinary experiments. He claims there are epistemological differences between experiment and simulation even though the former may not be intrinsically more epistemically powerful than the latter. Although both types of activities face epistemic challenges, he argues that the kinds of challenges each faces are fundamentally different. Essentially what distinguishes the two is the character of the argument given for the legitimacy of the inference from object to target and the character of the background knowledge that grounds that argument. In a simulation, the argument that the object can stand in for the target and that their behaviours can be counted on to be relevantly similar is grounded in certain aspects of model building practice. If we are studying the dynamics of some target system then the configuration of the object of investigation will be governed by the constraints used to model the target system. The reliability of those model building principles will provide the justification for the external validity of the simulation. Although this practice is also common in ordinary experimentation, Winsberg claims that in experiment we are interested in modelling what he terms "the object" under study (the experimental setup) rather than the target system, and hence the model building principles are used to justify the internal validity of the experiment.[17] In simulation we are interested in the target system and its relation to the outside world, hence external validity is what we are concerned with (2008, 24).

In the end Winsberg concludes that none of these conditions means that simulation has less potential to make strong inferences back to the world. In fact, a simulation of the solar system that relies on Newton's laws is epistemically stronger than virtually any experimental setup, simply because the ability to construct good models for this type of system is not in question. Hence, it is the quality, not the kind, of background knowledge and the skill involved in manipulating it that is important for grounding inferential practices in both simulations and experiments.

While I certainly agree that simulation is equally able to make inferences back to the world, it is not clear to me that the distinction between experiment and simulation should be grounded in the difference between internal versus external validity. Moreover, emphasising such a difference has implications for both the kind and strength

17. I take it that "object" here means apparatus, whereas in CS the object is the simulation run on the digital computer.

of the inferences we make about the world based on the results of experiment and simulations. When establishing a claim or hypothesis about a physical system, the internal validity of the experiment is simply the first step in that process. Without that, we have no basis for assuming the legitimacy of the result. But external validity is crucial in assuming that experimental findings are true of the physical world and not just the shielded environment of the experiment. Focusing only on internal validity when characterising experiment leaves us without any methodology for making the type of inferences required to extend experimental results.

In addition, if one locates the justification for inferential practices with the models used in each context, then the types of inferences made in both experiments and CSs begin to appear very similar. This becomes especially apparent when one looks at the way that models are used in an experiment, where both the object and target systems are modelled. For example, in particle physics we often do not directly observe the object being measured in an experiment, as in the case of electron spin or the polarisation of a photon. Instead, extremely complex equipment is used, together with a theoretical model that describes its behaviour by a few degrees of freedom interacting with those of the microscopic system being investigated/observed. It is by means of this model that the behaviour of the apparatus is related to the assumed (modelled) properties of the microscopic system. In other words, it is this type of comparison that constitutes a measurement, with the model of the target system and the model of the apparatus playing an essential role. Moreover, in simulation a great deal of emphasis is placed on calibration, where we test not only the precision of the machine (the computer) but the accuracy of the numerical procedure   both of which rely on calibration models to establish external and internal validity.[18]

---

18. I will have more to say about the process of calibration in chapter 7.

To illustrate these points in more detail, let me introduce the notion of a "simulation system" and compare it with two different types of experiment, one that is rather straightforward and the other less so. What I will show is that the way models function as the primary source of knowledge in each of the three contexts is not significantly different; hence we have no justifiable reason to assume that, in these types of cases, the outputs of experiment and simulation are methodologically or epistemically different. As I will show, the causal connections between measurement and the object/property being measured that are typically invoked to validate experimental knowledge can also be represented in simulations. Consequently, the ability to detect and rule out error is comparable in each case.[19]

CONNECTING SIMULATION WITH EXPERIMENT

The kind of "simulation system" I want to focus on is CS using particle methods.[20] This involves tracing the motion of tens of thousands of particles and is typically used for evolutionary calculations—for the temporal development of an initial value/boundary value problem. The initial state of the system at time t = 0 is specified in some finite region of space on the surface of which certain boundary conditions hold. The simulation involves following the temporal evolution of the configuration. What is central to CS, and something that both Winsberg and Parker stress, is the importance of representing the target system in terms of an appropriate theoretical/mathematical

19. Chapter 7 will deal exclusively with the notion of error and uncertainty in simulation and how those difficulties are dealt with and, where possible, overcome.
20. For an extensive treatment of simulation using particle methods see Hockney and Eastwood (1994). A good deal of my discussion of this method borrows from their account. I introduce the notion of a "simulation system" as a way of isolating what I take to be the crucial features of the particle method.

model. The particle method provides an appropriate way of discretising the theoretical model for cases where we have a corpuscular system or the system is succinctly described by a Lagrangian formulation.[21] Some examples of physical systems appropriate for particle methods include semiconductor devices, ionic liquids, stellar and galaxy clusters, and many others.

What, then, is the relation between this discretising method, the target system, and the simulation itself? We can think of the process as involving a bottom-up framework that begins with the phenomenon or target system and a theoretical/mathematical model of that system. We then use a specific approximation method to discretise that model in order to make it amenable to numerical solution. These discrete algebraic equations describe a simulation model, in this case a particle model, which can then be expressed as a sequence of computer instructions (an algorithm) that yield the simulation programme. In other words, the simulation model is the result of applying a particular kind of discretisation to the theoretical/mathematical model. The representation provided by the simulation model is an important feature in developing the algorithm out of which the programme is constructed. A trade-off between the quality of the representation and computational costs/power needs to be established in order for the programme to fulfill certain conditions like ease of use and modification. What I call the "simulation system" consists of the computer, the simulation model, and the programme and allows us to follow and investigate the evolution of the model physical system (i.e., the theoretical model/representation of the target system).

There are several reasons for characterising this type of investigation as an experiment, or more properly, a computer experiment. First of all, we can think of the simulation system as encompassing

21. Other methods of discretisation include finite difference approximations and finite element approximations.

both the apparatus and the object under investigation. Considered as an apparatus, it allows us to create the kind of controlled environment where one can vary initial conditions, values of parameters, and so on. In that sense it functions like a piece of laboratory equipment, used to measure and manipulate physical phenomena. Unlike traditional experiments, the situation is not constrained by conditions such as linearity, symmetry, or large numbers of degrees of freedom. The properties of the physical system being modelled are represented in accordance with the limitations of the discrete representation on the computer, the particle/simulation models. To clarify, the experimenter can represent certain features of the target system in the simulation models, which are then investigated using the computer and programme. One could refine the distinction even further by isolating the computer plus programme as the apparatus and the simulation model as the object under investigation.

It is tempting to object here that in referring to what is being investigated I am equivocating between the model-representation and the properties of the material system. In a CS, unlike an experiment, one is not directly manipulating a "material object," unless of course we think in terms of the materiality of the digital computer itself in the way that Parker (2008) suggests. Strictly speaking the model is what is being investigated and manipulated in a simulation. However, that model functions as a representation of a physical system via its relationship to the theoretical/mathematical model of the target, so to that extent the target system itself is also the object of inquiry.[22] As I will show, this type of model/system relation is not

22. There are issues here about the degree of departure between the discretised simulation model and the mathematical model, that is, whether the former is an accurate representation of the latter. To some extent these issues are practical problems resolved via calibration and testing and hence are not reasons for general scepticism regarding the representational capacity of the simulation model itself. I will discuss this issue in greater detail in chapters 7 and 8.

simply a peculiarity of CSs but is also present in more traditional forms of experimentation. One might object here that in experiment there is a material constraint whose state gets interpreted by models, whereas in a simulation no such constraint exists—there are only models; hence the simulation cannot really provide the same kind of knowledge as an experiment. While this characterisation is certainly true, I want to claim that the conclusion needn't be, unless of course one is prepared to rule out as nonempirical a good deal of contemporary investigation that relies on simulation. For example, how should one think about results from disciplines like astrophysics and cosmology, where the object of investigation is primarily a simulation model, yet the information the models yield is thought to be of the physical system that the model represents? Put differently, scientists understand simulation results as being about physical systems and/ or measuring parameters associated with those systems; so what do we need to presuppose in order to justify that practice?

The picture I am arguing for differs from other accounts of simulation and comparisons of simulation with experiment (e.g. Humphreys 2004; Parker 2008) because it does not locate the materiality in the machine itself but associates it with the simulation model and the system it represents. What justifies this assignment? In most applications using particle methods, the particles in the simulation model can be directly identified with physical objects (via the theoretical model of the system). Each computer particle has a set of attributes (mass, charge, etc.), and the state of the physical system is defined by the attributes of a finite ensemble of particles, with the evolution determined by the laws governing the particles.[23] In molecular dynamics simulation, each atom corresponds to a particle, and

---

23. For more details see Hockney and Eastwood (1994, 3). As they point out, one advantage is that a number of particle attributes are conserved quantities, so there is no need to update the system as the simulation evolves.

the attributes of the particle are those of the atom, while in simulation of stellar clusters, stars correspond to particles. The relationship between the physical particles and the simulation particles is determined by the interplay of finite computer resources together with the length and time scales that are important for the physical systems. The trick is to devise a model that is sufficiently complex that it reproduces the relevant physical effects but without making the calculation too onerous. There are different types of particle models, each of which is useful for particular types of problems.[24]

I should add here that the emphasis on particle methods is an important part of my argument, since I do not want to claim that every type of simulation enjoys the same status with respect to the data it produces. Particle methods enable an identification with the physical system in ways that are sometimes not possible with other types of simulation. Typically, the particles are viewed as objects carrying a physical property of the flow that is simulated through the solution of ordinary differential equations. The latter determine the trajectories and the evolution of the properties carried by the particles, such as the locations and velocities, as well as density, temperature, vorticity, and the dynamics of the simulated flows. Particle simulations are well suited to a Lagrangian formulation of the continuum equations and can be extended to the mesoscale and nanoscale regimes using techniques such as molecular dynamics and dissipative particle dynamics, which are inherently linked to the discrete representation of the underlying physics. In fact, particle methods enable a unifying formulation that can produce systematic and robust multiscale flow simulations. What is especially important about particle methods is that their computational structure involves a large number of abstractions that help in their computational implementation, while at the

---

24. The decision to use a particular method depends on a variety of factors, including the size of the system, whether the forces are long-range, nonzero interaction, smoothly varying, etc.

same time these methods are inherently linked to the physics of the systems that they simulate.

While this is not a case of 'materiality' in the sense of experiment, it is the type of representation of materiality that is appealed to when simulated data are used to draw conclusions about physical systems. It is also important to stress that I'm not claiming that simulations can replace experiments tout court but rather that we need to broaden the category of experimental knowledge in order to make sense of the practice of using simulation as experimental data against which other simulations are compared, and as a form of theoretical prediction against which other empirical data are compared.[25]

These kinds of conclusions can be drawn more convincingly with particle methods because the simulations mimic the physical world down to the interactions of individual atoms. But in virtue of the enormous detail and attention to the physical constraints of the target system, this kind of mimicking goes well beyond simple modelling. Simulations can not only reveal new physics but also guide the setup of new experiments and assist in understanding results of past experiments. In fact, we can think of simulations as electronic experiments that replicate scaled models of experiments that would be too difficult or expensive to perform or would raise environmental or safety issues. For example, one of the motivations behind increasingly realistic simulations has been the U.S. Department of Energy's National Nuclear Security Administration programme, which ensures the safety of stockpiled nuclear weapons. Other projects that involve extensive simulation include designing anticancer drugs, developing detection systems for protein toxins, and investigating the mechanisms of DNA repair and replication. All of these

---

25. The other strand of the argument, which I spell out in the next section, highlights the way that information provided by materiality constraints is so heavily model dependent that it ceases to do any epistemological work.

simulations involve molecular dynamics software that mimics how individual atoms interact. Simulations also enable one to address questions that are difficult to answer even with advanced experiments; one such example is the propagation of a shock front in liquid deuterium. Learning that the propagation of the front is related to the front's electronic excitation allowed better planning for future experiments and a greater understanding of past experiments, since it was the first time a shock in a molecular liquid could be described in such detail.

Similarly, quantum simulations provide simultaneous access to numerous physical properties, such as structural, electronic, and vibrational, and allow one to investigate properties that are not accessible for experiments. An example is microscopic models of the structure of surfaces at the nanoscale, which cannot yet be characterised experimentally with current imaging techniques. The characterisation of nanoscale surfaces and interfaces is important for predicting the function of nanomaterials and their eventual assembly into macroscopic solids. Another example involves the simulation of 20-million-atoms to study crack propagation in the fracture of brittle materials. These studies unexpectedly showed the birth of a crack travelling faster than the speed of sound, a result that contradicted theory. Because it is impossible to "observe" cracks forming and spreading during experiments, the simulations were able to serve as a type of computational microscope that revealed processes at the atomic scale. Not only are simulations essential in the design of modern experiments as I will show in the discussion of the LHC in chapter 8, but they are now of sufficient resolution and size and contain enough physics that their results can be directly compared with experimental results, providing a way to increase the understanding of physical phenomena involved in experiment. In that sense, there is every reason to see simulations not only as a supplement to experiment but as providing a type of experimental knowledge.

The motivation for claiming that a simulation model can function as the 'material' under study arises not only from the aforementioned examples but also from the necessity that simulation models be physically meaningful, as is the case with molecular dynamics simulations/particle methods. In that sense, the "physical" success of the CS rests, ultimately, with the simulation model.[26] This together with the similarities between these investigations and those in astrophysics and cosmology serves as a basis for epistemically associating simulation data with certain types of 'experimental' results.

In their book on particle simulation models Hockney and Eastwood (1994) draw some comparisons between simulation, characterised as a "computer experiment," and more traditional types of experiment. For them, the computer experiment occupies a middle ground where the gap between theoretically and experimentally realisable objectives is difficult to bridge. Theory requires a vast number of simplifications and approximation techniques, a small number of parameters, and so on, and laboratory experiments are forced to deal with enormous complexity, making measurements difficult to both make and interpret. The computer experiment, in its ability to overcome these difficulties, becomes the "link between theory and experiment."[27]

They claim that computer experiments, like their material counterparts, can be divided in roughly three categories. The first involves simulations designed to predict the workings of complex devices, allowing different configurations to be evaluated before the apparatus is actually constructed. The second involves the collection/production of data that are not obtainable using ordinary laboratory techniques, as in the simulation of galaxies. The third involves what

---

26. Provided of course that the other relevant calibrations on the machine have been performed.
27. Winsberg (2003) has suggested a similar view in his claim that simulation, like experiment, has, to use Hacking's phrase, a life of its own.

Hockney and Eastwood call the "theoretical experiment," which is intended as a guide for theoretical development in that it enables us to examine complex situations by dissecting them into smaller components with an eye to obtaining a clearer theoretical picture of the target system. The film output from the computer experiment provides a more precise picture of the dynamics than the mental images/thought experiments of the theoretician. Hockney and Eastwood claim that the computer experiment, in conjunction with theory and physical experiment, provides a more effective way of obtaining results than either approach or pair of approaches together. Theory uses mathematical analysis and numerical evaluation; experiment—apparatus and data analysis, and computer experiment—uses simulation programme and computer. Taken together, they constitute a sophisticated methodology for scientific investigation.

While Hockney and Eastwood want to situate simulation squarely in the experimental camp, their characterisation of different types of computer experiment applies equally well to modelling, especially when we think of how models provide a link between theory and experiment.[28] But we can take the similarities much further. Just like simulations, models are often constructed before building an apparatus or physical structure; they are sometimes the focus of investigation when the target system is inaccessible; and they often provide the stimulus for new theoretical hypotheses. There are, of course, the computational resources of simulation which make it different from modelling, but given the various functions of simulation I have outlined, one could certainly characterise it as a type of "enhanced" modelling. I should note here that despite these similarities, I want to stress the unique role that simulation plays in the methodological landscape. Comparing its results to those of experiment doesn't entail that its character is somehow

---

28. This, of course, is just the sense in which models function as mediators between theory and material systems. I will have more to say about the specifics of this link later.

identical to experiment; rather the issue is one of epistemic parity of the outputs or results, with the similarities intended to provide evidence for that claim.[29]

There are many reasons why the picture of simulation as modelling may seem attractive. Earlier I discussed the various ways in which models, both mathematical and what I have called the 'simulation models,' play a role in the CS of the target system. Indeed many of those who have written on simulation have stressed the link with models. Winsberg (2003, 107), for example, claims that simulation "provides a clear window through which to view the model-making process." He uses the term "simulation" to refer to the process of building, running, and inferring from computational models. Simulations themselves, he claims, are based on models insofar as they incorporate model assumptions and produce models of phenomena. And, as I have pointed out, he also sees the justification for simulations as directly related to the strength of the underlying model of the target phenomenon/system and the legitimacy of the modelling techniques themselves. Humphreys (2004) also emphasises the role of computational models and has provided a helpful characterisation in terms of a computational template that provides the basic form of the model, other construction assumptions, output representation, as well as other factors. Computational science is then defined in terms of the development, exploration, and implementation of computational models.

While this characterisation seems relatively unproblematic in one sense, it raises the following concern: if we identify simulation with modelling, then how can we account for the experimental features typically associated with simulation? Moreover, it we understand

29. What this means is that I also disagree with the analysis provided by Frigg and Reiss (2008) who claim that the methodological issues related to simulation are the same as those relating to modelling more generally. My discussion in chapter 7 sheds light on why that is not the case.

model manipulation as calculation, then there is no basis whatsoever for linking simulation with measurement.[30] To successfully argue for the experimental status of CSs requires more than just an appeal to the fact that intervention with and manipulation of models and machines are involved. Similarly, to categorise CSs simply as 'numerical' experiments narrows their scope to cases where their primary function is calculation. More principled arguments are required to establish robust epistemic similarities between experimental results and those arrived at using CS, arguments that turn on the similarity of methodology and evaluation of results.

As I mentioned earlier, many of the arguments that favour a strong distinction between experiments and simulations rely on the epistemic priority of materiality that is characteristic of physical experiment. Locating the materiality of computer experiments in the machine itself, however, carries with it no epistemological significance because the conclusions one draws are about the computer itself rather than the model or system being investigated.[31] Although I have briefly discussed the materiality issue already, I would like to return to it now to explore its philosophical implications more fully. While the argument from materiality has intuitive appeal, I will show why it is extremely difficult to motivate philosophically. The reason for this is the pervasive role of models at all levels of experimental practice. Earlier I claimed that models are experimental tools capable of functioning as measuring instruments, but they are also objects of inquiry in cases where they, rather than physical systems, are being directly investigated and manipulated.[32] What

30. Consequently, we would be unable to capture many of the uses of CS in experimental contexts, specifically astrophysics and cosmology.
31. One might want to claim that 'experimenting' on the machine can provide evidence that it gives reliable outputs, which in turn provides increased confidence in the simulation results, but this needn't be an epistemic consideration in the sense that it legitimates the simulation model itself.
32. The use of the term 'direct' is important here. It is not that the target system is not being investigated in contexts where there is a strong reliance on models, but rather there is no direct (or even indirect) access to the target system making the model the immediate object of inquiry.

this suggests is a close connection between models and experiment, and as I will show, it is this link that figures prominently in establishing the experimental character of simulations. In other words, arguments illustrating the experimental features of models can also establish the experimental nature of simulation.

In what follows, I describe how models act as measuring devices and how this role is crucial in defining their experimental character. The association with these types of modelling practices also underwrites our ability to classify the outputs of CS as measurements. Put slightly differently, in contexts where the modelling features of simulation are coextensive with its experimental character, epistemically relevant differences between experimental and simulation data become difficult to articulate.

MEASUREMENTS, MODELS, AND MEDIATION

In discussing the "experimental" features of models, it is important to distinguish between models that are used to classify or organise experimental data and what I refer to as experimental models. The former are discussed (albeit in a slightly different form) in some of the early work in statistics (Pearson 1911) and, among other places, in the literature on the semantic view of theories, particularly Suppes (2002, 7). He describes the relation of theory to data as a process that puts experience "through a conceptual grinder" and produces experimental data in canonical form. These data constitute a model of the experimental results that, given its discrete and finite character, is a different logical type than a model of a theory. Statistical methodology then relates the model of the experimental results to some designated model of the theory. In order to do this, there needs to be a theory of experimentation in place that can not only adequately connect the two but also enable us to estimate theoretical parameters in the model of the theory from models of the experimental results (or data). This is the famous model selection problem in statistics, and there are many different approaches one can take to these issues (Akaike information criterion, Bayesian methods, classical Neyman-Pearson statistics, etc.). However, my concern here is to focus on how we should understand the more general relation between models and experiment; that is, how models enable us to extract information from our apparatus and how we should understand their role in experimental practice more generally.[33]

I will look very briefly at two different types of experiments, the measurement of gravitational acceleration and spin measurement. Although each of these might appear to involve different types of measurement, one more direct than the other, this in itself is not significant. In both cases, and indeed in most experimental measurements of physical quantities or effects, models occupy centre stage. The first example I consider is the measurement of gravitational acceleration using a simple plane pendulum.[34] This is the kind of experiment one usually does in the lab as a student, and although it may seem relatively straightforward, a good deal of theoretical modelling is required in order to achieve an accurate result.

We begin with a theoretical (model) object—the ideal point pendulum—supported by a massless, inextensible cord of length l. From Newton's laws we know the equation of motion for oscillations in a vacuum and for the period. If the cord length and period are known, we can solve for the acceleration of gravity. So the experimental problem is to measure l and T_0. However, once the measurements are made on the physical apparatus, a vast number of corrections must be applied, since the equation used to solve for g

33. As I will show in chapter 8, this notion of modelling is especially important in the case of the LHC, where every aspect of the experiment has to be modelled and simulated in order to construct its actual features and understand the results.
34. See Morrison (1999) for more details.

as a function of l and T_0 describes a pendulum that deviates significantly from the physical one used in the measurement.

The period of oscillation of the real pendulum T is related to its idealised counterpart T_0 using a series of corrections depending on the desired level of accuracy. They involve (1) finite amplitude corrections; (2) mass distribution corrections which take account of the bob, the wire connection, and its mass and flexibility; (3) effects of air, which include buoyancy, damping, added mass, and theoretical damping constants; and (4) elastic corrections due to wire stretching and motion of the support. Some of these corrections, especially (1) and (2), are relatively straightforward, but the others involve rather complex applications of modelling assumptions and approximation techniques.[35] The level of sophistication of the experimental apparatus determines the precision of the measurement, but it is the analysis of correction factors that determines the accuracy. In other words, the way modelling assumptions are applied determines how accurate the measurement of g really is. This distinction between precision and accuracy is very important—an accurate set of measurements gives an estimate close to the true value of the quantity being measured, and a precise measurement is one where the uncertainty in the estimated value is small. In order to make sure our measurement of g is accurate we need to rely extensively on information supplied by our modelling techniques/assumptions.

The point I am making here is not just the well-known one of requiring a model in order to apply the law of harmonic motion. Rather, it is that using the physical pendulum as an experimental apparatus requires us to have in place a very sophisticated model of that apparatus, together with extensive approximations; only then

---

35. This is a different issue from the kinds of considerations required for measurement by, for example, the National Bureau of Standards, where it is necessary to take into account variation in temperature, change in length due to atmospheric pressure, etc. Those kinds of considerations are over and above the correction factors just described.

does it function as a measuring instrument. In other words, the corrections applied to the model pendulum in order to describe the physical system are the source of the knowledge and reliability associated with the measurement. While we tend to think about theory or models as informing our interpretation of experimental data or results, we often ignore the specific role that models play in informing the entire activity, including how the apparatus is used.[36]

Obviously, this is not just an issue that concerns the pendulum. In exploration gravity surveys, field observations usually do not yield measurements of the absolute value of gravitational acceleration. Instead, one only derives estimates of variations of acceleration. The primary reason for this is not a lack of sophisticated equipment but rather the difficulty in characterising/modelling the recording instrument well enough to measure absolute values of gravity down to 1 part in 50 million. Simply put: without models there is no measurement.

This brings me to a related issue—the status of the measurement of g. As I have shown, from values of the cord length and period we can obtain a value for gravitational acceleration. If we take the view that models are abstract symbolic entities, then questions arise about where to draw the line between measurement and calculation. In other words, how do we determine when the manipulation of models counts as measurement and when it is simply calculation? The standard definition that comes from measurement theory does not help us here. It tells us that measurements are mappings from objects being studied to some numerical representation called a variable. Calculation on the other hand is usually defined as involving the transformation of inputs into outputs. Both seem to be satisfied in our pendulum example.

---

36. A "theory or model of the apparatus," which involves the theoretical knowledge required to build a machine that will function in the desired way, is somewhat distinct from the use of a model to measure. However, I should also point out that in designing machines like the LHC, CSs of particle paths provide crucial data for the alignment of magnets, etc.

One possible way of differentiating the two involves the distinction (which goes back to Carnap 1950) between fundamental and derived measurement. Fundamental measurements deal strictly with observing relations among physical objects, performing operations on those objects, and using some type of counting procedure to quantify or assign numbers to those relations. Derived measurements incorporate these procedures but also involve abstract calculation of the sort used to measure, for example, the instantaneous acceleration of a body. In this latter context there is no observational counterpart for the mathematical operations. Although this gives us an intuitive way of differentiating measurement and calculation, where only the former is based on observation, virtually none of the measurements performed in modern physics can be classified in this way. Even the measurement of gravitational acceleration done with our plane pendulum does not qualify as an observation in the sense I have described.[37] As Luce and Tukey (1964) point out (albeit for slightly different reasons), fundamental measurement is largely a theoretical property.

There is, however, a methodological counterpart of this distinction that appeals to direct versus indirect measurements.[38] The latter are simply those that presuppose prior measurements, while the former do not. In the pendulum case, we solve for g if we know the length and period, which seems to satisfy the conditions for indirect measurement. Indeed many of the quantities we typically 'measure' are the products of indirect measurement or involve what are sometimes referred to as indirect variables. Velocity, for example, is defined as

37. Batitsky (1998) argues that even things like length measurements cannot be justified solely on the basis of our perceptual interactions with the world. Hence, the notion of fundamental measurement is essentially an empiricist's myth.

38. Sometimes this distinction is absorbed or collapses into the fundamental/derived distinction. Causey (1969) defines a derived measurement as one that has dimensions expressed in terms of previously given fundamental quantities. Fundamental measurements are those that can be made independently of the possibility of making any other measurements.

the distance covered per unit time, while the notion of a force field is something that is only measurable in virtue of its effect. This distinction requires that there be fundamental quantities like mass, length, and time, with other quantities being monomial functions of these. Although the representational theory of measurement is formulated on the basis of this distinction, it is questionable whether there really are any truly direct measurements. Even if there were, it does not solve the problem I have referred to: defining the boundary between indirect measurement and calculation.[39]

The issue becomes more complicated in the second example I want to consider—the measurement of spin, an intrinsic angular momentum associated with the electron and other elementary particles. Although most physics texts tell us that the Stern-Gerlach experiment was the first experimental observation of spin on a beam of neutral silver atoms, it was not identified as such at the time because the spin hypothesis had not yet been put forward.[40] However, one of the most peculiar things about the Stern-Gerlach experiment was its failure to be associated with electron spin by its discoverers, Goudsmit and Uhlenbeck (1926) and by Pauli himself, who first proposed the idea of a fourth quantum number. Moreover, both Pauli and Bohr claimed that it was impossible to observe/measure the spin of the electron separated fully from its orbital momentum by means of experiments based on the concept of classical particle trajectories (Pauli 1932, 1958). In other words, it is questionable whether the claim that the free electron really has a spin can ever be decided on the basis of experimental measurement.

Renewed attempts to 'measure' electron spin took place in the 1970s, with the results being described as an improvement of three or four orders of magnitude in the accuracy attained in magnetic

39. I come back to this point later.
40. The experiment did however measure the magnetic moment of the silver atoms.

moment measurements. But this is not really a measurement of spin in the sense discussed by Bohr and Pauli. Moreover, since the experiments were different from classical quantum measurements, questions arose as to how to theoretically interpret them. Various approaches involving generalisations of QM and nonlinear stochastic Schrödinger equations have been suggested, but none has proven satisfactory. That said, this is not just a problem of how to interpret the experiments themselves. As in most 'measurements' of microscopic systems, what is involved is the comparison of different models. A theoretical model is constructed where the behaviour of the macroscopic equipment is described using a few degrees of freedom, interacting with those of the microscopic system under observation. By means of this model, the observed behaviour of the apparatus is related to the observed properties of the microscopic system.[41]

My claim is not that this is inherently problematic, or that it should not qualify as measurement; rather, what the example emphasises is the importance of the point mentioned earlier: in order to have any understanding of what is happening in these experiments, one requires highly sophisticated models that are themselves sometimes hypothetical. Spin measurement now involves electron spin resonance techniques and scanning tunnelling microscopy, extremely effective methods for detecting precession frequencies of spin. But even here it requires about 10^{10} electrons to get a measurable signal. In addition, MRI techniques are useful, but the spatial resolution of MRI is limited, partly because it takes around 10^{15} nuclei to generate a detectable signal. In none of these cases are we actually measuring the spin of a single electron.

Despite these considerations, no one would claim that spin is not a measurable property of certain types of elementary particles. Nor would one say that the extensive use of modelling assumptions

41. For a detailed discussion of these measurements see Morrison (2007a).

and corrections somehow undermines the claim that we can measure the acceleration of gravity to four significant figures of accuracy using the pendulum. So what are the implications of this? Clearly the use of models in these examples is not sufficient to characterise the activity as simply calculation. With respect to spin, the Dirac equation is thought to provide the requisite *calculation* of electron spin, and as I have shown, Maxwell's equations furnished a calculated value for the propagation of electromagnetic waves. Neither of these could, under any interpretation, be called a measurement. To that extent, we have a distinction between measurement and calculation that matches our intuitions—what we do in manipulating mathematical equations is calculation; measurement involves another type of activity. More specifically, measurement involves some functional relation to instruments that generate data from some physical source. In that sense, a measurement, even one that is indirect, bears some type of connection to the property being measured. Although various calculational techniques are undoubtedly part of the measurement process, the activity of measuring involves an additional set of constraints. The accurate measurement of g requires a model as the primary source of this knowledge. But it is the intervention with the model and the accompanying interplay with the physical pendulum that we use to characterise the measurement process.[42]

Given this depiction of the role of models in experiment and experimental measurement in particular, what, if anything, differentiates the outputs or results in these experiments from the kind of

---

42. In the pendulum case, we are interested in both precision and accuracy and hence concerned not only with the status of the physical pendulum as a measuring device (internal validity) but also with its ability to measure the true value of g (external validity). The correction factors applied to the idealised model are relevant for both. Hence, contrary to the distinction introduced by Winsberg, the modelling involved in experimental contexts relates to both internal and external validity and includes the physical system under investigation as well as the object being manipulated.

'computer measurement' produced in a simulation? Can we claim that simulation also involves measurement, even though it seems to lack the kind of functional relation we typically associated with measurement? The cases of experimental measurement I have discussed illustrate the centrality of models in acquiring knowledge of the relevant parameters; questions about 'materiality' or some type of direct comparison between object and target system based on 'materiality' do not play a justificatory role. And in the case of spin measurements, what is allegedly measured is the value of spin via inferences based on modelling assumptions. Indeed, such is the case with most measurements on elementary particles like quark masses. Experimental measurement is a highly complex affair where appeals to materiality as a method of *validation* are outstripped by an intricate network of models and inference. In other words, making claims about "the same stuff" or invoking some ill-defined notion of material manipulation in effect simply begs the question, or at best invokes a long-outdated view about the nature of experimental practice. Appeals to materiality as a kind of *self-evident* justification for the priority of material experiment have the same force as Dr. Johnson famously kicking the stone as a refutation of Berkeley's idealism.

If we look at the practice of CS, we see that the relation to modelling is strikingly similar to what we find in experiment. We start with a mathematical model of the target physical system and apply the appropriate discretising approximations, which replace the continuous variables and differential equations with arrays of values and algebraic equations. This yields the simulation model, which together with various numerical algorithms produces the programme, which is run on the computer. This translation of the discrete simulation model into a computer programme involves devising a sequence of operations that constitute the numerical algorithm and is expressed as a series of computer instructions. When these operations are performed, they solve for the unknowns of the discrete model equations.

The quality of the algorithm is judged by the number of arithmetic operations required to solve a given set of algebraic equations. The programme itself is tested and calibrated to ensure that it reproduces the behaviour of the target system (as described in the theoretical/ mathematical model) in a reasonably accurate way before it is put to work in actual experiments. In that respect it functions like an apparatus or piece of machinery in a typical laboratory experiment. As in an experiment, we can trace the linkages back to some material features of the target system that are modelled (theoretically) in the initial stages of investigation.

So, while we have a theoretical link to specific features of the target, we don't have the 'material' link described above. If the goal is to provide evidence for the *existence* of a particular particle or effect, then it seems patently obvious that some type of material dimension is required.[43] However, if we are interested in determining or measuring the value of a parameter, then the situation is not so clear, especially given the nonjustificatory role that materiality, taken in itself, plays in the experimental process, together with the epistemic burden shouldered by models. For instance, measuring the values of critical exponents in second-order phase transitions is typically done via simulations. Given that simulation is capable of generating enough data to take account of an extremely large number of scenarios and conditions, it would seem that it can provide a much more reliable way to determine or measure the values of parameters than experiment, even when the latter might be possible.

Simulations also serve as the basis for the construction of sophisticated experimental equipment. For example, the computing project developed to handle the vast amounts of data generated by the

---

43. However, as I will show in the discussion of the Higgs boson, materiality in and of itself proves nothing without the simulation knowledge that gives it meaning.

LHC was started to support both the construction and calibration of the machine. As I will show in chapter 8, it involves simulating how particles will travel in the tunnel, knowledge that determines how the magnets should be calibrated to gain the most stable "orbit" of the beams in the ring. In that sense, the simulation acts as a piece of "experimental" data required for determining the proper operation of the collider. In other words, it provides us with various possible setups against which to test the theoretical aspects that are embedded in the machine.

The framework for CS also allows for a natural division between calculation and measurement, a distinction that can be used to further motivate the notion that simulation outputs can be treated like experimental data. The simulation involves the evolution of the configuration/system in temporal increments by what is called the timestep DT; DT is an important modelling parameter and should be as small as possible, consistent with the requirements of the problem and computer time available. This timestep cycle constitutes the main part of what we can call the 'calculation,' and typically a few thousand timesteps are required to get useful results from a computer experiment. The calculation generates a large amount of data, requiring that they be appropriately modelled in order to render them interpretable. Only by doing that can we say that the computer experiment, like an ordinary experiment, has measured a particular quantity. In both cases models are crucial.[44]

44. And, just as in the pendulum example, where we are interested in both precision and accuracy, similar concerns arise for simulation, where the precision of the machine and the accuracy of the programme must be tested. This can be done by using the apparatus (machine + programme) to reproduce known results, as in simulating a model that is analytically solvable.

MATERIALITY REDUX

Before closing, let me return briefly to the issue of materiality, in particular a well-put objection by Giere (2009) which represents a direct challenge to the "simulation as measurement" thesis. I claimed earlier that although models may play an important role in the experimental context, the goal in some simulations still involves a type of comparison with laboratory experiments, as in the case where we want to determine the existence of a subatomic particle. So what is the justification for classifying simulations as experiments if the *ultimate test* remains the more traditional type of experimental confirmation? There are of course the examples of simulations used to test theories in ways that laboratory experiments cannot. For example, molecular dynamics simulation has been widely used to study phase changes, particularly glass formation and melting in ionic systems. Here the simulation can test microscopic features of theory that are not possible in the laboratory, features like the hardness of the ions, which can be varied independently of their radii. Because different theories of melting predict different dependencies of the melting point on hardness, it is fair to say that the simulations provided new and independent experimental tests.

However, in cases where simulations are stand-ins until laboratory experiments can be performed, any comparison of the two needs to take account of whether the structure of experimental knowledge differs in any way from that produced in a simulation. At this point, our intuitions incline toward the 'materiality' of experiment and the notion that this somehow confers epistemic legitimacy and priority on the outcome. As I mentioned, Morgan (2005), for example, argues for the epistemic priority of material experiments, claiming that inferences about target systems are more justified when both the experimental and target system are made of the same stuff. Parker (2008) challenges this view and claims that when comparing

CSs with experiments, the emphasis on materiality is misplaced. The justification of inferences about target systems depends on having good reasons to think that the relevant similarities, whether material, formal, or some combination of the two, between the experimental and target systems hold.

Giere (2009) has given what is perhaps the most apt version of the "materialist" objection, which can be summarised as follows.

> One constructs a computer model of a well-known system such as the solar system. Since the laws governing the gravitational interactions are exceedingly well established, the outputs of the simulation can reliably be substituted for actual measurements on the solar system. In fact, the results of the simulation might be more accurate than most actual measurements. But these outputs do not count as measurements on the solar system according to traditional accounts of experimentation. They are just the results of calculation. A substitute for a measurement is not a measurement, which traditionally requires causal interaction with the target system. (2009, 60–61)

Giere goes on to point out that in such a case, *actual measurements* on a real system of particles are impossible, but the simulation can determine the detailed evolution of the system from its assumed initial state. But again, one has only a reliable substitute for an experiment, not a traditional experiment, and consequently no actual measurement. While this may be termed a "computer experiment," there is no interaction with and no new information about the target system. He claims that the "epistemological payoff" in the case of traditional experiments is greater (or less) confidence in the fit between a model and a target system, something that is due to the causal connection with the target system. Because computer experiments are not connected to actual data, they fail to confer any additional confidence in the fit (or lack thereof) between the simulation model and the target system.

While Giere undoubtedly raises an important issue here, questions about the nature and evolution of scientific knowledge also need to be considered in any evaluation of his claim. Experimentation in modern science, especially physics, is significantly different from the sort of table-top experiments that characterised its past; this, in turn, raises philosophical questions about the description and interpretation of the practice itself. For example, is the causal connection Giere refers to an essential feature of modern experimentation and if so, what does that connection consist in? What constitutes interaction with the target system in an experimental environment, and is it reasonable to claim, as he does, that no new information exists without this interaction? In the various examples discussed throughout this chapter and in the ones that follow, I have tried to show that the notion of material interaction, while intuitive and seemingly straightforward to invoke, is often difficult to substantiate in contemporary experimental contexts, as in the case of spin measurement. My claim throughout this chapter has not been that CS is just like traditional experiment, or that it somehow bears the same causal connection to the target. Instead, my argument has been designed to show that in many cases of traditional experiment the causal connection to the target is not what is doing the epistemological work. In other words, the modelling assumptions play an integral role in what we take to be the causal information gleaned from the experiment and from simulation as well.

Giere does address this point in a discussion of my pendulum example, saying that while the "pendulum is the instrument which interacts causally with the Earth's gravitational field, the models used to correct the measured period of the pendulum are abstract objects which don't interact causally with anything." Hence, there is no reason to extend the notion of a measuring instrument to include abstract models, even in a functional way, and no basis for saying that computer experiments are epistemologically on a par with traditional experiments. Again, my claim here is not that models are "interacting" with anything but that the notion of interaction in and of itself, and the appeal to the physical independence of the pendulum as an instrument, provide no foundation for any epistemic claims without the accompanying models. Simply saying that experiment is epistemically superior due to a causal interaction with the target and that the models are somehow peripheral begs the epistemological question in the same way that arguments emphasising the materiality of the target system beg the question against simulation.[45]

Giere goes on to claim that in climate modelling we use simulation models to investigate, within the confines of the model, aspects of future climate changes that are inaccessible to any actual measurements. Here, he says, the qualification "within the confines of the model" is all-important. If the simulation allows us to investigate aspects of climate change, then we need to ask ourselves what the epistemic status of that investigation is, especially if simulation occupies the rather impoverished role Giere attributes to it. Nobody would dispute that the information gleaned from a simulation depends on the constraints of the model, but this is not necessarily a reason to undervalue its epistemic worth. In the case of climate modelling, policy decisions need to be made on the basis of evidence that

---

45. One of the referees suggested that it is possible to state Giere's argument in a slightly different way, claiming that while simulation results may be as trustworthy or enjoy the same justificatory status as measurements, they lack the defining feature of measurement, which is causal interaction. As I see it, this would turn the argument into a terminological dispute about the defining conditions for measurement. While I have no particular difficulty with this, it isn't clear to me how it advances the debate. The important issue is whether simulation data can replace experimental measurement in certain contexts. If they are as trustworthy and justified as measurements, then presumably they can, and if not, then we are still left with the question of how to epistemically classify simulation outputs and the task of providing reasons for that classification. Nothing in particular turns on "measurement" as a label, but everything turns on the role that simulation data can play in the larger scientific context.

comes largely from simulation. That in itself doesn't establish epistemic superiority, but it does point to the fact that scientific information is becoming increasingly linked to simulation data. As a result philosophers need to begin looking seriously at the methodological and epistemological implications of this, rather than criticising simulation because it fails to meet conditions that have been used to characterise more traditional forms of experimentation. Indeed, as I will show in chapter 7, there is a robust methodology in place for evaluating the status of simulation knowledge. While these methods are by no means unproblematic, the restriction to the confines of the model can, in most situations, be reasonably accounted for in the same way that laboratory restrictions on experiment can also be successfully generalised.

Giere is certainly right in saying that it is central to the traditional notions of experiment and measurement that it involves interaction (however indirect) with a target system, but my claim is that careful examination of both experimental and simulation practices suggest that the traditional notions need to be rethought. It is no longer "interaction" per se that provides the appraisal of the representational adequacy of the models used in these contexts, as Giere suggests. Nor do my claims imply that simply running a simulation provides a basis for evaluating the representational adequacy of the simulation models. Doing so would be to ignore the complex methodology involved in validating simulation models, something Giere ignores in his remarks about the dangers in misleading consumers of simulation results into thinking that their simulation models are epistemologically better founded than they in fact are.

Although the emphasis on the materiality of laboratory experiments appeals to our intuitions about empirical verification, I have argued that, the sense in which experiment and the knowledge gained therein provides a "causal connection" with concrete physical systems is typically via models. Consequently, the comparisons are not between a directly accessible physical system and a hypothesis but between various levels of modelling. I have also stressed that one cannot determine the existence of physical phenomena using CSs; only material experiment is capable of that. But the ability of such experiment to establish ontological and epistemic claims about those phenomena requires a complex network of modelling assumptions that are an inseparable part of the experimental practice. In that sense, the appeal is not to materiality as the source of justification but to the model of that materiality that best accounts for the data. But this is also true of CSs, in that we typically begin with a material target system that we want to investigate. To reiterate, my point is not to deny the role of materiality in establishing ontological claims but only to point out that in complex experimental contexts, materiality is not always an unequivocal standard that functions as the way to epistemically distinguish simulation outputs from experimental results.

In this context, it is worth noting that simulations frequently function as the confirmation of experiment. For example, CSs of particle collisions provide data that enable researchers to deduce the nature of the debris produced in a collision. These results are then compared with actual experiments as a way of determining what exactly the experiment has shown. In that sense, the 'measurements' produced by the simulation provide an important source of data that are crucial features of the discovery process. This comparison between a computer experiment and a laboratory experiment seems no different in kind from the comparison of a model of the apparatus with a model of the target system that occurs in a laboratory experiment. In each case we adjust the parameters and calibrate the instruments to ensure the legitimacy of the agreement. Given the dependence on CS in these and other contexts, like astrophysics and nuclear weapons storage, there seems no justifiable reason (provided certain conditions are met) to deny the products of simulation the same epistemic status as measurement, or indeed not to identify them as measurements.

It is important to stress, once more, that this does not involve an abandonment of empiricism. The hierarchy of modelling that is characteristic of CS experiments begins with a mathematical model of the physical target system that is then discretised to produce the simulation model. While the CS may represent states of a system that have not yet occurred, our ability to determine how the system will evolve under certain conditions plays an important role in the way scientific knowledge is put to practical use. And, unlike Kelvin's models of the ether, there is a theoretical link with the target system via simulation methods such as molecular dynamics, similar to the theoretical links that form the foundation of a material experiment.

Finally, I have shown how models function as both the object of investigation and as a type of experimental tool in different kinds of investigative contexts. The physical apparatus, while an important part of experimental investigation, is only one feature of the overall measurement context; models are required to extract meaningful information about both the apparatus and the target system. The conclusion, that some forms of simulation can attain an epistemic status comparable to laboratory experimentation, involved showing its connections with particular types of modelling strategies and highlighting the ways in which those strategies are also an essential feature of experimentation.[46] The role that models play in these contexts highlights the difficulties in justifying (epistemically) any intuitive appeal materiality might have in elevating traditional experiment over CS.

---

46. A general epistemological issue that emerges from this discussion concerns the changing nature of both measurement and experiment. In the end, it may be that the account of CS I have argued for is one that is more appropriate to the natural rather than the social sciences. However, given the complex nature of measurement in the social sciences, I am inclined to think that the two contexts may be remarkably similar in certain respects. Justification of that intuition will have to wait for another time.

So I am not arguing for the experimental status of simulation *tout court*; instead I want to push the more modest proposal that in some cases and with specific types of simulation techniques we can be reasonably justified in claiming that simulation outputs can function as measurement. In some sense it really doesn't matter whether we can characterise a simulation as an experiment; what matters is that their outputs can enjoy the same epistemic status when suitable conditions are met. However, the argument(s) in favour of that conclusion need to be supplemented by a careful evaluation of issues related to assessment of the reliability of the simulation itself, both as a model of the target system and as a numerical tool. In chapters 7 and 8 I discuss some of the problems and solutions associated with simulation reliability, as well as the ways in which simulation knowledge can acquire the legitimacy necessary for it to function as an indispensable part of scientific inquiry.

7

Legitimating Simulation

Methodological Issues of Verification and Validation

An important question that motivates much of the philosophical literature on CS is how we should evaluate the data produced by this practice. This question has given rise to a series of subquestions about where exactly we should locate CS on the methodological landscape, questions of the sort I addressed in chapter 6, such as: is CS a form of experimentation or just an enhanced version of modelling? Are there new epistemic questions that arise in the context of CS that are different from those related to modelling and experimentation? An obvious characterisation is that CS is some type of hybrid activity that involves aspects of modelling and experimentation and as such occupies a middle ground. The result is that data produced via simulation have an epistemic status that is less robust than that of experimental data but greater than that of the results obtained from the mathematical manipulation of or calculation with models.

While the hybrid view is an attractive one, as a general picture of CS it is rather unhelpful, since it is obviously not the case that we can simply generalise about the nature of computer simulated data or the methodological aspects of CS itself. Nor does the notion of a hybrid tell us very much about where to locate CS data on the epistemological landscape. One of the reasons for this is that there are a number of different types of CS that use different methodologies and are used in different experimental contexts, so to simply classify simulation as a hybrid activity is not a helpful solution. Similarly, rehearsing a long list of similarities and differences with both experimentation and modelling accomplishes little in establishing any epistemological conclusions. Instead, the focus should be directly on CS outputs, how they are generated, and how they are used, in order to evaluate their epistemic status.

In chapter 6 I claimed that in some cases CSs could be considered epistemically on a par with experimental measurements. My intention was not to argue that simulation is just like experiment but rather to emphasise that the conditions under which we have faith in experimental data are sometimes also replicated in CS. In other words, simulations outputs are, in some cases, akin to experimental measurement. One of my goals in this chapter is to extend that argument by highlighting a number of different issues that seem to be misplaced or misguided in the process of evaluating CS data. The other is to highlight the role of simulation in experiment and to show how simulated data, considered in their own right, play an increasingly significant role in the justification of experimental results. In that sense, CS data function as an integral part of experiment, not something distinct from it.

The first and perhaps most often cited objection to the robustness of simulation data is that we cannot learn anything genuinely novel from CS, since we get out only what we put in. In other words, unlike experiment where nature can "push back" with results that are both conceptually and ontologically distinct from the experimental setup, CS only gives us the consequences of what has been programmed into the computer. While this claim is in some sense trivially true for deterministic simulations, it misses the larger and more important point about CS, which is that it allows us to extract information that is not otherwise apparent, and would likely never be apparent, until the simulation has run. The objection is rather like saying that we don't learn anything new from mathematically based arguments in physics since all the information is already contained in the equations we want to solve; but few, if any, would deny that new knowledge is produced as a result of mathematical argumentation. In that sense the importance of the objection for assessing simulation outcomes is both exaggerated and misguided. Simply put, the computational power provided by CS allows us uncover features of physical systems that may be implicit in the equations but would otherwise remain unknown. And, perhaps more important, in the case of stochastic simulations the outputs are just as uncertain as experiment.

In order to properly assess the status of simulation knowledge our focus should include the degree of uncertainty inherent in simulation outputs, uncertainties that result from an information loss in the discretisation process, as well as those associated with input parameters in the theoretical model. Related to the question of uncertainty are the methodological issues surrounding V&V, particularly the validation hierarchy and the notion of a validation metric used to compare simulation results with experimental data. A close examination of these various aspects reveals that while simulation clearly has links to methodological features of both experiment and modelling, it ought not to be assimilated with one or the other, nor should it be considered a hybrid.[1] The methodological structure associated with CS provides us with a type of knowledge that is uniquely generated and raises its own epistemological concerns, concerns that require a careful and subtle approach when assessing epistemic warrant. However, any evaluation of simulation data and their application

---

1. Frigg and Reiss (2008) claim that no new issues arise in the context of simulation; the problems are simply the same as those that arise in modelling contexts. Humphreys (2008) has a convincing reply to these arguments.

in experimental contexts needs to address questions regarding the methodology used for justifying simulation results and whether that methodology is itself problematic in certain respects. Note that this is a different question from whether we should consider simulation results on a par with experimental data. In that sense, my immediate concern in what follows is to investigate the processes involved in legitimating simulation data, taken in their own right.

The methodology of V&V is designed to legitimate simulation as a source of knowledge. As I will show, what distinguishes it from the sort of hypothesis testing characteristic of experiment is that it introduces new approaches for addressing epistemic questions about the accuracy and reliability of simulation. Despite this methodology, worries arise regarding what is actually entailed by the process of validating a simulation, as well as the relationship between verification and validation. Technically, verification is a precondition of validation and involves ensuring that the code accurately represents the problem of interest; only then can validation supposedly be carried out. Winsberg (2010) has recently argued that these processes are rarely carried out sequentially and V&V are typically done together in a rather ad hoc way, with the focus more on successful results rather than methodological justification.[2]

Although Winsberg provides little if any concrete evidence for these claims, his remarks raise interesting questions regarding the role of V&V, especially with respect to the focus of chapter 8, which is a discussion of the use of simulation in the discovery of the Higgs boson at the LHC. For example, what exactly does it mean to validate LHC simulations performed at a time when very few data were available and when a great deal of important data were yet to be produced. Validation at the LHC is an ongoing process, so it is important to

---

2. Winsberg (2010, ch. 2).

determine exactly what was validated, when, and how this determination relates to the discovery aspects of the experiment.

I begin with a discussion of some of the different ways simulation can "go wrong" and how isolating those problems allows us to gain a better understanding and focus for assessing how simulation can produce new knowledge. The production of such knowledge is of course intimately connected with the justificatory methods used in its evaluation. In the second section I discuss the methodology of V&V and the reasons behind our trust in simulation knowledge. It is important to point out that when speaking about trust in computer-generated data and measurements I am referring not only to normative questions regarding philosophical justification but also to issues surrounding the use of CS outputs as experimental data. In other words, I want to look at how these outputs are used and what is presupposed in their use, as well as the degree of epistemic warrant that can be reasonably said to accompany that use. I conclude with some general remarks about the status of simulation knowledge and why, despite its various pitfalls, it remains an important part of our understanding of complex and otherwise inaccessible systems.

SIMULATIONS GONE WRONG: IDENTIFYING THE PROBLEMS

One of the most well-known simulation disasters was the *Columbia* shuttle accident. Damage from a broken piece of foam was judged, upon computations, as nonserious when it was, in fact, highly dangerous. This case is an example of a theoretical modelling problem: the model didn't properly consider the size of the debris. As a result, the wrong modelling parameters were fed into the simulation, which then produced an incorrect output. The foam-wing collision conditions were outside the range of validation for the computational model, CRATER, which was intended to model the impact of small objects, such as meteorites, on the shuttle tiles. The foam was more than 400 times the size of the impacting objects used in the CRATER validation tests.

A different type of problem arose with the Sleipner accident, where a gravity base structure of an offshore platform sank in the North Sea during a ballast test. Here the problem was numerical and directly related to the simulation itself—finite element analysis gave a 47 percent underestimation of shear forces in the critical part of the base structure. A third class of failures is exemplified by the Ariane 5 rocket that exploded 40 seconds after takeoff. In this case the problem was implementation of round-off errors, which is the difference between an approximation of a number used in computation and its exact (correct) value. In certain types of computation, round-off error can be magnified because any initial errors are carried through one or more intermediate steps. Essentially, the inertial reference system attempted to convert a 64-bit floating-point number to a 16-bit number but instead triggered an overflow error, which was interpreted by the guidance system as flight data, causing the rocket to veer off course and be destroyed. Although this type of problem is certainly simulation related, it is an example of a more general computer science problem, which results from dealing with floating-point numbers where exact values cannot be stored.[3] Finally there is the simple

3. Floating point values can be stored to many decimal places, and results calculated to many decimal places of precision, but round-off error will always be present. To ensure that results of floating-point routines are meaningful, the round-off error of such routines must always be quantified. In computing, floating point describes a method of representing real numbers in a way that can support a wide range of values. Numbers are, in general, represented approximately to a fixed number of significant digits and scaled using an exponent. The base for the scaling is normally 2, 10, or 16. The advantage of floating-point representation over fixed-point and integer representation is that it can support a much wider range of values. The floating-point format needs slightly more storage (to encode the position of the radix point), so when stored in the same space, floating-point numbers achieve their greater range at the expense of precision.

problem of human error. The Mars Climate Orbiter, which was lost in the Mars atmosphere, was the result of an unintended mixture of Imperial and metric units. Although this caused the inaccuracy in the simulations it was an error that was not simulation based.

From this brief list of examples we can see that while the issue of round-off error is important it is nevertheless one that is, with careful attention, controllable. The important sources of error where simulation is concerned are at the interface between the first and second types of problems—modelling error and numerical treatment error. The interface between these two is often where issues related to V&V arise. In order to clarify that relation we first need to define a "simulation structure," which will isolate each part of the simulation and how the various processes characteristic of each part are related. In chapter 6 I referred to this as a "simulation system," but here I want to emphasise the structure of this system in order to highlight the way that V&V concerns related to one part can affect other parts as well.

The foundation of a typical simulation problem is a conceptual or mathematical model of a target system that contains input data, such as coefficients of PDEs, boundary conditions, and so on, all of which must be well defined. In chapter 6 I also identified this as a theoretical model. The point is to distinguish between the model of the target system that has been constructed on the basis of theoretical principles and mathematical equations from the more formal model that results from applying discretisation techniques. The construction of the computational or simulation model essentially involves transforming a calculus problem into an arithmetical one by changing continuous differential equations into discrete difference equations. There are a variety of methods or techniques that can be employed to achieve this, such as finite element methods, finite difference methods, particle methods, and so on. The use of a particular method is often linked to the type of system or problem being investigated. For example, finite element is the method of choice for all types of analysis in structural mechanics (i.e., solving for deformation and stresses in solid bodies or dynamics of structures) while computational fluid dynamics tends to use finite difference methods or the particle methods associated with molecular dynamics. Once the computational model is constructed, it is mapped into software instructions. The simulation is run, and the programmed software is then mapped into a set of numerical solutions, with the raw numerical data transformed into a numerical solution representation. Both of the latter steps can give rise to errors: the first involves numerical solution errors, which are the result of epistemic uncertainties regarding the status of the solutions themselves, as well as further uncertainties that arise in the transition from raw data to the solution representation.

The aforementioned uncertainties typically result from uncertainties in input data that are transmitted through the process of constructing and running the simulation. They can be due either to theoretical modelling errors, errors that occur in the process of discretisation, or they can be the result of genuine physical uncertainties due to random processes that are uncontrollable. In the case of errors, one needs to distinguish between those that result from simple mistakes, such as programming errors (e.g. mistakes in source code) or incorrect use of input files, and the types of error that can be estimated, such as insufficient spatial discretisation.[4] Both types of error can result in uncertainties in different stages of the simulation construction, which can affect not only the accuracy of the description of the physical system being modelled but also the estimation of model parameters and the sequence of possible events in a discrete event representation. In other words, the uncertainties associated

4. I will distinguish below between this kind of error and the more technical use of the term, which refers to the deviation from the true value of a quantity.

with different kinds of error can be either physical or numerical. These distinctions can be further refined into two basic categories:

1. *Aleatory uncertainty*: physical uncertainty (variability or randomness) associated with the environment that typically can't be decreased or avoided. Usually represented by a probability distribution and includes things like damping in structures, random vibrations, and so on. The factors involved in aleatory uncertainty are often known and hence can be accounted for. The mathematical treatment of it typically involves a probability distribution, with the uncertainty's propagation through the modelling and simulation process represented by a well-developed probabilistic methodology. This type of uncertainty is what we typically associate with randomness found in SM.

2. *Epistemic uncertainty*: uncertainty that is due to a lack of user knowledge and can occur at any point in the process. While it can, in principle, be reduced, epistemic uncertainty is typically the result of or a combination of ignorance about the system in question or lack of knowledge regarding parameter values and/or how to construct an appropriate model or simulation, as is the case with modelling turbulence. While these sources of uncertainty can in principle be diminished, if one is unaware of the uncertainty (cases where the system is largely inaccessible, with very limited data leaving one unable to even isolate sources of uncertainty) it will propagate through the system leading to strong bias in the predictions. This problem, which is related to model selection, is different from the uncertainty that arises due to stochastic parameters that give rise to parametric uncertainty. While the latter can be an epistemic issue (when the value of a parameter is

unknown) it is often a reflection of the indeterminacy of the physical system and as such is more accurately characterised as aleatory uncertainty.[5] The quantification and propagation of epistemic uncertainty is much more problematic than that of aleatory uncertainty and is not usually defined within a probabilistic framework.

In light of this very general picture of the different types of uncertainties and error that affect simulation, the goal of V&V methodology is to manage uncertainties, especially those in input data, and evaluate their impact on the justification and use of simulation results. As I have noted, in cases where actual experimental data are sometimes scarce, V&V becomes especially important and, at the same time, correspondingly difficult. Epistemically, the important issue related to V&V is the degree of robustness in the methodology itself and the corresponding epistemic value of the conclusions it is able to underwrite. In that sense, the notion of accuracy is an important feature in V&V; but accuracy also presupposes that one can specify a measure of correctness that gives it meaning. But how do we determine the limits of accuracy when experimental data available for comparison are scarce? This is inherently problematic, for reasons I will discuss later. However, by distancing V&V from the methodology of hypothesis testing, we can come to appreciate its specific justificatory role in evaluating simulation data.

5. An important question regarding epistemic uncertainty is how to deal with uncertainty that arises as a result of decisions to idealise or ignore features of a system when constructing a conceptual or mathematical model. Since this is a constant feature of scientific practice, this type of uncertainty will always be present, regardless of whether the quantities in question are approximated or not. A similar situation arises when one discretises the mathematical model, since a loss of information will also accompany such a process. I will have more to say about discretisation error below in the discussion of V&V.

SHOULD WE TRUST SIMULATION?

Verification is the process designed to ensure that the theoretical or conceptual model is solved correctly by the discretised computational model. This is essentially a mathematical problem and in a sense concerns the relation between two different types of models. Validation, in contrast, is a physics problem and relates to the comparison between the computational simulation results and experimental data. Although the latter is supposedly a straightforward empirical issue, the technical literature on V&V sometimes describes validation as determining the degree to which the computational solutions are *adequate* for the problem of interest. Oberkampf, Trucano, and Hirsch (2004), who have initiated a good deal of the discussion of V&V in the literature, claim that this latter interpretation of validation is problematic, since adequacy for purpose is often ill defined. Different adequacy conditions may apply at different levels of modelling within a complex system, so there may be no uniform way to determine that a particular model that contains many submodels is valid for a particular problem.

A further difficulty, one they don't specifically mention, relates to the users and concerns the possibility that different individuals or groups will assess adequacy differently, some using more stringent criteria than others. I will return to the issue of adequacy, but for now let me focus on the more general problem of establishing the validity of a computational model in the absence of appropriate experimental data. One of the primary reasons for using simulation is the scarcity or lack of experimental data; hence if validation requires a comparative assessment, questions arise as to its overall legitimacy. In order to assess these issues, it is necessary to first examine the methodological differences between V&V to illustrate how each contributes to the epistemic warrant of simulation results.

Verification: a realisable goal? All validation activities are based on the assumption that the computational model provides a (reasonably) accurate solution to the theoretical model. Because mathematical errors can give the impression of correctness by furnishing the right answer for the wrong reason, it is absolutely crucial that a sufficient level of verification is achieved prior to any validation activity. There are several different steps in the verification procedure that focus on both the computer code itself and the solutions it generates. In the former case, the concern is to show that the code is able to compute an accurate solution. This requires finding and removing mistakes in the source code by determining that the numerical algorithms have been correctly implemented within the code, for example, determining that a spatial discretisation method will produce the expected convergence. The other aspect of code verification involves identifying errors in software. The problem inherent in code verification is that the process is largely holistic—very often the correctness of the algorithm cannot be determined independently of code executions that involve software implementation. Because algorithm verification is connected to individual executions of the code, it is usually achieved by comparing computational solutions with exact solutions to the mathematical/theoretical models or highly accurate solutions that function as 'benchmarks.' The notion of an exact solution refers to the solution to a mathematical model that is in closed form, that is, in terms of elementary functions or readily computed special functions of the independent variables.[6]

---

6. Analytical solutions are closed-form solutions to special cases of the PDEs that are represented in the conceptual/theoretical model and are often represented by infinite series, complex integrals, and asymptotic expansions and thus require numerical methods for their computation. The important point here is that the accuracy of these solutions can be quantified much more rigorously than can the accuracy of numerical solutions of the conceptual model.

The problem, however, is that analytic solutions exist only for very simplified physics or geometries, and scientific computing often involves complex systems of coupled PDEs that have relatively few exact solutions. As a result, the "method of manufactured solutions" is often used as a more general approach, and as the label suggests, this method involves manufacturing an exact solution to a modified equation. Because verification deals only with mathematical considerations, the manufactured solution needn't be related to a physically realistic problem. The general method is to choose a solution a priori and then operate the governing PDEs onto the chosen solution. The chosen solution is then the exact solution to the modified governing equations made up of the original equations plus additional analytic source terms. Essentially, it is a solution to a backward problem: given an original set of equations and a chosen solution, find a modified set of equations that the chosen solution will satisfy.[7] Although the solutions need not be physically realistic, they should obey physical constraints that are built into the code.

There are other benefits and drawbacks to manufactured solutions that are not especially relevant for this discussion, but it is important to note that there are many instances where physically realistic exact solutions are required; for instance, evaluating the reliability of discretisation error estimators. In these cases, there are methods for generating "realistic" manufactured solutions, such as using simplified theoretical models of the physical phenomena as the basis for a manufactured solution.[8] These kinds of problems indicate just how multifaceted verification can be.

---

7. For details of the method, along with a discussion of benefits and drawbacks, see Oberkampf and Roy (2010, 225–34).
8. There are also a variety of methods for approximating exact solutions, as in cases where a suitable transformation can reduce a system of PDEs to a system of ordinary differential equations.

Typically, when we think of epistemological problems associated with CS the focus is on the transition between the original model of the physical system and the discretised version, and whether the latter representation is sufficiently close to the theoretical model to guarantee the kind of physical results we desire. As one can see here, the problem is magnified because the processes involved in code verification—specifically, the equations used as a baseline for evaluating the accuracy of the numerical algorithm are themselves approximations in the sense that they are often solutions to different equations than those being simulated. What these difficulties highlight is that the goal of verification is not really to demonstrate accuracy but to provide *evidence* that the theoretical model is correctly solved by the discrete mathematics computer code. In that sense the process is an evolving one, but also one that may be open to interpretation. In other words, the degree to which the evidence supports the claim that the model is correctly solved may be interpreted differently by different practitioners.[9]

Because code verification is not sufficient, solution verification is also required in order to provide a quantitative estimation of the numerical accuracy of the computed solution.[10] Although code verification cannot achieve the status of a proof it is nevertheless presupposed that the numerical procedure is stable, consistent, and robust before solution verification is carried out. While there are some similarities in the methods used for code and solution verification, the important difference between the two is that the latter is an attempt

---

9. Further problems can arise when a rigorously verified code (i.e. to second-order accuracy) is applied in a new situation. In these cases there is no estimation of the accuracy, so the use of a verified code is not enough to guarantee an accurate result.

10. Verification of input data is also an important aspect of solution verification and includes such things as checks for consistency between model choices and verification of any software used to generate input data. Although these verification procedures are important, the issues they raise are less philosophically interesting than those associated with numerical error estimation

to approximate the numerical error for particular applications of a code when the correct solutions aren't known; hence the numerical errors must also be *estimated*, not simply evaluated. This determination is also highly subjective in that it is based on individual judgement.

The main sources of error here are spatial and temporal discretisation in the numerical solution of PDEs, as well as round-off errors that arise due to the use of finite arithmetic on a digital computer. Round-off errors are usually defined as the truncation of a real number to fit it into computer memory.[11] In certain types of computation, round-off error can be magnified since any initial errors can be carried through one or more intermediate steps. But, in cases where numerical errors can be estimated with a high degree of confidence, they can be removed from the numerical solutions in a fashion similar to the way well-known bias errors are removed from experimental measurements.[12]

Discretisation error is the most difficult to estimate and involves the difference between the exact solution to the discrete equation and the exact solution to the theoretical model equation(s), incorporating things like mesh quality and resolution, time step, and so on. The problem, as I have noted, is that in many cases exact solutions are simply unknown. The general worry about discretisation errors is that they are transported in the same manner as the underlying solution properties; and while there are several methods for estimating them, the estimators often rely on information from past numerical solutions where there may be no clear indication of whether the error is sufficiently small.[13] Consequently, since the true value of the error

---

11. This should not be confused with truncation error, which is a measure of the difference between a PDE and its discrete approximation.
12. Often the degree of error can be determined by running the simulation with different degrees of precision and comparing the solutions.
13. The details of these methods are not crucial for our discussion, but it is important to briefly mention that the reliability of the estimations requires that the underlying numerical solution(s) be in the asymptotic range, something that is not easily achieved. Confirmation

is often unknown, discretisation error is more commonly associated with epistemic uncertainty than with the more straightforward types of numerical errors.

From this brief discussion it becomes clear that because verification requires the identification as well as the demonstration and quantification of errors, together with establishing the robustness, stability, and consistency of the numerical scheme, it goes well beyond the methods provided by analytic or formal error analysis that one finds in the context of traditional experiment. A very different and more complex methodology is required. Although classified as a mathematical problem, the subjectivity involved in the estimation and evaluation of errors makes verification less than exact.

While the analysis of experimental data is not without its own problems, these differences between simulation and experiment with respect to the estimation and evaluation of error also point to the vulnerability of simulation to error propagation. I have distinguished between epistemic and aleatory uncertainty and the way these are related to different types of errors. I am now in a position to refine that analysis in a way that links error and uncertainty in the context of verification. Recall that at the beginning of the discussion I mentioned the well-known characterisation for distinguishing verification from validation—the former is a mathematical problem and the latter a physical problem. In addition, error and uncertainty can be assimilated to the distinction between mathematics and physics. Errors are associated with the translation of a mathematical problem or formulation into a numerical algorithm and a computational code. Here the known errors are round-offs, limited convergence of iterative algorithms, and so on, while the unknown ones might be due to, among other things, implementation mistakes. Uncertainties on the

that it is in that range requires at least three discrete solutions but this is also somewhat difficult to guarantee. For a full discussion see Oberkampf and Roy (2010, 317).

other hand are typically associated with the specification of physical input parameters required for defining the problem.

As I will show, uncertainty quantification is crucial in the validation stage of a simulation, but it is also important for verification. Typically, uncertainty is addressed in three stages of the simulation process: (1) the construction of the theoretical (conceptual) model and its mathematisation; (2) the discretisation and formulation of the simulation model; and (3) the computation of the results and the comparison with experimental data. Verification involves the first two but has important implications for the third, which concerns the validation stage. If we have uncertainties in either the assumptions or mathematical form of either the theoretical or simulation models, initial or boundary conditions for the PDEs, or the parameters occurring in the mathematical model, then the use or implementation of the computational model will result in the uncertainties being propagated or mathematically mapped to uncertainties in the simulation results. This will result in a compounded growth in uncertainties, as indicated by Trucano (2004): "an uncertain input parameter will lead not only to an uncertain solution but to an uncertain solution error as well."

The mathematical framework for propagating uncertainties is dependent on the representation of the data; for example, if they are represented using a probability distribution, then the propagation is probabilistic (either frequentist or Bayesian estimation), while a membership function requires fuzzy logic or set theory. I will have more to say about these methods in my discussion of validation, but the important point to glean from the present discussion is that none of these approaches seems entirely adequate if what we have in mind is a reasonably stringent sense of verification that can provide a foundation for validation practices. Not only does the legitimacy of the validation depend on a high degree of accuracy in the verification stage but the entire verification process depends on a standard of accuracy that assumes the correctness of the theoretical/mathematical model of the system. In that sense, the verification question—whether the computation model is solved correctly—is more than simply an internal mathematical problem.[14] Because at least some of the uncertainty associated with verification stems from input parameters or model form uncertainty, there is also a physical dimension that needs to be addressed. Due to the different forms of error and uncertainties embedded in the verification process and because the latter often involves an *estimation* of the degree of verification, rather than some definitive answer, there are clear and significant implications for the physics of validation. Hence the two are very closely linked.

This linkage, however, doesn't imply that the activities involved in V&V are carried out in an ad hoc way or that the process must involve tuning and parameter adjustment to obtain agreement. Nor does the interrelation of verification and validation imply that the process is nonsequential. If verification is not carried out prior to validation, the calculations involved in the latter may be subject to cancelling effects—algorithm deficiencies and inaccuracies in the numerical solution could cancel each other out in the validation calculation, giving the impression of an accurate solution where none exists. Of course it is true that coding and solution errors can be discovered during the process of validation, but this just means that one needs to go back and fix the errors before proceeding further; otherwise there is no way of knowing whether validation results are distorted due to coding errors or large solution errors.

Worries about V&V. So far I have introduced some of the basic features of V&V and their accompanying methodological problems. None of these need suggest systematic worries about the overall

---

14. All of the literature on simulation characterises the difference between verification and validation as that between a mathematics problem and a physics problem.

structure of V&V. Winsberg (2010), however, takes a more pessimistic view. He claims that V&V cannot be neatly separated in the way that simulationists suggest and that "rarely is one in the position of establishing that the results of a simulation model bear some mathematical relationship to an antecedently chosen and theoretically defensible model" (20). Moreover, he maintains that simulationists are also rarely in a position to give "good grounds, independent of the results of their solving methods, for the models they end up using" (20). These are rather bold statements, especially in light of my discussion here. Winsberg's remarks are grounded in the fact that he sees the epistemology of simulation as much closer to that of experiment than what the V&V structure can actually accommodate. He is also critical of claims that the reliability of computational techniques is underwritten by sound mathematical theory and analysis, emphasising instead the importance of relying on benchmarking against empirical data from experimental sources.

Whether well-established discretisation techniques qualify as "sound mathematical theory" is not a topic I intend to address here, especially since there are many issues regarding the use of different types of discretisation techniques that are important for assessing the merits of specific kinds of simulations. But a quick glance at the simulation literature reveals that practitioners themselves believe that a variety of different strategies are needed for V&V; one can't rely solely on mathematical argument.[15] Nor, contrary to what Winsberg suggests (2010, 20), does the presentation of V&V methodology indicate that the distinction between the mathematical aspects of verification and the more theoretical/empirical aspects of validation (the question of whether the right model has been chosen) are completely independent. From the foregoing discussion, and in what

15. Oberkampf and Roy (2010) is probably the most comprehensive review of the status of V&V, its various difficulties and attempts to remedy them.

follows, it is clear that V&V is highly complex, involving several different levels and techniques, with the goal of providing *evidence* for legitimating simulation results, not establishing conclusive proof.

Although mathematics alone isn't sufficient for 'verifying' a simulation result, it seems like an exaggeration to claim, as Winsberg does (2010, 21), that the mathematical techniques used to turn the original model equations into a final algorithm are based on very weak arguments. The reasons he cites are various failures encountered by numerical methods, failures that result from assuming that certain types of linearity conditions hold when, in fact, they are of no relevance to the conditions that interest the simulationist. But Winsberg's argument here is equally weak. The fact that errors have been made does not, in itself, mean that numerical methods are inherently problematic. As I have shown, there are a variety of ways that a simulation can fail to produce the desired outcome, but the point to keep in mind is that the complexity of V&V is designed specifically to combat various types of errors. Nothing is foolproof, and mistakes do not necessarily imply ad hoc strategies. Although verification is far from unproblematic, recognising the nature of its shortcomings will yield more efficient ways of rectifying the problems.

Winsberg claims that benchmarking and calibration are some of the ways that simulation models are sanctioned. This involves comparisons with experimental results as well as with other simulations. Undoubtedly these kinds of comparisons are often difficult, due to the differences not only in the form of the data but in the sources from which they are gathered. Winsberg goes on to remark that in the absence of the skilled judgement of observers who can compare images against images, there is "no metric of similarity between the different data sets that need to be compared" (2010, 22). Because visualisation is the most effective means of identifying characteristics within complex data sets, it is also the most effective means of judging the degree of benchmarking success of simulation against real data.

In the end the sanctioning of simulations, according to Winsberg, does not divide cleanly into verification and validation; instead, they are sanctioned all at once, with the simultaneous confluence of features such as fidelity to theory, physical intuition, mathematical rigour, and known empirical results. Winsberg claims he is not arguing that verification and validation are not separable activities in practice but simply warning philosophers not to overinterpret what is a "pragmatic distinction" among practitioners. Winsberg's worry is that philosophers will, as a result of the distinction, conclude that the principle work of evaluating a simulation is mathematical, as opposed to empirical, and that any conceptual clarity afforded by keeping verification and validation distinct is ultimately misleading.

While verification and validation are by no means problem free, Winsberg's characterisation ignores crucial aspects of the methodology and in doing so presents a distorted view of its goals and methods. His discussion suggests that V&V is rarely successful in any rigorous sense because the sanctioning of simulation is a rather piecemeal affair. However, as I have shown, there are well-developed techniques in place that not only address specific types of difficulties but reveal just how important the sequential nature of V&V is. Indeed the different aspects of V&V indicate the importance of both the mathematical and empirical features of the methodology—why they need to be separated but also how they work together. The idea that validation could proceed in any meaningful way in tandem with verification would render validation a completely meaningless undertaking. Moreover, as I will show, it is simply not true that the best way of judging the success of simulation against empirical data is visualisation; it is exactly because this is a highly subjective and ineffective approach that validation experiments and the notion of a validation metric have been established.[16]

---

16. There is a vast literature on V&V and its various aspects, many of which are by Oberkampf and various colleagues, as well as Roache (1997). For a full list see Oberkampf and Roy (2010).

In order to clarify the advantages of both the conceptual and practical elements of the sequential character of V&V, along with the techniques employed at each stage, let me now turn to a discussion of validation. Despite what might be construed as interactive aspects of the process, the separation of verification and validation is significantly more than a pragmatic matter.

VALIDATION: FROM MATHEMATICS TO PHYSICS

As I have shown, validation involves determining the degree to which the model is an accurate representation of the target system, or put slightly differently, the degree to which computational simulation results agree with experimental data. Here the word 'model' refers to the computational model that is the discretised version of the theoretical/mathematical model of the system. In the end what we want to know is whether the latter model agrees with experimental data, but this can only be determined via the solutions to the computational model. In contrast to verification, which concerns whether the equations have been solved correctly, validation centres on the physical question of whether the correct equations have been solved. The answer to this question involves two distinct issues: (1) a comparison between experimental data and computational results that focuses on accuracy, and (2) the adequacy of the comparisons for a specific purpose. Because validation is primarily a statistical issue, its proper domain is (1) rather than (2). What this means is that there ought to be an essentially objective aspect to (1), in that standards of agreement should be specified in a formal way. In the case of (2), different groups can reasonably adopt different standards for model validation depending on its intended purpose. For example, if the model provides the foundation for the design of a nuclear waste facility, then the standards of adequacy will need to be extremely strict.

How, then, should the type of objectivity required for (1) be defined or achieved? In addition to identifying and quantifying the uncertainty in the theoretical and computational models, as well as quantifying the numerical error in the computational solution, the experimental uncertainty needs to be quantified before the two can be compared. Typically the comparisons between computational results and experimental data are represented using graphs that plot a computational and experimental quantity over a range of some parameter. If the results generally agree with the experimental data over a range of measurements, the computational model is said to be validated. The problem with graphical comparisons is that there is no quantification of numerical solution error or uncertainties in experimental data that might arise from variability in experimental conditions, unknown boundary conditions, or other conditions simply not reported by the experimenter. Because experimental uncertainties are often considered free parameters in the computational analysis, they are frequently adjusted to obtain better agreement with experimental data. This of course can lead to disastrous consequences; but, as I will show, the methodology of V&V has been designed to accommodate these problems, at least in principle.

There is, however, a further and more important issue regarding the *kind* of experimental data needed for validation. Because the goal is to test the accuracy of a particular model, the initial conditions, boundary conditions, and other model input parameters need to be accurately specified, with all test conditions and other measurements fully accounted for. In the case of traditional experimentation the goals are often somewhat different—one is usually interested in improving understanding of a particular phenomenon or system, estimating values of model parameters or improving the model itself. As a result, the careful documentation or control of experimental parameters necessary for validation may not be performed or even necessary in traditional experimental settings. These shortcomings are often accompanied by inadequate measurement of system output quantities, as well as limited uncertainty estimates and documentation of random and bias errors. In addition to rectifying these problems and strictly adhering to specified standards, validation tests should produce a variety of data, so different aspects of the model can be assessed. Consequently, comparison with existing experimental data is insufficient to validate a simulation because many of the values for the requisite parameters are simply unavailable. In order to meet the specified requirements, specific validation experiments need to be performed.

The results of validation experiments are then compared with computational model solutions using a validation metric that is a quantitative measure of agreement between the computational results and experimentally measured data for a specific quantity. It is typically defined in terms of a difference operator that can yield a deterministic result that is a precise or an imprecise probability distribution. Oberkampf and his collaborators (Oberkampf and Trucano, 2002; Oberkampf and Barone, 2006; Oberkampf, Trucano and Hirsch, 2004; Oberkampf and Roy, 2010) were the first to draw attention to the need for validation experiments and validation metrics in the context of computational fluid dynamics, but it quickly became apparent, with the increasing use of CS, that this methodology was crucial for assessing the merits of simulated data. In order to fully understand how V&V is used to establish the credibility of simulation knowledge and to highlight the difference between this methodology and hypothesis testing used in traditional experimentation, three separate questions need to be addressed: (1) What is the methodology of validation experiments and how are they different from traditional experiments? (2) How is the metric defined? (3) How is this methodology carried out and how are comparisons made when data are scarce or unavailable? Issues related to (3) are interspersed in the discussion of (1) and (2) and also in chapter 8. Obviously the reliability of the metric will depend on the extent to which reliable data can be gathered from validation experiments. Because the latter are often carried out only in a limited way, the scarcity of data needs to be taken account of in the development and evaluation of validation experiments.

What is a validation experiment? Validation experiments are a relatively new type of experiment and, as mentioned earlier, are conducted in order to quantitatively determine the ability of the model and its representation in the computer code to simulate a particular physical process. Validation experiments are designed specifically so that data are sufficiently related to code calculations in a specific domain. Unlike traditional experiments, where the emphasis is on measurement of processes in a controlled environment, in validation experiments the emphasis is on the characterisation of the experiment itself, that is, measuring the various characteristics of the experiment that are needed for the simulation. Controlling the environment is less important than being able to accurately specify the surroundings in a precise way so that all the relevant features of the simulation model are contained in the experiment. As with traditional experiments, it is essential to determine the accuracy and precision of the data, and uncertainties in measured quantities should be estimated to ensure the legitimacy of comparisons with the computational model predictions.

Because the system being modelled or simulated is often large-scale and extremely complex, it is unfeasible and impractical to conduct experiments on the entire system. Moreover, the large number of components and/or nonlinear behaviour make it difficult to isolate problems. The degree of complexity can give rise to error cancellation among different levels of models, giving an erroneous appearance of validation. In other words, the system can be modelled at various levels of complexity, ranging from very simple models that don't include any interactions to more complicated modelling that encompasses physics and engineering models, with the more complicated type giving rise to a greater probability of errors. To counter these problems, a validation hierarchy is typically established that structures the ordering of validation experiments and how comparisons between various levels are carried out. This involves separating the system into tiers, with the lowest level exhibiting the least amount of complexity. Spatial dimensionality and the coupling of physical processes are the most common types of complexity that need to be separated. Nonlinear coupling is reduced or eliminated by conducting experiments with uncoupled and separate physical effects, and indeed the philosophy behind the hierarchical tiers is based on the assumption that increased accuracy of the "system" model can be determined by examining the parts. The purpose is not only to separate nonlinear couplings but to facilitate the evaluation of code from different types of inputs or disciplines (e.g., physics, different areas of engineering, computer science, etc.).[17]

The top level or "complete system" tier represents the entire system, with the hierarchy then divided into unit problems (the lowest level representing the simplest aspects of the system), benchmark cases, and subsystem cases. As we ascend up the hierarchy, we become less and less able to measure specific values of parameters because the system becomes increasingly complicated. When we reach the "complete system" level, complexity prevents carrying out full validation experiments. In some cases there may also be safety or economic restrictions that limit the performance measures, as in the case of testing nuclear devices. Part of the importance of validation experiments is the recognition that the quantity and accuracy of information varies radically over the different tiers. The quality and strength of inferences is inversely proportional to the complexity

---

17. For a complete discussion of validation experiments and the notion of a validation hierarchy see Oberkampf and Roy (2010).

of the system as a whole. Because the uncertainties increase as one moves up the hierarchy, there is no expectation that validation experiments performed at each level will result in a validated model of the complete system.

In most discussions of the validation hierarchy (see Oberkampf, Trucano, and Hirsch (2004, 362) it is perceived from a distinctly engineering perspective rather than a scientific or model-building one. As I have noted, the goal is to identify a range of experiments that involves the separation of coupled physics and levels of complexity related to an engineering system. This allows computer codes from different disciplines to be evaluated. Based on this characterisation, Oberkampf, Trucano, and Hirsch claim that the hierarchy is application driven, not code-capability driven. While it is certainly the case that engineering features such as isolating specific hardware aspects are crucial for designing validation experiments at the subsystem tier, distinguishing between epistemic and application aspects of the validation hierarchy seems misplaced, giving an incorrect impression of the motivation for these experiments. This is especially true if the goal of validation experiments in general, and the hierarchy in particular, is to determine the accuracy of the computational model as a representation of the system of interest. As I mentioned, the accuracy question must be answered before any application issues are addressed. In other words, the point of the validation hierarchy is to ensure, as far as possible, that the errors and uncertainties in the different computational models employed to represent the system are accounted for and quantified. This is especially important as one moves from the subsystem tier to the benchmark tier, since this marks the transition from the focus on hardware and components to physics-based problems. The physics-based tiers at the top of the hierarchy present the most difficult challenge for validation experiments, due in part to the difficulties in isolating different features of the system. To focus simply on application driven validation can result in an incorrect model being used simply because it gives the desired results for a specific problem.

Because validation experiments are designed to determine how well the model, embedded in the computer code, simulates a particular process, the code itself plays an important role in defining the expected results of the experiment and in the designing the experiment via its predictive function. At first glance this may give the appearance of circularity, raising the fear that validation experiments are not truly independent in the way that traditional experimental activity is, or that validation and verification are simultaneous activities. But this would be to mistake the important differences between the two types of experimental methodologies, differences that are crucial for establishing the legitimacy of validation experiments.

Oberkampf, Trucano, and Hirsch (2004) capture the distinction between traditional and validations experiments by focusing on two questions. In traditional experimental practice the typical question takes the following form: how will a respond given this specific experimental design and gauge location? In the case of validation experiments, the question involves specifying a particular outcome, such as locating gauge a at x, that is based on computational predictions and then asking whether that agrees with experimental data. We can see, then, that the code is already included as part of the validation experiment, but this in itself needn't be problematic; in fact, without it there is no way to define, design, or analyse the validation experiment. The code is used in a predictive sense in that it enables one to define the specific principles and goals of the experiment. In other words, specification of the initial and boundary conditions, material properties as well as other parameters are defined through code calculations. The success of the validation experiment will depend on the degree to which it matches the specifications defined by the code. The more complex the system, the less chance that the conditions required for a successful experiment will be met (365).

The overall goal of validation is to assess the accuracy of the computational model in a *blind* test with experimental data generated from validation experiments. This should be distinguished from calibration, where the goal is to adjust the model parameters to bring them in line with experimental data. To that extent, the data against which the model is compared must not have been used for calibration.[18]

From this brief description, it is clear that the goal of validation experiments is to establish a level of accuracy for the computational model; the question is how this accuracy gets defined. Recall that I defined accuracy as simply the comparison of the computational model solutions with experimental data. Whether the degree of accuracy is sufficient for a particular use of the model is another question, one that involves the notion of adequacy which is based on the judgement of the users. To that extent, the latter is a practical matter determined by specific preferences or assumptions, whereas the accuracy question requires an objective assessment. The way these comparisons are made is crucial in the overall evaluation of simulation data. Just as experimental methodology and principles related to design help to ensure the legitimacy of experimental results, so, too, with simulation. Ensuring that certain practices and standards are in place is a crucial part of the overall analysis of simulation as a source of scientific knowledge.

Validation metrics. During the past ten years or so, the simulation community has placed increasing emphasis on model accuracy assessment which involves constructing mathematical operators, known as validation metrics, that compute the difference between experimentally measured results and simulation

18. In addition, it is important that validation experiments do not produce data that depend, in any fundamental sense, on code *calculations* for critical data reduction tasks. Experimental data that require code calculations lack the requisite independence necessary for comparison. See Oberkampf et al. (2004, 366) for a discussion of these issues.

results.[19] The form of the validation metric should correspond with the quantity being assessed. For example, if both the computational and experimental quantities are probability measures, such as a probability density function or a cumulative distribution function, then the metric should also be a probability measure and should quantify both errors and uncertainties in the comparison between computational results and experimental data. This includes numerical error in the computational simulation, uncertainties and errors in the modelling process, estimates of random error in experimental data, computational uncertainties due to random uncertainty in experimental parameters, as well as uncertainty due to lack of experimental measurement of the necessary computational quantities.[20] Finally, it should incorporate the level of confidence in the experimental mean, not just variance or scatter in the data. This quantitative estimation of confidence is important for inferences that take us from validation domain to the application domain (where the simulation model will be used) and is especially important when there is a very small or no area of intersection between the two, as in the case of CRATER where the application domain far exceeded the validation range. If experimental uncertainties and numerical errors are not properly estimated and quantified, there is no way to distinguish numerical errors from modelling uncertainties in the computational-experimental comparisons. The point of the validation metric is that in the comparison between a collection

19. See Oberkampf and Barone (2006).
20. Experimental uncertainty estimation is typically divided into two parts: characterisation uncertainty, which is due to a limited number of measurements of the quantity of interest, and epistemic uncertainty that exists in the measurement itself. The former is usually referred to as sampling error; the latter may have many different sources. For more see Oberkampf and Roy (2010, 488).

of computational model predictions and experimental data, the metric will produce the same assessment each time.

Validation metrics are typically a function of all the input parameters to the computational model, even though the relevant quantity of interest will be dependent only on a few dominant ones. Because the simulation and experimental results are usually functions— probability distributions or p-boxes—rather than single numbers, the typical validation metric will be a statistical operator.[21] As I noted, validation experiments conducted at higher tiers in the hierarchy will have poorly characterised experimental data for inputs to the computational simulation. In these cases, validation requires a probabilistic treatment of uncertain parameters in the physics submodels, initial conditions or boundary conditions for the PDEs. This typically relies on probabilistic sampling techniques like Monte Carlo methods to provide values for the various parameters.

An additional problem is that physics models embedded in the computer codes are based on a number of approximations and are sometimes applied to regimes that are inaccessible experimentally. Consequently, one has to rely on a simulation of the underlying microphysics for the validation of the computational models. A simple example is the direct numerical simulation of material strength properties via a molecular dynamics description of the fundamental processes (i.e. interatomic potentials). The fact that the 'experimental' data themselves contain simulation data does not present a problem in principle, or indeed in practice. When asking whether the code or computational model passed a validation experiment, there is no assumption that the experimental measurements are more accurate than computational results. What is required is simply a basis for

---

21. A p-box is a special type of cumulative distribution function that represents the set of all such possible functions that fall within certain prescribed bounds. It can represent both epistemic and aleatory uncertainty with the simulation, the experimental result, or both. See Oberkampf (2010, 526–35).

comparison. Since all experimental data have random (statistical) and bias (systematic) errors, the notion of "correctness" is replaced with a "statistically meaningful comparison." It is this comparison that is represented in the validation metric.

There are three traditional approaches for quantitative comparisons of computational and experimental results: hypothesis or significance testing, Bayesian statistical inference, which often includes parameter estimation, and, finally, validation metrics, which can be based on a number of different methodologies. Before saying a bit more about these I should also note the importance of methods to represent, aggregate, and propagate uncertainty through computational models themselves.[22] Typically, this is done using probability theory, either frequentist or Bayesian approaches. Other approaches include fuzzy set theory and Dempster-Shafer evidence theory, but these are less well developed in the context of computational problems. Uncertainty propagation is typically concerned with questions of the sort: given an input (I) together with a probability distribution that measures its uncertainty, what is the probability distribution for the output (O)? The related question is, of course, how well the inferred distribution actually represents the uncertainty in (O). And, as philosophers of science are all too aware, uncertainty propagation by itself is unable to answer the latter question.

Sensitivity analysis is also an important aspect of uncertainty propagation, since it influences decisions about which uncertainties in the input data must be retained and which ones can be neglected. It usually involves multiple simulations from a code to determine the

---

22. It is important to point out that for any particular mathematical model of a system we should distinguish between parametric uncertainty and model-form uncertainty. The former can be entirely aleatoric, relating to stochastic parameters in the model. The latter is fundamentally epistemic and concerns actual changes in the model or the selection of one model in a class. Although they usually occur together, the concern here is parametric uncertainty only.

effect of the variation of an input parameter or modelling assumption on a specific output quantity. In other words, all other input quantities are held fixed, and the effect of the variation on the output quantity is computed. If the input consists of hundreds or thousands of parameters, then sampling strategies are very important. Monte Carlo–based methods are one way of approaching the problem, but in cases where the problems are complex and expensive, one needs more sophisticated sampling strategies. This raises the issue of the precise characterisation of the probability distributions associated with input parameters and whether probability theory can accurately capture the quantitative characterisation of uncertainty. Bayesian inference is a popular method for addressing these problems (i.e. the forward uncertainty problem).[23]

Earlier in the discussion of validation metrics I mentioned that the metric should include only an accuracy estimation of the computational model and not an assessment of the adequacy of the model for a specific purpose. The reason is because in many cases the latter involves subjective decisions by the user as to whether the degree of accuracy is good or bad given the appropriate levels of tolerance for in specific circumstances. The major difficulty, as I discuss below, is that decisions or strategies extraneous to a simple blind comparison are often embedded in the methodologies used for comparison.

Bayesian analysis is similar in many ways to parameter estimation, in that it is concerned with model updating or calibration. A probability distribution is constructed for each input quantity in the computational model that is chosen to be a random variable. One then

---

23. There is also the inverse uncertainty or backward problem, which attempts to reduce the output uncertainty by updating the statistical model using comparisons between computations and experiment. This might enable one to improve the original prior distributions that characterise the parameter uncertainty. The difficulties associated with these issues are problems specific to Bayesian statistical inference rather than computational problems per se. For a discussion see Trucano (1998).

conditionalises or updates, using Bayes' theorem, the previously chosen probabilities for the input quantities, based on comparison of the computational and experimental results. This also involves propagating input probability distributions through the computational model to obtain probability distributions for the specified quantities commensurate with those measured in experiment. As Oberkampf and Barone (2006, 10) point out, the updating of the input probability distributions using Bayes' theorem to get posterior distributions typically assumes that the computational model is correct, which of course is not necessarily the case.

A further and perhaps more important issue is that the point of validation metrics is not to tune the model to experimental results but to determine whether the existing computational model accurately represents the physics of the theoretical model. In doing this, validation metrics do not give priority to either experimental results or computational models; they are formulated to provide a blind comparison only. This issue is especially important for thinking about the relation between experiment and simulation. The fact that experimental results are not accorded special status as the basis for comparison indicates that experimental methods themselves are not considered more reliable than simulation. Because the goal here is validation of simulation outputs, it is tempting to see experiment as the 'benchmark' against which they are compared. However, that would be to unfairly judge the simulation as a priori more uncertain, which could result in adversely affecting the comparison. It is important to clarify here the status of experimental data. Validation experiments where all the parameters have been specified are obviously accorded a greater epistemic status, but as I noted above, this situation is extremely rare. In most cases validation experiments, especially at high levels of complexity, will have significant uncertainty associated with the various input parameters. And in cases where simulation data is compared with data from ordinary experiments, the situation is even more uncertain for the reasons I discussed above—reasons that necessitated the introduction of validation experiments in the first place.

One might think that hypothesis testing is the obvious choice, since it is a well-established statistical method for determining whether a model is consistent with an experimental result. With hypothesis testing, the focus is on obtaining a yes-no statement of the consistency between the computational model and experimental data for some specified level of significance. By contrast, the focus in constructing a validation metric is computing a metric that functions simply as a measure of agreement (or mismatch) between the computational and experimental results. Because the validation process involves providing evidence for the accuracy of a particular model rather than establishing a "true/false" conclusion, the methods of hypothesis testing are not altogether appropriate. In particular, information about the specific way in which numerical error and experimental uncertainties affect the measure of agreement or mismatch is not provided by the framework of hypothesis testing.[24] And, perhaps most important, probability measures in hypothesis testing represent both the accuracy estimate of the computational model and the level of confidence in the estimation of the accuracy. In other words, they are combined in the same measure. A true validation metric should not do this because, as I have noted, the confidence level that must be attained can be specified pragmatically, depending on the interests of the modelers; that is, depending on the degree of risk one is able to absorb for a specific application.[25]

24. An interesting discussion, but not one that I can go into here, would be the role of type 1 and type 2 errors in the validation process. See Oberkampf and Trucano (2002, 257) for a short account.

25. A mathematical metric should satisfy the following properties and be completely independent of decisions regarding adequacy for particular purposes: (1) nonnegativity: $d(x, y) \geq 0$; (2) symmetry: $d(x, y) = d(y, x)$; (3) triangle inequality: $d(x, y) + d(y, z) \geq d(x, z)$; (4) identity of indiscernibles: $d(x, y) = 0$ iff $x = y$. Ideally, it should allow us to compute, in a mathematically rigorous way, the difference between the computational and

One approach to the construction of validation metrics discussed by Oberkampf and Roy (2010) involves comparing the estimated mean of a computational result(s) with the estimated mean of the experimental measurement(s). A statistical confidence interval is then computed that reflects the confidence in the estimation of the model accuracy, given the uncertainty in the experimental data. The most accurate way of obtaining the mean in the case of the computational model is to propagate, using a sampling procedure, the uncertain inputs through the model to obtain a probability distribution for the computational result. The mean can then be computed, provided there is a sufficiently sampled distribution. This is then compared with the mean of a population of experimental measurements, for which only a finite set of measurements has been made. The initial focus is on the statistical nature of the sample mean, with an emphasis on the statistical procedure for estimating a confidence interval for the true mean of the population.[26] In hypothesis testing the confidence interval is computed for the difference between two hypotheses, but as Oberkampf and Roy (2010) point out, that embeds a stated level of agreement or disagreement in the difference operator. The details for constructing a validation metric, which can involve a variety of different methods, are somewhat complicated and not required for the main point, which is simply that comparisons between simulated and experimental data

experimental result for a specific quantity when those results exhibit both aleatory and epistemic uncertainties.

26. In some cases, the input quantities in the experiment may not be precisely known, so they are taken as random input variables for the computational model and are then propagated as uncertain quantities through the model to compute the value of the specified quantity. However, this value can also be characterised as a mean, when in fact it is only the mean or expected value of uncertain input parameters that is propagated through the computational model. This approach is best suited for linear models or nonlinear models where there is very little scatter associated with the random variables. The main difficulty is that one can get a mismatch between the model and the experimental data where the source of the disagreement is not the model itself but the inaccuracy of the computational mean that is based on the assumption of the mean of the inputs.

should be limited to assessments of accuracy without any accompany-ing measure of risk tolerance. [27]

SUMMING UP: PROBLEMS, PROSPECTS, AND WORRIES

Finally, regardless of how carefully one constructs the validation met-ric, fundamental problems arise regarding how to model uncertain inputs and formulate algorithms so that simulation output accurately reflects the propagation of uncertainty. As I discussed, validation experiments at higher tiers have poorly characterised or very little data input for computational simulations. This requires probabilistic treatment of uncertain parameters in the computational submod-els, initial conditions, or boundary conditions for PDEs, with their propagation through the computational model carried out via proba-bilistic sampling methods like Monte Carlo. But because quantita-tive specification of information flow *within* the hierarchy from the unit problem/benchmark tiers to the subsystem/system tiers may be highly uncertain, the result can be *second-order uncertainty* in the validation hierarchy.

What the discussion points to is that while V&V is concerned with quantitative accuracy assessments, the available epistemological resources are far from able to solve the problem of simulation cred-ibility. They contribute to the process by providing *evidence* that the simulation outputs are correct or accurate, but because of the com-plexity of the processes being simulated, there is often no computable

27. One of the ways to construct a validation metric is to compute the area between the prob-ability p-boxes resulting from the model data and the experimental measurements. The comparison in this case could be the shape between the two cumulative distribution func-tions, with the discrepancies capable of being measured. See Oberkampf and Roy (2010) for a full discussion of the development of the equations for a validation metric of this type.

reference value that can serve as a basis against which the simulation is compared. As a result, numerical error *estimation*, together with an *estimation* of the effects of all contributions to uncertainty in the system response, are the only options for evaluation; but these may be highly subjective in the way the data are interpreted. And there are always risks when a successful simulation model is applied to new situations.

In the case of verification, we sometimes have highly accurate solutions to mathematical models that are nevertheless limited in their application. In the context of validation, the benchmarks are particular parameters measured in carefully constructed validation experiments, but these are often used together with uncertainty estimations of all the quantities required to perform a simulation of the experiment. Hence, although the methodology of V&V can be highly specific, due to the enormous complexities involved, the goals of objectivity typically cannot be met in any strict sense. Like all other scientific activity, including traditional experiment, V&V relies heavily on human judgement and skill in the accurate assessment of the outcomes.

Despite these difficulties, one should see the methodology of V&V as an evolving practice, with the goals of legitimating simulation models in a variety of contexts. Indeed, because of the different ways that simulation is used in scientific investigation, V&V can involve a variety of techniques and strategies. None of that entails that this is a piecemeal activity in the way Winsberg (2010) suggests. The overall objectives, the methodological structure, and the successes of the process extend far beyond what we would expect from an ad hoc activity. Simulation is widely used as the basis for both scientific and policy decisions in areas as diverse as nuclear waste storage to the space programme. To suggest that the activities associated with V&V in these contexts are based on ad hoc decisions is not only inaccurate but undermines the creditability of simulation generally, as well as the goals of V&V. Exposing the problems should

COMPUTER SIMULATION: THE NEW REALITY

serve as a guide for improving the deficiencies in the practice, not as the basis for overall criticism. The history of scientific activity generally is replete with incidences of miscalculation, human error and the acceptance of theories, models and methods that later proved inaccurate or unjustified; simulation is and will be part of that history and as such subject to the similar sorts of difficulties.

In chapter 8 I want to focus on the role of simulation in the LHC experiment(s). Given the problems associated with V&V, an interesting issue arises as to how we should evaluate the status of the simulation(s) at the LHC, especially since dedicated validation experiments of the type I have described are generally not feasible. Nevertheless, the validation project is an important part of LHC physics, where the goal is to assess adequacy of both the simulation physics and the overall the environment in which the experiments take place. The discovery of a Higgs-like boson is, in some sense, a validation of all the various aspects of the simulation(s), since it indicates that the simulated physics and detector are reliable. However, as I mentioned at the outset, validation is an ongoing project.

In order to appreciate how the LHC simulations are evaluated in the context of V&V methods, I want to look at the different features of the simulation structure that forms the foundation of the experiments. Verification and validation at the LHC is interesting in its own right, insofar as it bears out the point I made earlier regarding different techniques and strategies. While much of the contemporary discussion of V&V and the development of the general methodology has its roots in computational fluid dynamics, that field is extremely different from high-energy physics. The importance of V&V in the latter context and its rather different features is evidence not only of the general significance of the methodology but also of its legitimacy and robustness across a broad spectrum of scientific investigation.

8

Without It There's Nothing

The Necessity of Simulation in the Higgs Search

One of the issues discussed in chapter 6 is whether experimental results were epistemically superior to simulation outputs/data or whether in some cases the latter could be viewed as having the same legitimacy as the former. Generally, the answer to the question will depend on the quality and kind of simulation in question, as well as the quality and kind of experiment. But, as I argued, there are some instances where simulation outputs should enjoy the same epistemic status as experimental results. The discussion in chapter 6 turned on the issue of modelling and the difficulties involved in isolating a notion of experimental measurement that was grounded in 'materiality' conditions, conditions that are often appealed to as the epistemic basis for the superiority of experiment over simulation. The problem, as I outlined it, is that 'materiality' in and of itself often plays no useful epistemic role in establishing the priority of experiment because in many cases one could not easily separate the so-called "material" component of a measurement result from the models used in the actual measuring process. The ability to separate the 'material' component of the measurement and to give 'materiality' some independent characterisation is necessary if the traditional argument from materiality is to succeed.

Perhaps not surprisingly, an analogous situation holds for cases where simulation plays a significant role *in* the experimental setting, as is the case in the various experiments carried out at the LHC, as well as others that rely heavily on data assimilation and so on. Here what I have in mind is the way knowledge gained via simulation literally makes possible not only the carrying out of the experiment but knowing what to look for and what the results mean. At first glance this may seem like an exaggerated claim, but a closer look at the LHC experimental context reveals that this is not the case. Although it is obvious that no simulation can prove that the Higgs particle exists, experiments and equipment designed to discover the Higgs rely heavily on knowledge produced via simulation. Hence, to say that the discovery of the Higgs was only possible using simulation is by no means to overstate the case. Again, not only is simulation required to process the experimental or 'signal' data but simulation provides the foundation for the entire experiment. To put the point in a slightly more perspicuous way, simulation knowledge is what tells us where to look for a Higgs event, that a Higgs event has occurred, and that we can trust the overall capability of the collider itself. In that sense the mass measurement associated with the discovery is logically and causally dependent on simulation.

There is, of course, an obvious reply to this characterisation, which is that the ultimate piece of evidence for the existence of the Higgs can only come from signal data and not simulation. This is a more specific version of the claim, often made against the significance of simulation, that nature can push back in an experiment (or fail to) in ways that simulation never can. Yet another variant of this argument is one I mentioned in chapter 6—that simulation can never yield anything new since we get out only what we put in. However, as I will show, this seems factually incorrect, given the role it plays in the LHC experiments. However, the point remains that although simulation can give us unexpected and novel results, they fail, in and of themselves, to establish existence claims. The question, though, is whether this 'ontological' effect, in and of itself, can translate into epistemic authority.

As I see it, the answer is no because the foundation for the epistemic authority of the signal data (in the case of the LHC experiments) is heavily reliant on simulation knowledge; in other words, the signal data are only jointly necessary for establishing the existence of the Higgs, and they are certainly not sufficient. Moreover, as I will show, simulation data are combined with signal data in the analysis of various events, rendering any sharp distinction between simulation and 'experiment' practically meaningless. The simulation is as much a part of the experiment as the signal data. Hence, the inability, in this context, to sharply distinguish simulation and experiment in the traditional way is especially significant, since the LHC experiments are often cited as the paradigm case where experiment affirms its authority over simulation. As I will show, the melding of the two suggests a shift not only in the way experiment and simulation are characterised but also in the way we evaluate the knowledge acquired in these contexts. Given the integral role simulation plays in the LHC experiment(s), the *contrast* with experiment is the wrong perspective from which to evaluate the role of simulated data.

What I want to explore in this chapter is how the extensive use of simulation in the LHC experiments can broaden our perspective on the role of simulation and the information it provides. In order to make that claim, however, it is important that the detailed role of simulation is made absolutely explicit. Too often we assume that although simulation is an important part of experimentation it nevertheless plays a secondary role. Undermining that claim requires close attention to the details so that the various uses of simulation are completely clear. The other equally important issue in this chapter concerns the methodology of V&V in the context of the LHC experiments, in particular how we evaluate the epistemic status of simulated data when there is a lack of experimental data available for comparison. Does this change the nature of validation where the LHC experiments are concerned?

CREATING THE EXPERIMENTAL CONTEXT

If we think of the typical requirements for any experimental measurement, there are two things that immediately come to mind. One is that the analysis must be designed to be maximally sensitive to the process being investigated; the other is that there must be a proper understanding the effects of the instrument on the measurements so that any effects can be compensated for when determining the value of a measured quantity. The ATLAS experiment at the LHC, which is designed to uncover mechanisms of electroweak symmetry breaking, consists of a 25- by 45-meter 7,000-ton cylinder of particle detection hardware with roughly 100 million readout channels. Hence meeting these requirements is nothing short of a herculean task.

New particles discovered at the LHC are typically unstable and rapidly transform into a cascade of lighter, more stable, and better understood particles. The particles travelling through the detector leave behind characteristic patterns, or 'signatures' which allow the particles to be identified, and the presence (or not) of any new particles can then be inferred. Forty million times per second, particles collide within the LHC, with each collision generating particles that often decay in complex ways into other particles, which move through layers of subdetectors. The subdetectors register each particle's passage, and microprocessors convert the particles' paths and energies into electrical signals, combining the information to create a digital summary of the "collision event." The raw data per event are around 1 million bytes (1 Mb), produced at a rate of about 40 million events per second. The 15 petabytes or so of data produced annually must be sifted through to determine if the collisions have thrown up any interesting physics. The experiment cannot store or process that amount of data, so a trigger system is used to reduce the number of events down to about 100 per second.

To accomplish this, a series of dedicated algorithms called 'triggers' are employed, with each trigger level selecting the data that become an input for the following level, which has more time available and more information to take a better decision. The first level is a hardware-based trigger that selects events with large energy deposits in the calorimeters. The initial calculation that results in a decision to keep an event is made in about one μs, and because this takes place online, once the data are rejected, they are lost forever. The second level is software based and selects events from a rudimentary analysis of regions of interest identified in level-1. The third level does a preliminary reconstruction of the selected events, which are then stored for offline analysis. As one can see, then, achieving the physics goals requires sophisticated algorithms that are applied successively to the raw data in an attempt to extract physical quantities and observables of interest that can be compared to theoretical predictions. The challenge is to continuously improve detector-calibration methods, and to refine processing algorithms to detect ever more interesting events. What is especially interesting about this situation is not simply that highly sophisticated algorithms are required to analyse the data but that decisions about where to look for so-called interesting events are fully determined by these algorithms as well. In other words, theory is used to develop simulations that are then used to construct and refine further algorithms for the triggers that pick out which data will be analysed in the search for possible Higgs events. In other words, the experiment is completely theory and simulation driven.

Prior to this stage, simulation also plays a crucial role in creating the context that makes data production possible. In order to build the detector(s) and understand measurements made with it, every aspect of the detector must be simulated as precisely as possible. The simulation framework involves a number of distinct processing stages, beginning with fundamental event simulation. The event generators are programmes that produce simulations of high-energy physics events for a number of aspects of the standard model. Included in these are specialised particle decay packages that simulate particle decays using the latest experimental data from other sources. There are several multipurpose event simulators with the most widely used being PYTHIA, HERWIG, SHERPA, which simulate simple hard processes, parton showering/quantum chromodynamics radiation, and hadronisation, as well as other underlying events. Many of the parameters for these simulations are tuned to data from the large electron-positron collider at CERN and from Tevatron, which was a proton-antiproton collider at Fermilab. ATLAS alone uses seven different types of event generators and several different decay packages. Each of the generators is used for a specific type of event. For example, Charbydis is used to simulate black holes; PYTHIA is used for quantum chromodynamics multijets and Higgs production. The different decay packages that simulate particle decay showers (TAUOLO, PHOTOS, etc.) are interfaced to work with the event generators.

A large simulation infrastructure is required to ensure that every aspect of the 'experiment' is accounted for. Once the fundamental events are simulated, interactions of the final state particles with the detector are simulated. In ATLAS this requires a number of different simulations: the simulation of charged particles in the position-dependent ATLAS magnetic field, modelling of the detector readout and electronics (including dead time and digitisation effects), the pile-up of pp interactions from the interacting proton bunches in the modelled event and its surrounding bunch, as well as background from other sources like cosmic rays that penetrate the rock above the detector. The data from all these simulations are then digitised to provide a representation that is equivalent to what is expected from the real detector.

The digitisation of data is obviously an extremely important aspect of the entire simulation process. At this stage the hits from a signal event (data from an actual run of the collider) are overlaid with background process hits, which include various types of "pile-up" interactions. The response of each subdetector element is then simulated in the required detail to create raw data object files equivalent to those from the readout drivers of the real experiment.[1] While most event types are simulated in the way I have described, some, such as cosmic rays, need more specialised treatment involving particular types of particle transport. There are also cases where statistics are needed but are unfeasible with full simulation, so approximate event simulation is used, which involves turning off the subdetectors and using only the inner tracker.

The final interpretation of the data and the understanding of the detectors require an equivalent amount of simulated event samples. Simulated and real data are reconstructed via the same process, with the simulated data also allowing for comparison to signal data. In that sense the simulated data serve as a kind of 'theoretical benchmark' against which signal data are compared; but simulated data also

---

1. There are several different kinds of data, including event summary data, reconstructed data from previous experiments, analysis object data, and event tag data. In many experiments the analysis framework only allows the user to read all events in a file one after the other. In order to select the wanted events, one has to apply a filter after the event data have been read into the memory, which results in an inefficient use of the computer resources. An event tag system reduces the time needed to perform an analysis by providing each analysis code only the events of interest as they are selected by the users. This event tag system is designed to provide fast preselection of events with the desired characteristics and involves imposing event selection criteria within the analysis code itself.

serve as 'experimental data' for determining the alignment of magnets and other technical specifications involved in the construction of the machine. In other words, theoretical principles that inform the engineering aspects are tested via simulation to ensure the most precise alignment of magnets and other design features. The goal is obviously to match, as much as possible, standard model physics with events seen by ATLAS (or the other experiments), and there is an active programme of event generator tuning within ATLAS and in the larger collider phenomenology community to facilitate that. Essentially, the task of the computer software is to filter data coming from the detector, monitor the performance of the detector, calibrate and align the detector components, simulate detector response from known physics processes, and carry out user analyses that lead to actual physics results. All of this relies on highly specific simulation to ensure that the final programmes are functioning accurately, programmes that form the foundation for the experimental searches.

The amount of data necessary to find a Higgs-type boson depends on how many Higgs signal events can be reconstructed from the detector, how many mundane background events are produced with the same "signature," and how well the Higgs signal events can be separated from the mundane (non-Higgs) background events. To assess the amount of data needed, simulations are used to determine the upper limit on the amount of Higgs bosons in the data, based on the expectations of the standard model. "Backgrounds" are other physics processes that produce events that look very similar to the Higgs. So, for instance, one might expect to be able to detect Higgs bosons in events with one electron, one neutrino, and two b quarks, but for every 10 Higgs events that have this "signature" there are thousands of backgrounds that have the same signature. Consequently, a particular event in the data cannot be determined to be signal or background with anything like 100 percent certainty. But if enough events are collected, one can study kinematic distributions such as the energy and masses of the particles in the events, and use this information to determine statistically whether there are Higgs bosons in a large data set. Hence the task is to collect sufficiently large amounts of data and study the kinematic distributions, amounts that are impossible without the addition of very large amounts of simulated data.

Complexity is one of the challenges in simulation of LHC events, not only because of the high energy and luminosity of the machine but also because of its intricacies. The high energy results in a large number of particles produced per interaction, and in the high luminosity mode there will typically be about 20 overlapping uninteresting collisions obscuring a signal event. Bunch crossing time of the LHC is 25 nsec, resulting in overlapping from subsequent bunch crossing in the signals of the slower detectors. Hence extracting information becomes very difficult. This has an impact on, among other things, the detector design. The LHC detectors must have fast response; otherwise there will be integration over many bunch crossings, resulting in a large "pile-up." The detectors must also be highly granular to minimise the probability that pile-up particles are in the same detector element as other interesting objects or events. This requires a larger number of detector channels, with the triggers for the experiments required to choose correctly at a level of 1 in 400,000 or better. As I noted, the high-level triggers are software based and so require extremely accurate simulation to ensure their robustness. Finally, the LHC detectors must be radiation resistant, since a high flux of particles from certain types of collisions results in a high radiation environment. All of this complex design and integration with the physics is possible only via simulation.

The simulation, reconstruction, and analysis programmes process one "event" at a time, with the event processing programmes composed of a number of algorithms that select and transform "raw" event data into "processed" (reconstructed) data and statistics. These algorithms often require additional "detector conditions" data (e.g. calibrations, geometry, environmental parameters, etc.), with the final data processing results given in statistical form (histograms, distributions, etc.). To illustrate the difficulties with these various tasks consider the information from jets gathered from SUSY-like events, where the goal is to distinguish between s-quark and gluino production. Several types of difficulties ensue that require very specific simulation; for example: (1) if mass splitting between the gluino and s-quark is small, then soft jets from gluinos will look like s-quark decay; (2) if weak bosons/Higgs are top in the decay chain, then additional jets will result that complicate jet counting; and (3) hard jets from quantum chromodynamics radiation can look like extra decay jets if they are not properly simulated. Precision simulation is absolutely necessary to get both jet numbers and energy variables right. So, in order to distinguish new physics at the LHC and to properly analyse the excesses, high precision event simulation, integrated with the various other simulations, is needed. All of these, taken together, constitute a simulated experiment, which is required for determining not only the proper functioning of the equipment but also what to expect and look for in the actual runs of the machine.

The final stage in the process involves raw data taken by the ATLAS detector (or CMS) and simulated data that are reconstructed together into streamlined event representations suitable for analysis. Like most high-energy physics experiments, ATLAS also uses roughly the same amount of simulated and signal events for many of their analyses that estimate detector response and efficiency. A generator programme is used to generate events of a certain physics process (e.g., top pair production, W boson production with leptonic decays), and that output is stored as raw data objects which contain information similar to detected raw data together with information about the underlying generated event. In addition to being necessary for physics analysis, simulated data were used to exercise and validate the ATLAS computing model, including reconstruction and analysis.[2]

To summarise: the first requirement in the LHC experiment(s) was a CS of Higgs bosons being produced and decaying according to calculations of the standard model. Next, an algorithm needed to be developed that would select all the interesting particles produced in the decays. Then all the other physics processes or "backgrounds" that can produce these same particles needed to be considered; this also required that they be simulated and selected. Once this was accomplished, a method had to be developed for telling the difference between the event and the background by comparing energies, momenta, angles, masses, and other quantities measurable in the detector. The data were then compared with the model of event and background processes, and calculations made to determine how much signal was in the data. The final step was the comparison of simulation data with data collected from actual runs of the detector, data that had also been processed using simulation. In other words, nothing is known without simulation.

So, in light of the previous discussion about the relation between simulation and experiment, what should we conclude from this enhanced use of simulation as a fundamental feature of the experimental investigation? First and foremost we can think of simulation as providing the "data" against which various aspects of the experiment are compared; but it also functions in a "theoretical" capacity insofar as it provides information about the nature of different types of physics events. In addition, simulation functions as a source of experimental data against which detector data are interpreted and against which various technological aspects of the detector are constructed and calibrated. Perhaps most

---

2. Because simulated data is produced for individual physics processes separately, event filtering is less important than for real data.

important from the epistemological perspective is the fact that since an extraordinarily large amount of data is required to detect a Higgs signature, signal data needed to be supplemented with equal amounts of simulated data. In that sense, the simulation functions as a source of both experimental and theoretical knowledge, each with its distinct role and specific methodological features. The presentation of the results of the Higgs discovery further indicates the prominent role played by simulation data in every aspect of the experiment.

THE DISCOVERY

The ATLAS and CMS announcements of the discovery of a Higgs-like boson in July 2012 were as follows:

> Clear evidence for the production of a neutral boson with a measured mass of 126.0 ± 0.4 (stat) ± 0.4 (sys) GeV is presented. This observation, which has a significance of 5.9 standard deviations, corresponding to a background fluctuation probability of 1.7×10^{-9}, is compatible with the production and decay of the Standard Model Higgs boson. (ATLAS *Physics Letters B* 716 (2012), 1–29)

> An excess of events is observed above the expected background, with a local significance of 5.0 standard deviations, at a mass near 125 GeV, signalling the production of a new particle. The expected significance for a standard model Higgs boson of that mass is 5.8 standard deviations. The excess is most significant in the two decay modes with the best mass resolution, $\gamma\gamma$ and ZZ; a fit to these signals gives a mass of 125.3 ± 0.4 (stat.) ±0.5 (syst.) GeV. The decay to two photons indicates that the new particle

is a boson with spin different from one. (CMS, *Physics Letters B* 716 (2012), 30–61)

The papers included a number of visual representations of data, including comparisons of simulated and signal data. Each of the experiments (ATLAS and CMS) have also produced a number of visual representations of simulated Higgs events. But what is important for my purposes here is the extensive reliance on simulated data in the images presented in the two discovery papers.

Figure 8.1 shows decay as reconstructed in the CMS tracking detector. Figure 8.2, from the ATLAS paper, shows the distribution of the four-lepton invariant mass, $m4l$, for the selected candidates, compared to the background expectation in the 80–250 GeV mass range, for the combination of the $\sqrt{s} = 7$ TeV and $\sqrt{s} = 8$ TeV data. The signal expectation for a SM Higgs with $m_H = 125$ GeV is also

Figure 8.1: A simulated event with the CMS detector featuring the characteristics expected from a decay of a Higgs boson into a pair of photons H → $\gamma\gamma$). The event could also be due to known standard model background processes. © CERN 2012.

COMPUTER SIMULATION: THE NEW REALITY

shown. The dots represent the actual data with error bars; all other background and event data are simulated.

As I mentioned, the (simulation) event generators are used to model the signal and background processes, with acceptances and efficiencies obtained mostly from full simulations of the detector (in this case ATLAS) using GEANT4. The simulations include realistic modelling of the pile-up conditions that are also observed in the data. Corrections obtained from measurements in data are applied to account for the small discrepancies between data and simulation. For example, large samples of W, Z, and J/ψ decays are used to derive scale

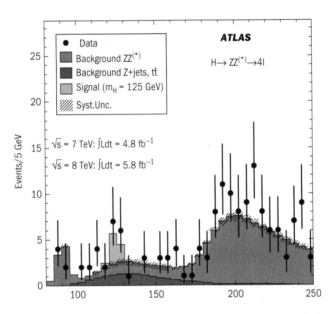

Figure 8.2: The distribution of the four-lepton invariant mass, m4l, for the selected candidates, compared to the background expectation in the 80–250 GeV mass range, for the combination of $\sqrt{s}$ = 7 TeV and $\sqrt{s}$ = 8 TeV data. The signal expectation for a SM Higgs with m_H = 125 GeV is also shown. © CERN 2012.

factors for lepton reconstruction and identification efficiencies. The expected background yields and composition are estimated using simulated data that are normalised to theoretical cross-sections for $ZZ^{(*)}$. Studies to determine potential bias were performed using large samples of simulated background events that were complemented by data-driven estimates. The potential bias for a given model was estimated by performing a maximum likelihood fit to large samples of simulated background events in the mass range 100–160 GeV for the sum of a signal plus the given background model.

Similar use of simulation is documented in the CMS paper. One of the things they highlight at the beginning is that their analysis of the 7 and 8 TeV samples with modified event selection criteria were performed in a "blind" way. In other words, the algorithms and selection procedures were formally approved and fixed before results from data in the signal region were examined. Because the Higgs mass is not predicted by theory and its production cross-section and natural width vary widely over the allowed mass range, the search was required to cover a large range of masses and diverse decay modes, such as photon pairs, Z and W bosons, b quarks, and τ leptons. In order to analyse all these channels, the detector needed to be capable of observing a Higgs boson at any point in this range. The amount of data and the type of analysis required as well as the construction and tuning of the detector simply would not have been possible without simulation. The event description algorithm used to reconstruct and identify each particle with an optimised combination of all subdetector information plays an important role in determining the particle momentum. As with ATLAS, the description of the Higgs boson signal is obtained from simulated data using decay modes and production processes provided by PYTHIA interfaced with other matrix element generators.

In the context of data analysis and statistical methodology, simulation is again crucial for what is called the "look elsewhere effect" (LEE). Recall that in the statement of the discovery the claim is that an excess of events was observed above the expected background with a local significance of 5.0σ at a mass near 125 GeV with a global p-value in the search range 110–145 GeV corresponding to 4.6σ. Further data reported by CMS put the p-value at 5σ, which is roughly a probability of 3×10^{-7} or about 1 in 3.5 million. What this means is that there is a 1 in 3.5 million chance of the background alone fluctuating up by this amount; or alternatively, only one experiment in 3.5 million would see an apparent signal this strong in a universe without a Higgs boson. The probability for a background fluctuation to be at least as large as the observed maximum excess is termed the local p-value, and an excess anywhere in a specified mass range is the global p-value. In order to evaluate the probability, sets of simulated data incorporating all correlations between analyses optimised for different Higgs masses must be generated. The global p-value for the specified region is always greater than the local p-value and is referred to as the LEE. In other words, the likelihood of finding something in the entire region you probed is greater than it would be if you had stated beforehand where the signal would be; there is a definite "probability boost" associated with looking in many places. However, with the use of simulated data, the LEE can be reduced in ways that are not possible simply on the basis of theoretical predictions alone.

Finally, the systematic uncertainties are also evaluated by comparisons between data and simulated samples of specific types of decay, for example, Z → ee; H → $\gamma\gamma$.

We can see from figure 8.3, representing some CMS results, that the observations of 7 and 8 TeV combine to give an observed limit with significant excess at m_H = 125 GeV. The local p-value is given as a function of m_H for the combined observations. The dashed line is the expected local p-value for the combined data set should a SM Higgs exist with a mass m_H.

So not only is simulation necessary for mapping the entire experiment(s) but it also figures importantly in generating the

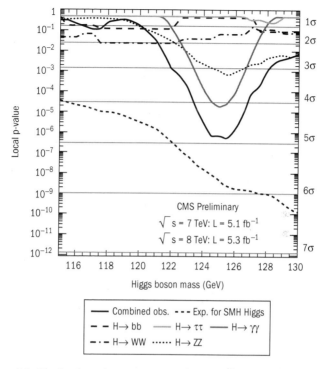

Figure 8.3: The local p-value is given as a function of m_H for the combined observations. The dashed line is the expected local p-value for the combined dataset should a SM Higgs exist with a mass m_H. © CERN 2012.

images associated with the reporting of data and the discovery process more generally.[3] Given its prominence, it is crucial that methods are in place to guarantee that simulated data are trustworthy and unproblematic. Consequently, any evaluation of simulation data and their application in experimental contexts needs to address questions

3. See Martina Mertz, "Data Handling through Imaging at the LHC," presentation at The Epistemology of Data Selection and Analysis Procedures in Physics Conference, Wuppertal University (7–9 March 2013) for an excellent discussion of the various types of imaging associated with the Higgs discovery and the importance of each for communicating specific kinds of information.

regarding the methodology used for justifying simulation results and whether that methodology is itself problematic in certain respects. Note that this is a different question from whether we should consider simulation results as on a par with experimental data. In that sense, the concern is to investigate the processes involved in legitimating simulation data, taken in their own right. As I discussed earlier, the methodology of V&V is designed to legitimate simulation as a source of knowledge by introducing new approaches for addressing epistemic questions about its accuracy and reliability. As I also noted, the methodology is not without problems, especially with respect to the processes involved in validating a simulation as well as the relationship between verification and validation. Given these general worries, further questions arise as to how we should assess the status of the simulation(s) at the LHC, especially since dedicated validation experiments of the type discussed in chapter 7 are generally not feasible.

The validation project is an important part of LHC physics, where the goal is to determine the adequacy of both the simulation physics and the overall environment in which the experiments take place. Because so much of the experimental infrastructure relies on simulation, and because that infrastructure had to be assumed to be largely reliable prior to the collection of signal data, issues naturally arise about the validation of various features of the simulation. As I pointed out in chapter 7, the goal of legitimating simulation data involves conducting *independent* validation experiments. But this is not possible in the LHC case because it is simply not feasible to conduct independent experiments capable of producing the kinds of high energy collisions that are being simulated; the simulation itself is what forms the foundation for the collection of experimental data once the machine is up and running. Because the validation must take place before any real jets are produced the problem is one of finding data that can serve as the basis for comparisons. And, because we have the rather peculiar situation of the experiment being only as good as the various simulations that make it possible, it is crucial that the validation procedure be as accurate as possible. The discovery of a Higgs boson is, in some sense, itself a validation of all the various aspects of the simulation(s) since it indicates that the simulated physics and detector are reliable.

But this is not sufficient for obvious reasons; validation must be carried out prior to and in order to guarantee the legitimacy of experimental results. The question, however, is whether the heavy reliance on simulation for the 'discovery' could in fact bias the effect in a way that threatens the outcome of the experiment. In order to answer this question and appreciate how the LHC simulations are evaluated in the context of V&V methods, let us take another look at the different features of the simulation structure that form the foundation of the experiments. The epistemic issues related to validation remain important even after the Higgs discovery, not only because other types of searches are carried out at the LHC which require the same reliance on simulation, but also because the machine is constantly being upgraded to run at higher and higher energies, something that is made possible only by very accurate simulations. Hence, validation is an ongoing process as long as the collider is operational.

VALIDATION AND THE LHC

As I have discussed, there are various aspects involved in simulation at the LHC. In addition to the specific experimental features that are simulated, it is also crucial that all the relevant physics processes are included in the simulation: ionisation, δ-ray production and propagation, multiple scattering, photon conversion, transition radiation and subsequent propagation of the X-rays in the detector material (relevant for ATLAS), synchrotron radiation (relevant mainly for

CMS), hadronic interactions, neutron interactions, and so on. The two aspects of the validation project for the LHC involve assessing the adequacy of simulation physics and the environment in which it occurs (detectors, etc.). This involves the validation of physics processes incorporated in detector simulation tools (the shower packages GEANT4 and FLUKA) as well as the simulation of hadronic interactions. Hadronic physics is not only a very broad but also a very difficult field because the underlying theory, quantum chromodynamics, cannot produce predictions for observables whose dominant energy range is outside the perturbative high-energy regime. The only current viable approach is to use different simplified models whose approximated validity is often restricted to particular incident particles, target material types, and interaction energies. As a result the simulation of hadronic interactions must rely on several different models for describing the showers and other phenomena/regions of interest.

In the GEANT4 simulation package a large set of hadronic models are available, and they can be chosen and combined according to different needs, according to application, precision, and computing time. To facilitate the choice, a certain number of "educated guess" Physics Lists, each of which is a collection of different (but consistent) models, are provided for use in different circumstances. Because of the different energies involved, each model is optimised for different applications. The adequacy and usability of the environment concerns the central processing unit (CPU), memory, Monte Carlo truth, and so on.[4] The overall goal is to prevent inadequate simulation

4. The CPU is the hardware in a computer that carries out the instructions of the programme by performing the basic arithmetical, logical, and input/output operations of the system. Monte Carlo truth is often defined in a variety of ways, some of which include: a snapshot of the event from the generator or a (simplified) snapshot of the event in the detector simulation. It is also described as a way of knowing what went into the detector or understanding the physics taking place in the detector.

models from leading to large systematic contributions to the physics; in other words, dominant or systematic error for the LHC shouldn't be due to imperfect simulation.

Two complementary approaches for validation are used. (1) Comparisons with test-beam data collected with the three LHC calorimeter modules or prototypes address shower features such as longitudinal, lateral, and time development, shower composition, and other features important for calorimeter measurements (energy resolution). The calorimeters are situated outside the magnet that surrounds the inner detector and measure energy from particles by absorbing it. (2) Benchmark studies—comparisons with experiments performed at nuclear facilities such as Los Alamos or Tevatron—provide tests of individual microscopic collisions like those occurring in the particle interactions with thin layers of LHC tracking detectors. The predictive power of detector simulation rests on the correct simulation of individual microscopic interactions between particles and detector material. These interactions can't be easily studied with a simulation of full LHC subdetectors where multiple interactions and showers are present. And, because of the complex phenomenology, there is sometimes an "averaging out" of problems at the microscopic level, hence the need for a validation hierarchy of the type described in chapter 7.

The various LHC experiments (ATLAS, CMS, etc.) all require the availability of more than one simulation package (i.e. FLUKA, G4) especially for the description of hadron interactions. The response of the various LHC subdetectors to electrons, muons, and pions can be studied with test-beam data over the energy range from few GeV up to 300 GeV. In addition, well-known physics decay samples can be used to understand and calibrate the detectors over a broader energy range than at the test beam (e.g., up to few hundred GeV for the ATLAS and CMS calorimeters). Because the detector response to very-high-energy particles (up to several TeV in ATLAS and CMS) cannot be directly checked with test-beam or collider data, it must be predicted by the simulation. The method to achieve accurate detector modelling consists of comparing the simulation packages to data over the accessible energy regions. This allows the physics content, the realism, and the reliability of the simulation to be validated and improved for the accessible regions. But simulation is required in order to predict the detector behaviour outside the range covered by test-beam and/or control data samples, so in that case the application domain for the simulation extends well beyond its validation domain.

It is possible to derive quantitative requirements for assessing simulation accuracy by looking at the most sensitive LHC physics channel(s) for each performance issue, such as calorimeter linearity, particle identification, and so on. It is typically calorimetric measurements that set requirements on global shower features. The validations of these features are performed, in both the experiments and in the Simulation Physics Validation Project, by comparing test-beam data with G4 and FLUKA simulations of the test-beam setup. The tracking devices are concerned mainly with individual microscopic collisions involving the interactions of low-energy particles with the sensitive thin layers of the detector. Because these are very granular, the process requires accurate modelling of individual microscopic collisions down to very low energies.

The environment inside the detector is also very crowded due to the high density of particles that produce hits in the active layers. Hence, if particle interactions are not accurately described, pattern recognition performance could be wrongly estimated by large factors. Here the simulation validation relies on both test-beam measurements and simple benchmark studies. A complete validation requires that the simulation packages describe not only a large number of relevant observables but also their correlations. High-quality test-beam data are required for accurate validation with any effects like beam contaminations and electronic noise, which also need to be fully quantified and understood in order to meet the precision requirements for the comparisons. Although these are not validation experiments in the sense of being constructed specifically to validate the simulation, there are nevertheless very stringent analyses of the experimental data. In that sense, assessments of the quality of the simulation depend, to a great extent, on the quality of the test-beam data; but these measured data are certainly not immune from problems as well.

Although these procedures do not qualify as 'validation experiments' in the sense specified by the V&V methodology, the important issue is the extent to which they can be said to fulfill the role of validation conditions. In the contexts where experimental data relevant for LHC are available (Los Alamos data—e.g. pion absorption below 1 GeV) these are the chosen benchmarks. It is also extremely important to focus on the underlying physics in order to prevent the programmes from developing into a set of experiment-specific tools with plug-in parameterisations. The problem, however, is that the underlying physics contains a number of free parameters, so how should these be handled? Several of these parameters that occur in various aspects of event generator codes need tweaking if the generator is to describe experimental data. Nonpurtabative hadronisation processes account for many of these cases, since the models are deeply phenomenological. As a result, a tuning process needs to be performed against a wide range of experimental analyses. This is primarily because some parameters may be insensitive to selective analyses, resulting in a 'nonphysical' impact on observables that are not considered in the analyses.

As I stressed in the discussion of validation in chapter 7, tuning was not a desirable aspect of uncertainty analyses, but in the LHC case it seems unavoidable. That said, a number of different highly technical approaches have been developed to deal with the tuning problem.

One of these is Rivet, a library of experimental analyses and tools for calculating physical observables. Its main problem is that it contains no intrinsic mechanism to improve the quality of the tune, and tuning 'by eye' is unsatisfactory. A solution is to define a goodness of fit function between generated and referenced data and then attempt to minimise the function. But this, too, has its problems. A true fit function is not analytic, and an iterative approach to minimisation will require an evaluation at each new parameter-space point which requires more runs of the generator. The solution to these difficulties is 'Professor,' a programme that parameterises the fit function with a polynomial. The details of the process are rather complicated, but the outcome is a predicted 'best tune,' which should then be further checked with Rivet.

Several levels of validation are required, especially for hadronic physics, such as calorimetry, where pion test-beam data collected with LHC calorimeters are compared with G4/FLUKA/(G3). In the tracking detectors, hadronic interaction test-beam data collected with LHC tracking detectors are also compared with G4/FLUKA/(G3) and finally there needs to be comparisons between G4/FLUKA/ (G3) for the simulation of the radiation background in the caverns of the LHC experiments. The level of agreement between data and simulation or between different simulation packages provides feedback for improved algorithms in the codes, as well as guidance for LHC experiments in selecting the best physics models for their needs.

This feedback to both the verification component and the theoretical model choice is not the same as one might find in typical validation contexts, but what it does do is tell us that certain features of the simulation packages are reliable and can be trusted not to produce systematic error in the larger experiment. The process involves a blind test with experimental data, where the accuracy of the comparisons is limited by the systematic error of the available data and their relevance for LHC processes. Although there is an element of tuning involved, this is necessary given the lack of fundamental theory in the development of the physical models.

The validation procedure in the LHC case doesn't directly address the predictive capability for the (larger) experiment, that is, it doesn't function like a simulation used to predict aspects of climate change, nor does it tell us what kind of physics beyond the standard model that might be revealed.[5] But what the LHC simulations do predict, or provide information about, is what a Higgs event will look like and its various identifying features. Unlike traditional validation experiments, the simulation validation at the LHC functions more like a second-order experiment that provides information used to further refine what we can think of as the experimental setup (the simulation codes/algorithms used to construct and run the machine, generate data, and illustrate what various background events will look like) as well as the choice of models used for the various aspects of the physics. Because simulation facilitates not only the design and functioning of the experimental equipment but also provides the information necessary for understanding the significance of the experimental data, constant refinement and updating is required. This process is facilitated partly via validation, and to that extent simulation, validation and experiment function almost as an integrated unit. The complete

---

5. For clarificatory purposes I should briefly mention the relation between validation and prediction. A prediction involves an application of a validated model to a domain outside the validation experiment/data. It uses assessed model accuracy as input and incorporates additional uncertainty estimation from extrapolation of the model beyond its experimental database. Another crucial feature is a comparison of the accuracy requirement of the particular application to the estimated accuracy of the model for that application. Validation, by contrast, presents the impact of uncertainty of experimental data on inferences drawn from the simulation validation process and makes no claims about the accuracy of a prediction. For prediction, the level of confidence in estimation of the accuracy should also be part of the metric (though separate from the estimation itself). If application and validation domains overlap, model uncertainty can be estimated on validation results. In cases where the accuracy comparison is deemed inadequate or validation isn't feasible, calibration becomes important. This involves adjusting the physical or numerical modelling parameters to improve agreement with data (parameter estimation, model tuning, updating).

integration of simulation and experiment, in the sense that the former is the foundation of the latter, changes the face of validation from something carried out independently to a process involving aspects of calibration. But, given the nature of the LHC experiment(s), it is difficult to see how it could be otherwise.

As I have stressed, it is important to point out the ways in which simulation goes beyond employing computational power in the processing of data. Although that is also a crucial aspect of the LHC experiment(s), the very decision about which data to even include in the analysis is made on the basis of simulation knowledge. Beamline simulations are also a crucial part of the experiment as well as background and radiation estimates, the development of physics analyses, and the determination of systematic errors. The representation of the experiment (geometry) is an important ingredient in the simulation as well as the event generators, particle transport, decays, interaction with other materials, and overall electronics responses. The validation of electromagnetic physics as well as hadronic physics (calorimetry, tracking, radiation background) and the overall simulation environment (Monte Carlo truth, shower parameterisation, CPU and memory requirements) are required to ensure that the predictive power of the detector simulation rests on correct simulation of individual interactions between particles and detector material. In that sense, simulation provides the entire foundation for the LHC experiment(s).

SUMMING UP

In chapters 6 and 7, I have shown how the problem of uncertainties in CS data is not just a reflection of discretisation uncertainties but includes a broad base of physical modelling assumptions, input parameters, data processing, experimental uncertainty estimations (aleatory and epistemic), and so on. The epistemic status of simulation data is the result of how that data are generated, assessed, and used. While the methodology of V&V goes some way toward ensuring the legitimacy of simulation knowledge in the LHC experiment, it is by no means an unproblematic process, with many of the decisions requiring estimations and evaluations that are somewhat different from the characterization of V&V outlined in chapter 7. But even the theoretical discussion of V&V methodology revealed the ways it can fall short of its stated goals and procedures. Realistically, what V&V provides is an evolving process that takes into account the various ways simulation can go wrong and works toward establishing practices that can overcome these difficulties. As in many areas of scientific practice, V&V relies on due diligence but in doing so provides a framework within which simulation knowledge can, in theory, and in many cases in practice, be evaluated.

Validation at the LHC is designed as a tool for, among other things, picking the right physics models. The process itself is too complex to fit well into the V&V framework described in chapter 7—a framework conceived largely for areas such as computational fluid dynamics to deal with situations that, while extremely intricate and complicated, lack the multifaceted complexity of both the theoretical and experimental constraints present in the LCH experiments. In that sense, then, the level of validation is restricted by the possibilities defined in the larger experimental context. However, the bases for these restrictions, specifically the enormous amount of data involved, the five sigma requirement on statistical significance, and the two independent experiments (ATLAS and CMS), also serve as validating conditions on the simulations, ensuring their legitimacy as the foundation for the larger experiment(s). But is this enough?

The fundamental problem at the heart of any evaluation of simulation data is understanding the assumptions and approximations involved in the simulations; understanding what is inside the

COMPUTER SIMULATION: THE NEW REALITY

programmes in order to answer questions regarding the effects produced by the simulation. In other words, is some particular effect due to different models, or approximations, or is it simply a bug? Is the quantity being measured a fundamental quantity or merely a parameter in the simulation code? If we consider only the detector simulation, for example, one needs to incorporate several different theoretical calculations such as interactions with atoms, some nuclear physics, and electromagnetic processes like scattering and pair production. Add to this the variety of empirical models (nuclear interactions, material dependencies, etc.), as well as data driven models of cross-sections and energy distributions, and already the detector simulation programme GEANT4 is beginning to take on the characteristics of a black box because it is simply too difficult to understand all of the underlying processes taken together.[6] Although electromagnetic interactions can be calculated from first principles, unlike hadronic interactions, the cross-sections and distributions of secondary particles are calculated in models. Some of these (those related to the nucleus) require input from empirical data, and the sheer number of processes that need to be accounted for involve significant computing time. Similarly, the hadronic-matter interactions are extremely complex and depend strongly on the particle type, the material, and the energy of the collision; different energies require different types of models. Indeed, the physics lists provided by GEANT4 contain many different models to describe the entire energy range of the interactions in a hadronic shower. Each list uses a different set of underlying models that have a smooth transition and are tuned to each other.

6. See Christian Zeitniz, "Validation of Detector Simulation," presentation at the Epistemology of Data Selection and Analysis Procedures in Physics Conference at Wuppertal University (7–9 March 2013).

What this points to is a use of simulation that certainly falls short of the transparency requirement for understanding the "inside" of the programme. But because of the complexity of the experiment, anything else is simply not possible; instead one must rely extensively on tuning and other types of controls to ensure that the validation is as accurate as the conditions will allow. What this means is that the distinction between accuracy and adequacy discussed in chapter 7 is essentially collapsed in the LHC validation context. But in some sense the demands of the experiment require it. The simulations are all done with specific goals and limits in mind; hence the validations are also performed in order to ensure that those goals are met. Unlike examples where a particular piece of hardware is simulated in order to gauge its behaviour under certain conditions, there are well-defined parameters involved in the LHC experiment(s) that need to be taken into account in the validation. The adequacy conditions and allowable margins of error are set by the constraints of experimental practice for discoveries in physics, not individual practitioners, and to that extent the adequacy conditions are built in, as it were, to the accuracy requirements. The complexity of the experimental context prevents us from fully understanding each aspect of the experiment and the simulation, which is the reason we require the extensive use of simulation in the first place!

My goal in this chapter has been to give the reader some sense of the extensive use of simulation in the LHC experiments and of how the information from simulation is evaluated and justified. Although I have only discussed this particular case, experiments in other areas of physics, as well as the natural sciences generally, are heavily simulation based. Exactly how simulation data contribute to the experimental outcomes will, of course, depend not only on the role they play but also the validation procedures associated with their use. In each case any philosophical conclusions about their epistemic status will depend heavily on the specific details of the case. Despite the

importance of specific details we can also draw some general conclusions about the role of simulation, conclusions regarding our overall
attitude toward its status as an instrument of scientific investigation.

As I mentioned in the introduction to this chapter, the use of
simulation at the LHC casts doubt on the very distinction between
experiment and simulation; the latter is simply an integral part of
the former. That said, there is still a distinction to be made between
signal data (or external data, if you will) and simulated data. But,
as I showed with the LHC, the two are "processed" together; a five
sigma (σ) result simply would not be possible without simulation
data. While other experimental contexts may not mimic the LHC
with respect to the role of simulation, areas such as climate science,
astrophysics, and cosmology all rely heavily on simulated data for
establishing their results. Indeed, in some engineering contexts simulations are more realistic than traditional experiments, in that they
make possible the configuration of environment parameters relevant
for the operational application of certain types of instruments. One
such example involves simulating the surface of planets in prepara-
tion for NASA missions.

Hence, the general conclusions we should draw from the discussion are as follows. First and foremost, the claim that simulation is,
in essence, epistemically inferior to experiment is simply not true,
nor is the materiality condition that motivates it—the traditional
philosophical categories are out of sync with contemporary practice.
Second, the verification and validation of simulation data, while not
unproblematic, is far from a set of ad hoc practices maniupated in
order to get the results we want. The pervasive use of simulation in
many high risk contexts speaks not only to their importance but to
the philosophical legitimacy of conclusions one and two. Like every
area of scientific investigation, simulation and its legitimation is an
evolving process. Philosophical analysis needs to evolve with it!

REFERENCES

Baker, Alan. (2005). "Are There Genuine Mathematical Explanations of Physical Phenomena?" *Mind*, 114, 223–38.

Baker, Alan. (2009). "Mathematical Explanation in Science." *British Journal for the Philosophy of Science*, 60, 611–33.

Bangu, Sorin I. (2008). "Inference to the Best Explanation and Mathematical Realism." *Synthese*, 160, 13–20.

Bangu, Sorin I. (2009). "Understanding Thermodynamic Singularities: Phase Transitions, Data, and Phenomena." *Philosophy of Science*, 76, 488–505.

Bardeen, John. (1951)."Electron Vibration Interactions and Superconductivity." *Reviews of Modern Physics*, 23, 261–70.

Bardeen, John. (1973a). "Electron-Phonon Interactions and Superconductivity." *Physics Today*, 26, 41–46.

Bardeen, John. (1973b). "History of Superconductivity." In B. Kursunoglu and A. Perlmutter (eds.), *Impact of Basic Research on Technology*, 15–57. New York: Plenum Press.

Bardeen, J., Cooper, L., and Schrieffer, J. R. (1957). "Theory of Superconductivity." *Physical Review*, 108, 1175–1204.

Batitsky, V. (1998). "Empiricism and the Myth of Fundamental Measurement." *Synthese*, 116, 51–73.

Batterman, Robert. (2002). *The Devil in the Details: Asymptotic Reasoning in Explanation, Reduction, and Emergence*. Oxford: Oxford University Press.

Batterman, Robert. (2005). "Critical Phenomena and Breaking Drop: Infinite Idealisations in Physics." *Studies in History and Philosophy of Modern Physics*, 36, 225–44.

Batterman, Robert. (2010). "On the Explanatory Role of Mathematics in Empirical Science." *British Journal for the Philosophy of Science*, 61, 1–25.

Belot, Gordon. (2007). "Is Classical Electrodynamics an Inconsistent Theory?" *Canadian Journal of Philosophy*, 37, 263–82.

Beringer, Jurg. (2004a). "Physics Validation of Detector Simulation Tools for LHC." *Nuclear Instruments and Methods in Physics ResearchA* 534, 156–61.

Beringer, Jurg. (2004b). "Production Cross Sections: A Benchmark Study for the Validation of Hadronic Physics Simulation at LHC." CERN-LCGAPP-2003-18, March 9, 2004.

Beringer, Jurg, and Gianotti, Fabiola. (2003). "The Simulation Physics-Validation Sub-Project." LCG AA Review, October 20–22, 2003 (Powerpoint slides).

Berry, Michael. (1994). "Asymptotics, Singularities and the Reduction of Theories." In D. Prawitz, B. Skyrms and D. Westerstahl (eds.), *Logic, Methodology and Philosophy of Science IX*. Amsterdam: North Holland, 597–608.

Boltzmann, Ludwig. (1964). *Lectures on Gas Theory*. Berkeley: University of California Press.

Bouchard, Fredric, and Rosenberg, Alex. (2004). "Fitness, Probability and the Principles of Natural Selection." *British Journal for the Philosophy of Science*, 55, 693–712.

Brown, Bryson. (1992). "Old Quantum Theory: A Paraconsistent Approach." *Philosophy of Science* (PSA 1992 Proceedings, vol. 2), 397–411.

Brown, Bryson. (2002). "On Paraconsistency." In Dale Jacquette (ed.), *A Companion to Philosophical Logic*, 628–50. Oxford: Blackwell.

Buckley, Andy. (2010) "Simulation Strategies for the LHC ATLAS Experiment." in Nuclear Science Symposium Conference Record (NSS/MIC), IEEE.

Butterfield, Jeremy. (2011a). "Emergence, Reduction and Supervenience: A Varied Landscape." *Foundations of Physics*, 41, 920–59.

Butterfield, Jeremy. (2011b). "Less is Different: Emergence and Reduction Reconciled." *Foundations of Physics*, 41, 1065–1135.

Callender, Craig. (2001). "Taking Thermodynamics Too Seriously." *Studies in History and Philosophy of Modern Physics*, 32, 539–53.

Callender, Craig, and Menon, Tarun. (2013). "Turn and Face the Strange. . . Ch-ch-changes: Philosophical Questions Raised by Phase Transitions." In R. Batterman (ed.) *Oxford Handbook of Philosophy of Physics*, 189–223. New York: Oxford University Press.

Carnap, R. (1950). *Testability and Meaning*. Graduate Philosophy Club, Yale University. New Haven: Yale University Press.

Cartwright, Nancy. (1983). *How the Laws of Physics Lie*. Oxford: Clarendon Press.

Cartwright, Nancy. (1989). *Nature's Capacities and Their Measurement*. Oxford: Oxford University Press.

Cartwright, Nancy. (1999a). *The Dappled World*. Cambridge: Cambridge University Press.

REFERENCES

Cartwright, Nancy. (1999b). "Fables and Models." In Cartwright, *The Dappled World*. Cambridge: Cambridge University Press.

Cartwright, Nancy. (1999c). "Models and the Limits of Theory: Quantum Hamiltonians and the BCS Models of Superconductivity." In M. Morgan and M. Morrison (eds.), *Models as Mediators: Perspectives on Natural and Social Science*, 241–81. Cambridge: Cambridge University Press.

Cartwright, Nancy, Shomar, Towfic, and Suarez, Mauricio. (1995). "The Toolbox of Science." In *Theories and Models of Scientific Processes*, Poznan Studies in the History and Philosophy of the Sciences and the Humanities, 44, 137–44. Amsterdam: Rodopi.

Causey, Robert. (1969). "Derived Measurement, Dimensions and Dimensional Analysis." *Philosophy of Science*, 36, 252–270.

Cebeci, Tuncer. (2004). *Turbulence Models and Their Application*. Berlin: Springer.

Cebeci, T., and Cousteix, J. (2005). *Modelling and Computation of Boundary Layer Flows*. Berlin: Springer.

Cook, Norman. (2006). *Models of the Atomic Nucleus*. Berlin: Springer.

Cooper, Leon. (1956). "Bound Electron Pairs in a Degenerate Fermi Gas." *Physical Review*, 104, 1189–90.

Cooper, Leon. (1973). "Microscopic Quantum Interference in the Theory of Superconductivity." *Physics Today*, 31–39.

de Regt, Henk W., and Dieks, Denis. (2005). "A Contextual Approach to Scientific Understanding." *Synthese*, 144, 137–70.

De Roeck, A., Gianotti, F., Morsch, A., and Pokorski, W. (2004). "Simulation Physics Requirements from the LHC Experiments." CERN-LCGAPP-2004-02. March 15, 2004.

Duhem, Pierre (1977). *Aim and Structure of Physical Theory*. New York: Atheneum.

Duhem, Pierre. (1954). *Aim and Structure of Physical Theory*. Princeton: Princeton University Press.

Earman, John. (2004). "Curie's Principle and Spontaneous Symmetry Breaking." *International Studies in the Philosophy of Science*, 18, 173–98.

Edwards, Anthony W. F. (1994). "The Fundamental Theorem of Natural Selection." *Biological Review*, 69, 443–74.

Ewens, Warren. (2004). *Mathematical Population Genetics*. Vol. 1: *Theoretical Introduction*. New York: Springer.

Fisher, Ronald A. (1918). "The Correlation between Relatives on the Supposition of Mendelian Inheritance." *Transactions of the Royal Society of Edinburgh*, 52, 399–433.

Fisher, Ronald A. (1922). "On the Dominance Ratio." *Proceedings of the Royal Society of Edinburgh*, 42, 321–41.

Fraser, Doreen. n.d. "Renormalization Group Methods in Quantum Field Theory and Statistical Mechanics: Analogies and Applied Mathematics." Unpublished manuscript.

French, Steven, and Ladyman, James. (1997). "Superconductivity and Structures: Revisiting the London Account," *Studies in History and Philosophy of Science Part B*, 28, 363–93.

French, Steven, and Ladyman, James. (2003). "Remodelling Structural Realism: Quantum Physics and the Metaphysics of Structure." *Synthese*, 136, 31–56.

Friedman, Michael. (1974). "Explanation and Scientific Understanding." *Journal of Philosophy*, 71, 5–19.

Frigg, Roman. (2006). "Scientific Representation and the Semantic View of Theories," *Theoria* 55, 49–65.

Frigg, Roman, and Reiss, Julian. (2008). "The Philosophy of Simulation: Hot New Issues or Same Old Stew?" *Synthese*,169, 593–613.

Frigg, Roman. (2010a). "Fiction and Scientific Representation." In Roman Frigg and Matthew Hunter (eds.), *Beyond Mimesis and Nominalism: Representation in Art and Science*, 97–138. Berlin: Springer.

Frigg, Roman. (2010b). "Models and Fiction." *Synthese*, 172(2), 251–68.

Frisch, Matthias. (2005). *Inconsistency, Asymmetry, and Non-Locality*. Oxford: Oxford University Press.

Frohlich, H. (1950). "Theory of Superconducting State 1. The Ground State at the Absolute Zero of Temperature." *Physical Review*, 79, 845–56.

Galilei, Galileo. (1623). Il Saggiatore. Rome. Trans. Stillman Drake and C. D. O'Malley as *The Assayer, in The Controversy on the Comets of 1618*. Philadelphia: University of Pennsylvania Press, 1960.

Gayon, Jean. (1998). *Darwinism's Struggle for Survival: Heredity and the Hypothesis of Natural Selection*. Cambridge: Cambridge University Press.

Gell-Mann, Murray, and Low, Francis E. (1954). "Quantum Electrodynamics at Small Distances." *Physical Review*, 95(5), 1300–12.

Gell-Mann, Murray, and Ne'eman, Y. (Eds.) (1964). *The Eightfold Way*. New York: W. A. Benjamin.

Giere, Ronald. (1988). *Explaining Science: A Cognitive Approach*. Chicago: University of Chicago Press.

Giere, Ronald N. (1999). *Science without Laws*. Chicago: University of Chicago Press.

Giere, Ronald. (2006). *Scientific Perspectivism*. Chicago: University of Chicago Press.

Giere, Ronald. (2009). "Is Computer Simulation Changing the Face of Experimentation?" *Philosophical Studies*, 143, 59–62.

Gilbert, N., and Troitzsch, K. (1999). *Simulation for the Social Scientist*. Philadelphia: Open University Press.

Gitterman, Moshe, and Halpern, V. (2004). *Phase Transitions: A Brief Account with Modern Applications*. Singapore: World Scientific.

Godfrey-Smith, Peter. (2006). "The Strategy of Model-Based Science." *Biology and Philosophy*, 21, 725–40.

Goudsmit, Samuel, and Uhlenbeck, George. (1926). "Die Kopplungsmoglichkeiten der quantenvektoren im atom." *Zeitschrif fur Physik*, 35, 618–25.

Greiner, W., and Maruhn, J. A. (1996). *Nuclear Models*. Berlin: Springer.

Guala, Francesco. (2002). "Models, Simulations, and Experiments." In L. Magnani and N. J. Nersessian (eds.), *Model-Based Reasoning: Science, Technology, Values*, 59–74. New York: Kluwer.

Hartmann, Stephan. (1995). "The World as a Process: Simulations in the Natural and Social Sciences." In R. Hegselmann (ed.), *Simulation and Modelling in the Social Sciences from the Philosophy of Science Point of View*,77–100. Theory and Decision Library. Dordrecht: Kluwer.

Hempel, Carl G. (1965). "Aspects of Scientific Explanation." In Hempel, *Aspects of Scientific Explanation and Other Essays in the Philosophy of Science*, 331–489. New York: Free Press.

Hockney, R. W., and Eastwood, J. W. (1994). *Computer Simulation Using Particles*. Bristol: Institute of Physics Publishing.

Hughes, R. I. G. (1999). "The Ising Model, Computer Simulation and Universal Physics." In M. Morgan and M. Morrison (eds.), *Models as Mediators: Perspectives on Natural and Social Science*, 97–145. Cambridge: Cambridge University Press.

Humphreys, Paul. (1990). "Computer Simulations." In A. Fine, M. Forbes, and L. Wessels (eds.), *Philosophy of Science Association Proceedings*, 2:497–506. East Lansing, MI: Philosophy of Science Association.

Humphreys, Paul. (2004). *Extending Ourselves: Computer Science, Empiricism and Scientific Method*. Oxford: Oxford University Press.

Humphreys, Paul. (2008)."The Philosophical Novelty of Computer Simulation Methods." *Synthese*, 169 (3), 615–26.

Jones, Martin. (2005). "Idealization and Abstraction: A Framework." In M. Jones and C. Cartwright (eds.), *Correcting the Model: Idealization and Abstraction in the Sciences*, 173–218. Amsterdam: Rodopi.

Kadanoff, Leo P. (1966). "Scaling Laws for Ising Models Near Tc." *Physics*, 2, 263.

Kitcher, Philip. (1989). "Explanatory Unification and the Causal Structure of the world." In P. Kitcher and W. C. Salmon (eds.), *Scientific Explanation*, 410–505. Minneapolis: University of Minnesota Press.

Krantz, D. H., Luce, R. D., Suppes, P., and Tversky, A. (1971). *Foundations of Measurement*. Vol. 1: *Additive and Polynomial Representations*. New York: Academic Press.

Krantz, D. H., Luce, R. D., Suppes, P., and Tversky, A. (1989). *Foundations of Measurement*. Vol. 2: *Geometrical, Threshold, and Probabilistic Measurements*. New York: Academic Press.

Krantz, D. H., Luce, R. D., Suppes, P., and Tversky, A. (1990). *Foundations of Measurement*. Vol. 3: *Representation and Axiomatisation*. New York: Academic Press.

Kuhn, Thomas. (1977). "Objectivity, Value Judgements and Theory Choice." In *The Essential Tension*, 320–39. Chicago: University of Chicago Press.

Kuper, C. G. (1959). "The Theory of Superconductivity." *Advances in Physics*, 8, 1–44.

Ladyman, James. (2002). "Science, Metaphysics and Structural Realism." *Philosophica*, 67, 57–76.

Landau, Lev. (1937). "On The Theory of Phase Transitions." Translated and reprinted in Landau, L. D., *Collected Papers*, vol. 1, 234–252 (Moscow: Nauka, 1969). Originally published in Zh. Eksp. Teor. Fiz. 7, pp. 19–32.

Leggett, Anthony J. (1997). "The Paired Electron." In M. Springford (ed.), *Electron: A Centenary Volume*, 148–81. Cambridge: Cambridge University Press.

Leng, Mary. (2005). "Mathematical Explanation." In C. Cellucci and D. Gillies (eds.), *Mathematical Reasoning, Heuristics and the Development of Mathematics*. London: King's College Publications, 167–89.

Leng, Mary. (2010). *Mathematics and Reality*. Oxford: Oxford University Press.

Lesne, Annick. (1998). *Renormalization Methods: Critical Phenomena, Chaos, Fractal Structures*. New York: Wiley.

London, Fritz. (1950). *Superfluids*. New York: Wiley.

London, Fritz, and London, Heinz. (1934). "The Electromagnetic Equations of the Supraconductor." *Proceedings of the Royal Society*, A149, 71–88.

Luce, R. D., and Tukey, J. W. (1964). "Simultaneous Conjoint Measurement." *Journal of Mathematical Psychology*, 1, 1–27.

Matthen, Mohan, and Ariew, Andre. (2002). "Two Ways of Thinking about Fitness and Natural Selection." *The Journal of Philosophy*, XCIX, 55–83.

Maxwell, James Clerk. (1954). *Treatise on Electricity and Magnetism*. (1873). Oxford: Clarendon Press; reprint (2 vols.). New York: Dover.

Maxwell, James Clerk. (1965). "On Physical Lines of Force." (1861–62). In W. D. Niven (ed.), *The Scientific Papers of James Clerk Maxwell*. New York: Dover.

Maxwell, James Clerk. (1965). *The Scientific Papers of James Clerk Maxwell*. Ed. W. D. Niven. New York: Dover.

Mayr, Ernst. (1976). "Where Are We?" (1959). Reprinted in Ernst Mayr, *Evolution and the Diversity of Life*, 307–28. Cambridge, MA: Harvard University Press.

Mayr, Ernst. (1982). *The Growth of Biological Thought: Diversity, Evolution, and Inheritance*. Cambridge, MA: Harvard University Press.

McMullin, Ernan. (1985). "Galilean Idealisation." *Studies in History and Philosophy of Science*, 16, 247–73.

Meheus, J. (Ed.). (2002). *Inconsistency in Science*. Dordrecht: Kluwer Academic.

Moeller, P., Madland, D. G., Sierk, A. J., and Iwamoto, A. (2001). "Nuclear Fission Modes and Fragment Mass Asymmetries in a Five-Dimensional Deformation Space." *Nature*, 409, 785–790.

Morgan, Mary. (2002). "Model Experiments and Models in Experiments." In L. Magnani and N. J. Nersessian (eds.), *Model-Based Reasoning: Science, Technology, Values*, 41–58. Dordrecht: Kluwer.

Morgan, Mary. (2003a). "Experiments without Material Intervention: Model Experiments, Virtual Experiments and Virtually Experiments." In H. Radder (ed.), *The Philosophy of Scientific Experimentation*, 216–35. Pittsburgh: Pittsburgh University Press.

Morgan, Mary. (2005). "Experiments vs. Models: New Phenomena, Inference and Surprise." *Journal of Economic Methodology*, 12(2), 317–29.

Morrison, Margaret. (1992). "Some Complexities of Experimental Evidence." In D. Hull, M. Forbes, and K. Okruhlik (eds.), *Philosophy of Science Association Proceedings*, 1:49–62. East Lansing, MI: Philosophy of Science Association.

Morrison, Margaret. (1998). "Modelling Nature: Between Physics and the Physical World." *Philosophia Naturalis*, 35, 65–85.

Morrison, Margaret. (1999). "Models as Autonomous Agents." In M. S. Morgan and M. Morrison (eds.), *Models as Mediators: Perspectives on Natural and Social Science*, 38–65. Cambridge: Cambridge University Press.

Morrison, Margaret. (2000). *Unifying Scientific Theories: Physical Concepts and Mathematical Structures*. Cambridge: Cambridge University Press.

Morrison, Margaret. (2002). "Modelling Populations: Pearson and Fisher on Mendelism and Biometry." *British Journal for the Philosophy of Science*, 53, 39–68.

Morrison, Margaret. (2006a). "Emergence, Reduction, and Theoretical Principles: Rethinking Fundamentalism." *Philosophy of Science*, 73, 876–87.

Morrison, Margaret. (2006b). "Scientific Understanding and Mathematical Abstraction." *Philosophia*, 34, 337–53.

Morrison, Margaret. (2007a). "Spin: All Is Not What It Seems." *Studies in History and Philosophy of Modern Physics*, 38, 529–57.

Morrison, Margaret. (2007b). "Where Have All the Theories Gone?" *Philosophy of Science* 74, 195–228.

Morrison, Margaret. (2008a). "Fictions, Representations, and Reality." In M. Suarez (ed.), *Fictions in Science:Philosophical Essays on Modelling and Idealisation*, 110–35. London: Routledge.

Morrison, Margaret. (2008b). "Models as Representational Structures." In S. Hartmann, L. Bovens, and C. Hoefer (eds.), *Nancy Cartwright's Philosophy of Science*, 67–90. London: Routledge.

Morrison, Margaret. (2012). "Emergent Physics and Micro-Ontology." *Philosophy of Science*, 79, 141–66.

Morrison, Margaret. (forthcoming). "Complex Systems and Renormalization Group Explanations." *Philosophy of Science*.

Morrison, Margaret, and Morgan, Mary. (1999). "Models as Mediating Instruments." In M. Morgan and M. Morrison, *Models as Mediators: Essays on the Philosophy of the Natural and Social Sciences*, 10–37. Cambridge: Cambridge University Press.

Muller, Fred A. (2007). "Inconsistency in Classical Electrodynamics?" *Philosophy of Science*, 74, 253–77.

Norton, B. J., and Pearson, Egon S. (1976). "A Note on the Background to and Refereeing of R. A. Fisher's 1918 Paper 'On the Correlation of Relatives on the Supposition of Mendelian Inheritance.'" *Notes and Records of the Royal Society*, 31, 151–62.

Norton, S., and Suppe, Fred. (2001). "Why Atmospheric Modelling Is Good Science." In C. Miller and P. N. Edwards (eds.), *Changing the Atmosphere: Expert Knowledge and Environmental Governance*, 67–105. Cambridge, MA: MIT Press.

Oberkampf, William L., and Barone, M. F. (2006)."Measures of Agreement between Computation and Experiment: Validation Metrics." *Journal of Computational Physics*, 217, 5–36.

Oberkampf, William L., and Roy, C. J. (2010). *Verification and Validation in Scientific Computing*. Cambridge: Cambridge University Press.

Oberkampf, William L., and Trucano, Timothy. (2002)."Verification and Validation in Computational Fluid Dynamics." *Progress in Aerospace Sciences*, 38, 209–72.

Oberkampf, William L., Trucano, Timothy, and Hirsch, Charles. (2004). "Verification, Validation and Predictive Capability in Computational Engineering and Physics." *Applied Mechanics Review*, 57(5), 345–84.

Parker, Wendy. (2008). "Does Matter Really Matter: Computer Simulations, Experiments and Materiality." *Synthese*, 169, 483–96.

Pauli, Wolfgang. (1932). In *Proceedings of the Sixth Solavy Conference 1930*, 183–86; 217–20; 75–80. Brussels: Gauthier-Villars.

Pauli, Wolfgang. (1958). In S. Flugge (ed.), *Handbuch der physik*. Berlin: Springer.

Pearson, Karl. (1896). "Mathematical Contributions to the Theory of Evolution, III: Regression, Heredity and Panmixia." *Philosophical Transactions of the Royal Society of London A* 187, 253–328.

Pearson, Karl. (1904). "Mathematical Contributions to the Theory of Evolution, XII: On a Generalized Theory of Alternative Inheritance with Special Reference to Mendel's Laws." *Philosophical Transactions of the Royal Society of London A* 203, 53–86.

Pearson, Karl. (1909a). "On the Ancestral Gametic Correlations of a Mendelian Population Mating at Random." *Proceedings of the Royal Society B* 81, 225–29.

Pearson, Karl. (1909b). "The Theory of Ancestral Contributions in Heredity." *Proceedings of the Royal Society B* 81, 219–24.

Pearson, Karl. (1911). *The Grammar of Science*. 3rd ed. London: Black.

Pincock, Christopher. (2007). "A Role for Mathematics in the Physical Sciences." *Nous*, 41, 253–75.

Pincock, Christopher. (2012). *Mathematics and Scientific Representation*. Oxford: Oxford University Press.

Portides, Demetris. (2005). "Scientific Models and the Semantic View of Theories." *Philosophy of Science*, 72, 1287–98.

Portides, Demetris. (2006). "The Evolutionary History of Models as Representational Agents." In Lorenzo Magnani (ed.), *Model-Based Reasoning in Science and Engineering*, 1–20. Amsterdam: Rodopi.

Portides, Demetris. (2011). "Seeking Representations of Phenomena: Phenomenological Models." *Studies in History and Philosophy of Science*, 42, 334–41.

Priest, Graham. (2002). "Paraconsistent Logic." In D. Gabbay and F. Guenthner (eds.), *Handbook of Philosophical Logic*, 2nd ed., 6:287–393. Dordrecht: Kluwer Academic.

Provine, William B. (2001). *The Origins of Theoretical Population Genetics*. Chicago: University of Chicago Press.

Psillos, Stathis. (2001). "Is Structural Realism Possible?" *Philosophy of Science*, 68 (supp. vol.), S13–S24.

Psillos, Stathis. (2006). "*The* Structure, the *Whole* Structure and Nothing *But* the Structure?" *Philosophy of Science*, 73, 560–70.

Rickayzan, G. (1965). *Theory of Superconductivity*. New York: Wiley.

Rimoldi, A. (2011). "Simulation Strategies for the ATLAS Experiment at LHC." Atlas Software Proceedings-2011-016.

Roache, P. J. (1997). "Quantification of Uncertainty in Computational Fluid Dynamics." *Annual Review of Fluid Mechanics*, 29, 123–60.

Rueger, Alexander. (2005). "Perspectival Models and Theory Unification." *British Journal for the Philosophy of Science*, 56, 579–94.

Saatsi, Juha, and Vickers, Peter. (2011). "Miraculous Success? Inconsistency and Untruth in Kirchhoff's Theory of Diffraction." *The British Journal for the Philosophy of Science*, 62, 29–46.

Salmon, Wesley C. (1984). *Scientific Explanation and the Causal Structure of the World*. Princeton: Princeton University Press.

Sarukkai, Sundar. (2005). "Revisiting the `Unreasonable Effectiveness' of Mathematics." *Current Science*, 88, 415-23.

Schrieffer, John R. (1973). "Macroscopic Quantum Phenomena from Pairing in Superconductors." *Physics Today*, 23–28.

Seigel, Daniel. (1991). *Innovation in Maxwell's Electromagnetic Theory*. Cambridge: Cambridge University Press.

Shapiro, Stewart. (1997). *Philosophy of Mathematics: Structure and Ontology*. Oxford: Oxford University Press.

Smith, Crosbie, and Wise, Norton. (1989). "Energy and Empire: A Biographical Study of Lord Kelvin." Cambridge: Cambridge University Press.

Sober, Elliot. (1984). The Nature of Selection: Evolutionay Theory in Philosophical Focus. Cambridge, MA: MIT Press.

Stanley, H. E. (1999). "Scaling, Universality, and Renormalization: Three Pillars of Modern Critical Phenomena." *Reviews of Modern Physics*, 71, S358–66.

Steiner, Mark. (1978)."Mathematical Explanation." *Philosophical Studies*, 34, 135–51.

Suarez, Mauricio. (2003). "Scientific Representation: Against Similarity and Isomorphism." *International Studies in the Philosophy of Science*, 17, 225–44.

Suppes, Patrick. (2002). *Representation and Invariance of Scientific Structures*. Stanford, CA: CSLI Publications.

Thomson, William. (1984). *Baltimore Lectures*. Reprinted in P. Achinstein and R. Kargon (eds.), *Kelvin's Baltimore Lectures and Modern Theoretical Physics*, Cambridge, MA: MIT Press. 1987.

REFERENCES

Thomson, William. (1891). *Popular Lectures and Addresses*. Vol. 1. London: Macmillan.

Trucano, Timothy. (1998). "Prediction and Uncertainty in Computational Modelling of Complex Phenomena: A White Paper." SAND98-2776. Albuquerque, NM: Sandia National Laboratories.

van Fraassen, Bas C. (1980). *The Scientific Image*. Oxford: Clarendon Press.

van Fraassen, Bas C. (2006). "Structure: Its Shadow and Substance." *The British Journal for the Philosophy of Science*, 57, 275–307.

van Fraassen, Bas C. (2007). "Structuralism(s) about Science: Some Common Problems." *Proceedings of the Aristotelian Society*, 81, 45–61.

van Fraassen, Bastian C. (2008). *Scientific Representation: Paradoxes of Perspective*. Oxford: Oxford University Press.

Vickers, Peter. (2008). "Frisch, Muller, and Belot on an Inconsistency in Classical Electrodynamics." *British Journal for the Philosophy of Science*, 59, 767–92.

Waddington, C. H. (1957). *The Strategy of the Genes*. London: Allen and Unwin.

Walsh, Denis. (2000). "Chasing Shadows: Natural Selection and Adaptation." *Studies in History and Philosophy of Biological and Biomedical Sciences*, 31, 135–53.

Walton, K. (1990). *Mimesis as Make-Belief: On the Foundations of the Representational Arts*. Cambridge, MA: Harvard University Press.

Weinberg, Steven. (1983). "Why the Renormalization Group Is a Good Thing." In A. Guth, K. Huang, and R. L. Jaffe (eds.), *Asymptotic Realms of Physics*, essays in honor of Francis Low, 1–19. Cambridge, MA: MIT Press.

Wilson, Kenneth. (1971). "The Renormalization Group (RG) and Critical Phenomena 1." *Physical Review B*, 4, 3174.

Winsberg, Eric. (2003). "Simulated Experiments: Methodology for a Virtual World." *Philosophy of Science*, 70, 105–25.

Winsberg, Eric. (2008). "A Tale of Two Methods." *Synthese*, 169, 575–92.

Winsberg, Eric. (2010). *Science in the Age of Computer Simulation*. Chicago: University of Chicago Press.

Wright, Sewell. (1922). "The Effects of Inbreeding and Crossbreeding on Guinea Pigs." *U.S. Department of Agriculture Bulletin*, 1090, 1–63, 1121, 1–49.

Wright, Sewell. (1929). "Evolution in a Mendelian Population." *Anatomical Record*, 44, 287.

Zinn-Justin, Jean. (1998). "Renormalization and Renormalization Group: From the Discovery of UV Divergences to the Concept of Effective Field Theories." In C. de Witt-Morette and J.-B. Zuber (eds.), *Proceedings of the NATO ASI on Quantum Field Theory: Perspective and Prospective*, NATO ASI Series C 530, 375–88. Les Houches, France: Kluwer Academic.

INDEX

abstraction, 4–6, 20–35, 38–41, 45–46, 81,
  113–117; *see also* idealisation
accuracy/adequacy distinction, 315
  Duhem's view of, 116
  and idealisation, 41, 46, 49, 90–92, 116
  mathematical, 6, 19–21, 45–46, 85–86
  other views, 21
accuracy, 255, 259fn6, 264–265, 269–276,
  280, 282–284, 311fn5, 315
  estimation, 280
adequacy, 152, 258, 269, 282
adequacy conditions, 258, 315
algorithm, 154, 212–213, 219, 259–261,
  284, 291
  numerical, 237, 263
allele frequencies, 32–33, 35–39, 44, 46,
  86–87, 113–115
analogies, 65, 86, 99–100, 134
analytic solutions, 259–260
anlagen, 37
Ampere's law, 103–105, 110–111
apparatus, 203–204, 216–217, 220, 226,
  230–232, 239, 243–246
applicability, 4, 38, 89, 110–114
Ariane 5, 253
assumptions, 32–38, 42, 44–47, 86–88,
  113–115, 117, 163, 166, 168–169, 177–181,
  185–192, 231, 235–237, 242, 312–313

astrophysics, 22, 202, 210, 214, 221, 228, 245, 316
asymptotic behaviour, 29, 58, 68
ATLAS (experiment), 290–292, 294, 296–301,
  305–307, 313

Baker, A., 4, 51–53
Bangu, S., 4, 51, 68
Bardeen, Cooper, and Schrieffer (BCS) preface,
  6, 26, 120–121, 130–132, 135–154, 182
Batterman, R., 4, 31, 51, 68, 131
Bayes's theorem, 281
Bayesian statistical analysis/methods, 230,
  264, 279–281
benchmark(s), 259, 266–267, 274, 281,
  284–285, 293, 307–309
  studies 307–309
beyond the standard model (BSM), 120, 311
biology, 16, 23, 31–34, 42; *see also* population
  genetics
Bohr, N., 154, 234, 235
Bose particle, 148
Bose-Einstein condensation, 69, 147
boson, 3, 10, 182–183, 294–305
  weak, 296
  Higgs, 3, 238fn43, 251, 290, 295, 302, 305
  Higgs-like, 251, 286, 294–295
boundary layer (n,a), 165–169, 173
Brown B., 156–157